THE COURT
OF
VIRTUE

JOHN HALL

THE COURT

OF

VIRTUE

(1565)

Edited
and with an Introduction by
RUSSELL A. FRASER

LONDON
Routledge and Kegan Paul

This edition published 1961
by Routledge and Kegan Paul Ltd
Broadway House, 68–74 Carter Lane
London, E.C.4

Made and printed in Great Britain by
William Clowes and Sons, Limited
London and Beccles

Copyright Russell A. Fraser 1961

Never . . . had any man a wit so presently excellent, as that it could raise itself; but there must
come both matter, occasion, commenders, and
favourers to it. If this be true, and that the fortune of all writers doth daily prove it, it behoves
the careful to provide well towards these acci-
dents; and, having acquired them, to preserve
that part of reputation most tenderly, wherein
the benefit of a friend is also defended. Hence it
is, that I now render myself grateful. . . .

BEN JONSON, 1607

PREFACE

The Court of Virtue is, of all the poetical miscellanies published in the
Tudor period, the most encyclopedic in kind. John Hall the author
touches on plants: one thinks of the herbalist, Turner. He inveighs
against contemporary dress: one calls to mind the tirades of Nashe
and Philip Stubbes. His religious verses summon up the Primer and
Prayer Book. His verses on astronomy redact the manuals of Proclus,
or Sacrobosco, or Recorde. He dislikes astrology: so does John
Calvin. He is enamoured of proverbs and semblables: so, too, are
Baldwin, and Palfreyman, and Erasmus. In short, there is nothing
in Hall or his book that would not have seemed familiar to an Elizabethan reader, nothing that does not touch on some aspect of
Elizabethan life. There is no reason why Thomas Marshe, who
printed the book in the early years of Queen Elizabeth's reign, should
not have entitled it *Speculum Mundi*.

Though portions of the text have appeared from time to time, in
articles and anthologies, it has not been reprinted entire until now.
The text offered here is based primarily on the Huntington Library
copy of *The Court of Virtue*. Since, however, this copy (like the other
three that survive) is imperfect, I have completed it, so far as is
possible, by reference to the British Museum copy. I have not
attempted to reproduce, in the bibliographical descriptions, the
exact typography of the originals. Neither have I sought, when
quoting from printed books of the fifteenth and sixteenth centuries,
to approximate the peculiar abbreviations and contractions found
frequently therein. I have, however, preserved the very common
use of a straight mark or double curve (the Spanish *tilde*) above a
letter, denoting the omission of a nasal following or preceding that
letter (*quoniā = quoniam*; *eīm = enim*), the omission of a combination
of nasals with a vowel (*aīa = anima*), and, often, an arbitrary abbre-
viation (*ē = est*).

I have altered, for the sake of consistency, the spelling and
punctuation of running titles throughout the text. In this reprint,
the left headline is made to read: *The Courte*; and the right headline: *of Vertue*. Catch words and folio numbers omitted by the
printer have been supplied. The position of page numbers in the
original edition, of catch words, and of signatures, has been stabilized.

I have corrected silently all typographical errors (punctuation, indentation of stanzas), and all misprints, but have recorded those misprints in a separate Table. Sometimes the printer ignores the customary distinction between the use of letters *u* and *v*. I have emended, to preserve the distinction. The letters *i* (I) and *j* (J) are rendered always as *i* (I), except in combinations: *xiiij*.

Musical notation accompanies many of the poems; I have transcribed it in modern form. Some of the songs which, in the original text, extend over two pages, are comprised here in less space. Thus a number of catch words have, necessarily, been changed. These changes are noted in the Table of Misprints. Hall, on occasion, commences a song without indicating a key signature, and then abruptly, in the course of the song, rectifies his omission. I have supplied a key signature throughout, except when such addition would result in a plethora of accidentals, denoting momentary departure from the signature by the raising or lowering of a note by means of a sharp, flat, or natural. In the latter case, I have abandoned Hall's key signature, and have supplied in its place the requisite sharps or flats. The last tune in *The Court of Virtue* is written in four distinct parts: Triplex, Contra tenor, Tenor, and Bassus. I have rewritten the four parts as one piece. Hall's music embraces three pages in the original text (a2v–a3v); my transcription does also (thus retaining the look of a page for page reprint), though the matter of the transcription differs, necessarily, from that of the original. Hall's verses, though varying in spelling from part to part, are essentially the same for each of the four parts. It would be meaningless to repeat them; I have given, therefore, the first rendering only (Triplex).

I am grateful to many persons and institutions for help in preparing this edition of *The Court of Virtue*. I want especially to thank the staff of the Huntington Library, the Folger Shakespeare Library, the Bodleian Library, the British Museum, the Cambridge University Library, and the Victoria and Albert Museum. My work has been supported in part by grants in aid from Dartmouth College, Princeton University, the American Philosophical Society, and the American Council of Learned Societies, which assisted publication of this volume as a result of a contribution from the United States Steel Foundation. I wish, finally, to record my debt to the late Hyder E. Rollins of Harvard University.

'Nothing man has projected from himself,' asserted Pater, 'is really intelligible except at its own date.' I suppose one has got to concur. I hope, however, that *The Court of Virtue* will help to make a little clearer much that was current and popular once, and is now dead and disused.

RUSSELL A. FRASER

London, 1960

CONTENTS

TABLE OF SUBJECTS

THESE page numbers are cited to direct the reader to the Notes, in which each reference given here is amplified or discussed.

INTRODUCTION

I. THE AUTHOR

THE birth in 1529 of John Hall, poet and medical writer, is fixed
by an entry in the *Dictionary of National Biography*.[1] It is, however,
unlikely that the man whose translation of *The Proverbs of Solomon*
into English metre was published in 1549 was born but twenty years
before. That 1529 was the year of Hall's birth is inferred from the
evidence of a woodcut portrait of the author '*aetat* 35,' which
appears in the 1565 *Chirurgery*. But the portrait may of course have
been cut before the year of publication.

It is true that, in his dedicatory verses to 'master Thomas Cole
doctor of diuinitie, and arch deacon of Essex' (3.4–5), Hall refers
to his 'yong . . . and haltyng age' (3.28), and assigns to Dr. Cole the
credit of curing it. In 1552 Cole was master of Maidstone School[2]
where, one may reasonably assume, Hall incurred the debt of which
he writes. Moreover, *Alumni Oxonienses* enters, on October 22, 1554,
the B.A. degree for 'John Hall.'[3] These dates seem to tally with
that of 1529. But Cole may have come to the mastership of Maidstone earlier than 1552; and there is besides no certain warrant
for identifying the recipient of the Oxford B.A. with the author of
The Court of Virtue. Finally, if in contradictory fashion, Hall asserts
that his age did 'very nere agree' with that of Cole (4.15), who, as
master and archdeacon, was presumably no longer young. It is
possible, then, that John Hall was born not in 1529 but a good
many years before.

As practitioner of surgery at Maidstone, in Kent, Hall became a
member of the Worshipful Company of Chirurgeons. His zeal in
medicine is attested to by Thomas Warton, the literary historian,
who records that Hall was 'author of many tracts in his profession.'[4]
Of the 1550 *Proverbs* (*S.T.C.* 12631), Warton writes, 'By the
remainder of the title it appears, that the Proverbs had been in

---

[1] (1890), XXIV, 69f.
[2] *D.N.B.* (1887), XI, 273f.
[3] *1500–1714* (Oxford, 1891), II, 632.
[4] *History of English Poetry* (London, 1781), III, 181.

a former impression unfairly attributed to Thomas Sternhold.'[1] The 'former impression' in which Hall felt himself slighted was thought by Warton to be an edition in quarto dedicated to Edward VI and entitled *The Psalms of David, Translated into English Meter by T. Sternhold, Sir Thomas Wyatt, and William Hunnis, with Certain Chapters of the Proverbs and Select Psalms by John Hall.* It is a nice irony that Hall, who, in his violent censure of the popular poetical miscellany, *The Court of Venus*, attacked the poems of Wyatt appearing in that volume, should have been associated with him in a pious undertaking. But the *Psalms of David* appeared in 1551. The question therefore arises whether Hall's work was included, presumably without sufficient credit, in a book printed before 1550.

An undated edition of Hall's *Proverbs* does in fact exist: *The Proverbs of Solomon, Three Chapters of Ecclesiasties, The Sixth Chapter of Sapientia, the Ninth Chapter of Ecclesiasticus, and Certain Psalms of David,* assigned, incorrectly, to the printer Edward Whitchurch,[2] and dedicated to John Bricket of Eltham. Though the 1550 *Proverbs* attacks, in its preface to the reader, *The Court of Venus*, the undated edition does not. Neither does Hall's *Proverbs* of 1549. I infer that an edition of *The Court of Venus* was published in 1549–1550,[3] and that the undated edition of the *Proverbs* appeared before 1550. The undated edition may be the one given, incorrectly, to Sternhold, or, alternatively, that edition may have disappeared. Though Hall felt himself denied the notice that was due him, his psalms were highly praised, and were compared to the renderings of Sternhold and Hopkins.

In 1565 the printer Thomas Marshe brought out *The Court of Virtue* (*S.T.C.* 12632), Hall's most considerable work, and one that had engrossed his attention, apparently, from the 1550s forward. The attack direct on secular verse, characteristic of the *Proverbs*, and sustained in the Prologue to *The Court of Virtue* (15.26–16.3), gives way, for the most part, in the latter work, to a subtler form of censure. Redacting songs by Thomas Wyatt, and imitating, frequently and derisively, the manner of popular poetry, Hall went, for his models, to *The Court of Venus* and to Richard Tottel's *Songs and Sonnets*.[4] Either Tottel or his editor had anticipated this larcenous

---

[1] *Whych prouerbes of late were set forth, Imprinted and vntruely entituled, to be thee doynges of Mayster Thomas Sternhold, late grome of the Kynges Maiesties robes, as by thys Copye it may be perceaued. M.D.L.*

[2] On the authority of the *S.T.C.* Examination of a copy of this edition held by the Cambridge University Library (Pressmark Syn. 8.54.152) indicates that it is not the work of Whitchurch, but of Thomas Raynald, who printed the *Proverbs* of 1549 and 1550.

[3] *The Court of Venus*, ed. Fraser (Durham, N.C., 1955), pp. 56f.

[4] Cf. *The Court of Venus*, pp. 57–61.

courtesy by purloining two poems from the 1549 *Proverbs* (sigs. A5–7), or from the undated edition, and including them with only slight verbal variations in the celebrated miscellany.[1] Tottel entitles the two poems 'The wise trade of lyfe' and 'That few wordes shew wisdome, and work much quiet.'[2] Both poems are dropped from the 1550 *Proverbs*.

Hall wrote also *A Poesy in Form of a Vision . . . Against Necromancy, Witchcraft, Sorcery, Incantations, and Divers Other Detestable and Devilish Practices*, 1563; and *A Most Excellent and Learned Work of Chirurgery, Called Chirurgia Parva Lanfranci*, 1565, a translation in four parts of Lanfranc's *Chirurgery*. It is this book that contains the woodcut portrait, '*aetat* 35,' referred to before. *A Very Fruitful and Necessary Brief Work of Anatomy* was appended to the translation of Lanfranc, as was *An Historical Expostulation: Against the Beastly Abusers, Both of Chirurgery and Physic, in Our Time: with a Goodly Doctrine and Instruction . . . of All True Chirurgians*. This work denounced the quacks of Hall's day, and protested against the combination of magic, divination, and medicine with as much vehemence as Hall had attacked secular verse. The *Expostulation* was printed by the Percy Society in 1844 under the editorship of T. J. Pettigrew. Hall's rendering into English of treatises by Benedict Victorius and Nicholas Massa on *The Cure of the French Disease* reposes still, in manuscript, in the Bodleian Library, together with letters from John Hall to William Cunningham, M.D., of London. In 1563 Hall contributed commendatory English verses to Thomas Gale's *Enchiridion of Chirurgery*, and to the same author's *Institution of a Chirurgian*.

In the Stationers' Register for 1562–1563, there is the entry, 'Receuyd of William greffeth for his lycense for pryntinge of a ballett intituled *a Dyscription of the [a]natime of a byrchen brome . . .* iiij^d.'[3] Hall incorporates (and presumably alters) this ballad in *The Court of Virtue* (266.14–267.29). His title is 'The anotomy or particular description of a byrchē broome or besome: In the composition or makyng wherof, are conteyned, iii. notable Iustices or purgers of vices.' Another ballad-entry, in 1565–1566, is also connected with Hall: 'Receuyd of WYLLIAM LEWES for his lycense for prynting of *the monsterus chylde which was borne in Buckenham shyre.* iij^d.'[4] Hall may have written this ballad, a version of which occurs in *The Court of Virtue* (268.2–270.13) under the title, 'The description & declaration of a monstrous chyld, borne in the towne of Maydston

[1] H. E. Rollins, 'Tottel's "Miscellany" and John Hall,' *TLS* (January 14, 1932), p. 28.
[2] *Tottel's Miscellany*, ed. H. E. Rollins (Cambridge, Mass., 1928), I, 234.
[3] Ed. Arber (London, 1875–1894), I, 200.
[4] *S.R.*, I, 310.

in the Countie of Kent, in the yeare of oure Saluation. 1561.' In 1569–1570 Richard Jones entered in the Stationers' Register 'The Sixth Chapter of St. Mathew that We Should not Be Careful Of Worldly Vanities,'[1] a ballad taken from *The Court of Virtue* (97. 12–102.9). Hall's version is entitled 'The maner of true and perfecte prayer instituted by our sauiour Iesus Christe, the only sonne of God, the wisdom of the father, and seconde person in trinitie.' The poem begins 'The syxt of mathewe if ye reade' and concludes with a poetical rendering of the Pater Noster. Thus Hall's moralizing *Court* was influenced not only by *The Court of Venus* and Tottel's *Songs and Sonnets*, but by the manner of popular broadsides as well.

Hall died in 1566. Three decades later, Andrew Maunsell's *Catalogue of English Printed Books*, 1595, recorded, on sig. D2v, 'The *Court* of vertue, containing godly songes with notes, made by Iohn *Hall* chirurgion. Printed by Thomas Marsh 1565. 8.' The availability of Hall's most important work in the closing years of the century may indicate sustained popularity, or, quite simply, that the book failed to sell. *The Court of Venus* is not mentioned by Maunsell, though attacks on it continued until the end of Elizabeth's reign.[2]

2. THE PRINTER

In the Stationers' Register for 1564–1565 appears the entry, 'Receued of *Thomas marshe* for his lycense for pryntinge of a boke intituled *the Couurte of vertu contaynynge many holy or spretuall songes Sonettes psalmes ballettes shorte sentences as well of holy scriptures as others &c . . .* xijᵈ.'[3] Marshe printed the *Court* in 1565. It was not, by much, the most important book to come from his press. Between 1561 and 1564 he had printed *The Court of Venus*,[4] first, in its earliest version, of the poetical miscellanies of the sixteenth century. John Hall's *Court of Virtue*, a 'work inuaying against vice,'[5] was inspired almost certainly by Marshe's printing of *The Court of Venus*, a work it resembles, ironically, not only in its title, but also in its use of the same font of type.

Thomas Marshe began printing at the sign of the Prince's Arms

[1] I, 416.

[2] For references to John Hall, cf. Thomas Tanner, *Bibliotheca Britannica* (London, 1748), p. 372; William Thomas Lowndes, *The Bibliographer's Manual of English Literature*, ed. Henry G. Bohn (London, 1859), IV, 978; William Herbert, *Typographical Antiquities* (London, 1785), I, 550, 588, II, 805f., 854f.; John Holland, *The Psalmists of Britain* (London, 1843), pp. 178f.; Lily B. Campbell, *Divine Poetry and Drama in Sixteenth-Century England* (Berkeley and Los Angeles, 1959), pp. 47f., 62f.

[3] I, 268.

[4] For information on the printing and dating of this work, cf. *The Court of Venus*, pp. 10f., 24–26.

[5] As the introductory matter to Hall's *Chirurgery* describes it.

in Fleet Street, or, as it was also called, the King's Arms, in 1554.[1] He had apparently worked in partnership with John King before that date. The *Hand-Lists of English Printers 1501–1555* give two un-dated books to Marshe 'with J. Kynge' before 1554, and the address in the colophon of Skelton's *Certain Books* is 'Crede Lane,' which was King's house. An original member of the Stationers' Company, Marshe was taken into the livery in 1562, was an under-warden in 1575, and an upper-warden in 1581. Using as devices a monogram and, more rarely, a figure of Fortune, he issued a very considerable number of books. Privileged to print grammars, he did a good deal of important literary work as well. His behaviour in general is said to have been disorderly: he disregarded frequently the Company ordinances, and was often fined. Nor does his character appear to advantage in the controversy, begun in 1573 and renewed in 1579, with John Kingston, sometime partner of Henry Sutton, over the copyright of *Aesop's Fables*, *Holy Dialogs*, and *The Epitome of Collo-quies*. On another occasion, Marshe pretended to the title of *Tully's Epistles*, which the wife of the printer Vautrollier was printing while her husband was abroad on special affairs. The patent granted him on September 29, 1572, to print Latin books for use in English gram-mar schools[2] helped engender the protest of the poor and under-privileged stationers to the Lord Treasurer. The result was that the more privileged members of the Company were compelled to yield up their rights in certain particulars for the benefit of the poor of the Company.

Among the more significant books printed by Marshe, other than *The Court of Venus* and *The Court of Virtue*, are Sir Thomas Elyot's *Castle of Health*, 1561 (*S.T.C.* 7651), Elyot's *The Book Named the Governor*, 1565 (*S.T.C.* 7641), and John Fitzherbert's *Book of Hus-bandry* (*S.T.C.* 11001), printed, perhaps, between 1557 and 1560. Marshe printed continuously up to 1587, and died probably in 1591, for in June of that year Thomas Orwin had 'granted unto him, by the consent of Edw. Marshe, these copies . . . [a long list of books is subjoined] which did belong to Tho. Marshe deceased.'

3. THE BOOK

The Prologue to *The Court of Virtue* is conventional and familiar. The author, vaguely troubled, wanders in the country. Suddenly, and necessarily, in the manner of many other heroes of Chaucerian

---

[1] For information on Marshe, cf. E. Gordon Duff, *A Century of the English Book Trade* (London, 1905), p. 100; John Stow, *Survey of London*, ed. Strype (London, 1720), p. 222.

[2] Stow's *Survey*, p. 222.

dream-visions, he falls asleep. In his dream, a trinity of fair ladies accosts him. Madame Hope, the first lady, who resembles the Genius of the Prologue to *The Court of Venus*, offers consolation. The poet listens next to a sterner recital from the second dame, Lady Virtue, or Arete, who complains bitterly of the state of men, attacks 'Trim songes of loue' (15.20), and *The Court of Venus* in particular, and adjures her listener to make without delay a book of holy songs, indicting folly. Hall, accepting the charge, concludes his Prologue with traditional modesty:

> My wyt is rude, and small my skyll,
> To stande and supplie suche a place.
> Yet must I nedes walke in the trace,
> That vertue did assigne me in,
> Therefore in hyr prayse I beginne.
>
> (17.25–29)

And so, begin he does, with poems, deriving from Scripture, on the allegorical figures of the Prologue (pp. 18–51). These give place to redactions of the Psalms (51–92), to verses indebted largely to the Prayer Book (92–126), and to various Books of the Bible (126–59). There follow assorted laments and rebukes, employing often the techniques of secular verse (159–81). Poems of Wyatt are levied on, to undergo an enfeebling transformation.

His moral sense thoroughly ascendant, Hall passes now to the penning of invectives: against pride, envy, slanderous tongues (182–210). He moralizes the sweating plague of 1552 (210f.), recapitulates his early praise of virtue (211–14), embodies his own name in homiletic verses (214f.). Again the dour mood rises, manifest in a series of warnings, exhortations, complaints (215–42):

> Remember well, O man I say,
> Thou art wormes meate, and very clay
>
> (215.16f.),

tricked out often, if ironically, in the dress of a popular poem:

> My harte constraines my mouth to tell,
> the dutie of eche worldly wight.
>
> (225.23f.)

In preface to a garland of lugubrious gnomes, drawn, most of them (at least professedly), from classical writers (249–65), the poet ventures on a sequence of descriptions in verse, delineating man's life, and the virtues and vices that compound it (243–49). He is not above the imitation of ballads and broadsides (266–70). The wonted manner, of admonition, of indictment, is, however, more congenial; he returns to it soon (270–86). A jeremiad, in the form of a vision and dream, and autobiographical in part, treats of the abuses Hall descries, and decries, on every side (286–331). *Facit indignatio versum.* Pious songs and sayings (331–47); two pictures of woman: whore and modest matron (347–60), the second nothing like so compelling as the first; and a final exordium (361–64), a sort of Parthian shot, bring the book to a close.

Many poems in *The Court of Virtue* essay a short proem or introduction; a religious song follows after. Often, the song is given in the first person, not by the poet, but by a sanctified figure like Jonas, Jeremiah, God, or Christ. Thus Hall (in some sense) may be called a dramatic poet. His skill in versifying is not admirable; he is, however, master of many rhythmic variations. Though his reliance on doggerel couplets is marked and monotonous, the frequent interspersing of Biblical phrases and metaphors lends a modicum of dignity and beauty. Many poems employ a refrain: perhaps this characteristic links them with the 'profane' songs of *The Court of Venus*. Rime-royal, or a variation thereof, is resorted to throughout; the Prologue is written in 51 stanzas in the scheme of rime-royal, though employing iambic tetrameter. In one poem, at least, Hall writes macaronic verse, taking as his refrain the phrase '*Venite ad iudicium*' (178–81). 'A Ditie declarynge the stedfast hope and trust that the faythfull afflicted soule hath in Christ Iesu' (227–30) is written in a close approximation of Skeltonics.

The Court of Virtue is important in part for its redacting of poems by Thomas Wyatt. 'A dittie of the pen inueiyng against vsury and false dealyng' (191–93) makes over 'My penne take payne.' 'Blame not my lute' (164–69) departs less widely from the poem on which it is based. 'A song of the lute in the prayse of God, and disprayse of Idolatrie' (169–72) depends on 'My lute awake.' Sometimes one senses the presence of a secular lyric behind Hall's verses, though the source of the redaction is to seek. Thus (by way of example), a poem with the improbable title 'A short song exhorting all men to abstayne from the vse of false weyghtes and measures' (225–27) seems kindred in rhythm and form to the work of a courtly maker. The ababcc stanzaic pattern, and the interlocking of one stanza with another, suggest Wyatt or an imitator, though the poem may be of course no redaction at all, but merely an approximation of courtly technique put to uses quite uncourtly in kind.

The title of his work Hall chose, I assume, as a way of throwing down the gage to *The Court of Venus* and other collections of like character. The complete title of *The Court of Virtue: Songs, Sonnets, Psalms*, etc., glances perhaps at Tottel's book. Conceivably, the appearance of Arete (Lady Virtue) in 'A meruaylous dreame' (307) continues Hall's Prologue and so parallels the promised continuation of the Prologue to *The Court of Venus*. Again, in the poem beginning 'In sommer time when flowrs gan spryng' (160) the author, like the distraught lover of the Prologue to *The Court of Venus*, walks 'to recreat . . . [his] mynde,' and calls on Christ as the courtly narrator called on Venus. Yet Hall's book, after all, is not based on *The Court of Venus* nor does it levy on that work specifically, beyond the redacting of a few poems. *The Court of Virtue* is rather the literary apologia of a man whose life and writings had been a constant protest against the wickedness, real or fancied, of the non-Puritan, pleasure-loving regimen of many of his contemporaries.

It is also a monument to those contemporaries, and a mirror of the world they created. That Hall took for his province astronomy and astrology, botany and costume, proverb lore and religion, and classical myth, that he elected to give those subjects poetic dress, is fortunate now (if no part, then, of his conscious design), for the *Court* is made thereby a student's *vade mecum* to the world of the Tudors.

So Hall describes at length the dress and cosmetics and even the manner of coquetry in vogue among women of all classes. Not spawned of a sea maid nor begot between cod-fish, he is constrained to turn away:

> Loke not to longe vpon a mayde,
> Least with hir forme thou be dismayde.
> (94.14f).

Like St. Cyprian (253.2–13) and, I suppose, his editor, Erasmus, he believes that women should be seen and not heard. Like Juan Vives,[1] he is sure that they are much the frailer of the sexes, wanton by temper, and safest perhaps when not seen at all. Unhappily for Hall, the sayings of the wise were no longer availing. Neither were the sumptuary laws. In his youth, all was different. Now, 'The fashion is changed' (351.14):

> Eche lasse lyke a lady is clothed in sylke,
> That dayly doth go to market with mylke.
> (353.22f.)

Here, purportedly at least, is the picture of a society rushing on destruction, a picture eked out in the writings of Tom Nashe and Philip Stubbes, of John Stow and Stephen Gosson.

Here also, presented with vivid detail, is the Elizabethan gentlewoman (and those who presumed to her estate). Her face is boldly painted, as if to be sold; her hair is worn curled, and tricked out

---

[1] *Vives and the Renaissance Education of Women*, ed. Foster Watson, London, 1912 (a translation of Vives' *De institutione feminae Christinae*, 1523), pp. 84–9, 94–102.

with ornaments; the upper part of her figure is squeezed so tightly by a doublet as to stop the blood and cause fainting; her frock swells out with 'buttocks most monstrously round.'

> There are boulsters likewise for the buttocks as wel as the breast,
> and why forsooth? The smaller in the wast, the better handled.
>
> (350.23–25n.)

Great hoops encircle her feet:

> A bombe lyke a barrell, with whoopes at the skyrte.
>
> (350.23–25n.)

Her breasts are exposed ('These naked paps, the Deuils ginnes'); her hair laid down wantonly to the eyes (350–52). So wroth is the poet that he ventures to take issue with Scripture:

> For though God to pryde haue geuen his curse,
> I esteme sluttyshenes to be muche worse.
>
> (352.14f.)

There is this wan consolation: so ridiculous do women cause them selves to appear, so quick are they to throw over one fashion for the next, 'chaunging (as it were) with the Moone,' that England, 'the Players stage of gorgeous attyre, the Ape of all Nations superfluities,' has become a 'laughing stocke to all the worlde.'

Item by item the dress of Tudor ladies is remarked, corroborating and adding to the record of a host of contemporary books, and the collection of costumes in the Victoria and Albert Museum. One reads of the cassock, or loose outward coat; the frock, for indoor wear; the farthingale, a round petticoat of canvas, distended with whalebone; the smock, or chemise; the kirtle, a jacket to which the skirt was attached; the partlet, or neckerchief; the rich overgown of silk or velvet; the common cap trimmed with fur, to the scandal of law-givers, who prohibited its use by any below the rank of knight or dame; the French hood, popularized by Mary Stuart; and the 'childishe gewgawes, and foolish trinkets,' clogged 'with gold, siluer, or silke lace,' that characterize a time when 'by theyr apparell none can now know,/ The hygh estate from the most poore and low.' (353.20f.)

Botany, also, attracts Hall's attention. This science, highly esteemed by the sixteenth-century reader, whose application of it was nothing if not catholic, is entered through the poet's catalogue of more than fifty plants and flowers. Often the cataloguer gives the scientific name for a flower. He does so not because of a preoccupation with botany for itself, but because he is a practising physician: for botany is a branch and helpmeet of medicine. No doubt it is of

interest to note that common yarrow 'hath very many stalkes ...
about which stande long leaues,' and that 'the flowers whereof are
either white or purple.' What is much more to the point, however,
is that yarrow will close up wounds and staunch the blood, and on
being put up to the nose will work in just the opposite fashion,
inducing nose-bleed. It is also the sovereign remedy for pelvic
disorders: 'This hath beene prooued by a certaine friende of mine,
sometimes a fellow of Kings Colledge in Cambridge, who lightly
brused the leaues of common Yarrow with Hogs grease, and applied
it warme vnto the priuie parts, and therby did diuers times helpe
himselfe, and others of his fellowes, when he was a student, and a
single man liuing in Cambridge.'

Again, consider the inconspicuous addergrass, which may be
described as to appearance, temperature, and virtue. For the first,
one may go to the poet. For the second, to the herbalist, who speaks
of a 'temperature hot and moist ... [of] much superfluous windi-
ness.' For the virtues of this plant, we learn from the physician, indebted himself to Dioscorides, that if men do 'eate of the great full
or fat rootes ... they cause them to beget male children: and if
women eate ... they shall bring foorth females.' Lastly, there is the
province of the enterprising 'chemist': 'The women giue the tender
full roote to be drunke in gotes milke, to mooue bodily lust ... Our
age vseth all the kindes of ... [addergrass to] stirre vp venerie, and
the apothecaries doe mixe any of them indifferently with compositions seruing for that purpose.' (Gerard, *Herball*, 1597, pp. 915, 158.)

Hall on astronomy is no less instructive. From his metaphorical
descriptions of the planets and stars and their movements, one
advances to an understanding of this pre-Copernican science which,
to the sixteenth-century reader, bore incalculably on human destiny. With a number of kindred subjects Hall is similarly acquainted;
in their lore he acts instructor to those who will attend. There is
necromancy, 'whiche science constrayneth the enemye the fende to
be taken and holde prisonner'; natural astrology, which predicts
the motions of the heavenly bodies; judicial astrology, a 'strumpet
counterfeit,' which studies the influence of the stars on human history; geomancy, the art of divination by means of signs derived
from the earth; augury or soothsaying; witchcraft; chiromancy,
which 'dothe facion in the palme of the hande seuen mountaines,
accordinge to the number of the planets: and supposeth that shee
is able to knowe, by the lines ... [a man's life]'; physiognomy; and
the interpretation of dreams.

Now as each of Hall's references is explored for its meaning and
possible indebtedness, a composite picture forms. It is compounded
of books, those that were read by a literate but quite conventional

representative of the middle class in the period just anterior to Shakespeare's. The picture shows, when seen as a whole, the standard Tudor library and, behind it, the popular culture of an age separated from our own by much more than a mere gulf in time.

So from books like Richard Taverner's *Prouerbes* (1552) and William Baldwin's *Morall Phylosophie* (1547), Hall gathered his political theory, which exalted submission to authority: 'the thynges that be aboue vs, belonge nothynge vnto vs ... it becometh not Iacke strawe to reason of princes matters'; and insisted on the maintenance of order: 'Cut of [f] the stealers handes. Hang vp theues and robbers, that the hygh wayes may be the surer. Burne the Sodomytes. Stone the adououterers. . . . Suffre not the swearers to escape vnpou[n]ysed.'

For astrology Hall resorted to works like *The Kalendar & Compost of Shepherds* (1st English edn., 1503), a fascinating account of the influence of the planets and zodiacal signs on the different parts of the body. The intimate if curious lore he found there has been dramatized by Shakespeare in *Twelfth Night*: '*Sir Andrew.* Shall we set about some revels? *Sir Toby.* What shall we do else? were we not born under Taurus? *Sir Andrew.* Taurus! that's sides and heart. *Sir Toby.* No sir; it is legs and thighs.' In fact, as Shakespeare knew, it was neither.

If Hall were to wonder—he did rather more—what opinion a Christian should entertain on this vexed and controversial subject, there was Calvin's scathing *Admonicion against Astrology Iudiciall* (1561), which, once read, precluded further doubt. Astronomy, in contrast, was a reputable science, and from works like the encyclopedic *Mirror of the World* (1480) Hall absorbed truths more sober and solid. He learned that at the centre of the universe was Hell, enclosed by Earth, the final repository for all the dregs and purgings of the spheres; and this knowledge contributed to his view of the nature of man. From Palingenius, whose *Zodiacus vitae* was the most popular astronomical poem of the English Renaissance, and from the *Sphaerae* of Proclus and Sacrobosco, the two principal Latin texts on elementary astronomy, his cosmos was elaborated. Its pinnacle was the Heaven Celestial, the domain of the Creator. But descending to the Earth in immutable order were other spheres: Heaven Imperial, home of the angels; the Firmament, containing the stars, among which the twelve constellations called the Zodiac were chief in virtue; the Pure Air, through which the seven planets pursued their orderly way. What precept was there for man in so harmonious a scheme, but deference to things as they were?

For his views on education, Hall went to Vives; for his botany, to William Turner. His style he formed on those 'Parables and semblables' whose popularity bemuses a contemporary reader: 'Lyke as to a shrewde horse belongeth a sharpe brydle: so ought a shrewde wyfe to be sharply handeled.' Thus he was himself a minor contributor to the development of Euphuist prose. If he would cultivate 'wisdom' (and he would), 'that is to saie, prompte, quicke, wittie and sentencious saiynges, of certain Emperours, Kynges, Capitaines, Philosophiers and Oratours, as well Grekes, as Romaines,' he had to hand a series of well-worn florilegia: the *Adagia* of Erasmus (1508), and the *Apophthegmes* (in Udall's translation, 1542); the *Vita philosophorum* of Walter Burley (printed 1515), based itself on Diogenes Laertius; and, most valuable of all, the *Polyanthea* of Nannius Mirabellius (1507), a collection of saws and sayings on every conceivable topic, and thus a mirror to popular thought.

Still other subjects find a place in the *Court*: mythology, for example, for a knowledge of which Hall drew on the lexicons of Stephanus and Suidas and Cooper, or on the Greek grammarian Apollodorus, or the *Fabularum liber* of Hyginus. The printing of music for many of the songs enhances the attractiveness of Hall's book.[1] In fact *The Court of Virtue* is the first work of its kind in English to include printed musical notation with the text. In some instances Hall omits the notation, but indicates the tune to which his poem is to be sung by giving the title of another refrain. Thus he will instruct the reader: 'Syng this as, I am the man whome God. &c.'

Religion, of course, was at the core of all he wrote; and indeed one discovers that first the Bible, and then the Primer and Prayer Book, were the books which John Hall—and, by inference, his contemporaries—knew best and used most. Thus *The Court of Virtue* versifies the Psalms and Proverbs, the Pater Noster, Creed and Ten Commandments, passages from Matthew and Luke, and from the Books of Daniel, Esdras, Tobit, Judith, Job, Ecclesiasticus, Isaiah, Jeremiah, Sapientia, and Hosea. Hall very probably owned both 'Matthew's Bible' (Tyndale-Coverdale) of 1537, and a revision of it, printed by John Day in 1551, and offering a new translation of Judith.

His indebtedness to the Prayer Book is almost as pronounced: the violent invectives which characterize the *Court*, and so many other works of its time, are all of them on subjects against which the primers inveighed. And if Hall and his co-religionists seem unwontedly sober, one need only refer to the church services they attended, services in which the conviction of death and decay, of fleshly lust, and the body as a whited sepulchre, is all-pervasive.

---

[1] See, for discussion of Hall and his music, R. A. Fraser, 'An Amateur Elizabethan Composer,' *Music & Letters*, XXXIII, no. 4 (October, 1952), 329–32; and 'Early Elizabethan Songs,' *Musica Disciplina*, VII (1953), 199–203.

Hall's predilection for versifying Scripture results, for the most part, in something less than poetry. Often the subject is degraded in a misguided attempt to improve it. Sometimes the poet begins prosperously but ends in a lame and disappointing manner:

> Out of the womb of hell
> To the when I did crye,
> My voyce thou heardest well,
> And holpe me louyngly.
>
> (157.9–12)

Yet Hall is capable, in flashes, of fine verse:

> Remember earth thy first estate,
> Thy lyons harte it wyll abate.
>
> (216.2–3)

It is the Hebraic mood that dominates and gives tone to *The Court of Virtue.*

Hall's sense of the corruption of contemporary life makes him to smart and agonize at every pore. The time is out of joint: that is the burden of his book.

> Presumpteous boldnes in vnshamfast wayes,
> Is termed courage or audacitie,
> But shame to sinne is counted now a dayes
> Great folyshnes, and doltysh dastardy,
> So ryfe so rype is nowe iniquitie.
>
> (269.30–270.4)

The Court of Virtue might, with propriety, have taken for its title that appended to a 'Godly new Ballad' of the time, one showing 'the manifold abuses of this wicked world, the intolerable pride of people, the wantonnesse [of] women, the dissimulations of flatterers, the filthinesse of Whoredome, the vnthriftines of Gamesters, the cruelty of Landlords, with a number of other inconueniencies.' And written, it is pleasant to record, to the tune of *Greensleeves.*[1]

In the rotten society Hall never wearies of indicting, money is the root of all evil.[2] Astrologers, fortune tellers, glozing prophets, conjurers, jugglers, minstrels, highwaymen, and, a piquant if mystifying interjection, 'rat catchers, And suche as teethe dyd drawe' (301.6f.): all render homage to Mammon. Hall excoriates them all.

---

[1] *The Pack of Autolycus*, ed. H. E. Rollins (Cambridge, Mass., 1927), pp. 3–6.

[2] Pp. 288–305 recite a multitude of ills worked by lust for gold. The gloom and acerbity of the poet in the face of those ills are paralleled by the temper of a host of contemporary broadsides. Cf. Henry Huth, *Ancient Ballads & Broadsides* (London, 1867), pp. xxxii–xxxvi.

What is interesting, and significant, is the impartiality of his hatred:
it is easy, and not particularly audacious, to inveigh against

> The cobler, tynker, and the smyth.
>
> (291.22)

To hold up the mirror to their betters is more courageous, or more
foolish. Hall is courageous, and foolish. The merchant, the man of
law, the learned leech incur his ire. So, too, do the clergy (190.2–9),
and those

> That euery houre
> Do Christe deuoure,
> And his poore flocke oppresse.
>
> (223.5–7)

Premier among them are the rich, who, exalting wealth above
commonwealth, grind the faces of the poor (290.18–25).

Hall's criticism is exciting and portentous. It is not, however,
really shrewd (which is to say, economic), but ethical and moral in
content. In this, it is emphatically of its time: the criticism of
Fortescue, and Elyot, of Richard Morison, of Latimer, and Dudley,
and a hundred other polemicists and prelates is informed by the
same ethical bias.[1] But Hall, if in homiletic fashion, goes beyond the
conventional homilist, ventures to look into the sun. So 'A ditie
shewyng the office of all estates' (172.4–175.23) treats, inferentially,
of the malpractice of princes:

> Let not rulers be rude and vayne.   (174.26)
> Let kynges . . .
> Supporte no more iniquitie,
> Nor mainteyne suche as are peruart. . . .
>
> Or els surely
> The lord God whiche is kyng of all,
> Your glory turne to shame he shall
> Moste ryghteously.
>
> (174.5–14)

Like York and Gaunt, in *Richard II*, John Hall would not presume to
lift an arm against the King, God's minister, the deputy anointed by
the Lord. And if the King err: Vengeance is Mine. But—it is amusing, and instructive—Hall anticipates that vengeance, broods on it,
savours it: '. . . the last day is not farre hence' (311.8). Portents and
prodigies betoken its coming.

---

[1] Cf. Arthur B. Ferguson, 'Renaissance Realism in the "Commonwealth"
Literature of Early Tudor England,' *Journal of the History of Ideas*, XVI, no. 3
(June, 1955), 287–305.

> Wherfore the day,
> At hande I say,
> Of force muste nedes appere,
> This worlde to burne,
> That thus dothe turne,
> To worse from yere to yere.
>
> (286.2-7)

When that day comes, the faithful party 'electe of Christe' (12.11), 'outcastes ... nowe' (151.26), 'hated for the truthe' (220.13): Hall's party, the Puritan party, will have its reward. So, infallibly, will 'Eche lorde and lady, kyng and quene' (180.8):

> In payns of hell thus shall they crye
> That nowe doe Christ his flocke oppresse.
>
> (181.20f.)

It is all unexceptionable, this summons, replete with warning, to the good life, this paeon to responsibility, and degree. Hall does not —I dare say, could not—think to go beyond it. But in his moral fulminations, latent, unwished, and unrealized, is a summons, afar off, to Marston Moor.

THE COUURTE OF VERTUE

Contaynynge
Many holy or spretuall
songes Sonettes psalmes ballettes
shorte sentences as well of holy scriptures as others &c

In Effigiem JOHANNIS HALLI CHIRURGI
RODOLPHI M. CARMEN

Quem graphice pictor pinxit liber explicat Hallum,
    Effigiem cernas ingeniumque simul.
At si Halli uultum uelles perspicere uiuum,
    Haec sua scripta legas, quae explicuere animum.
Triginta is Vixit quatuor non amplius annos,
    In Lucem quando hoc aedere corpit opus :
Effigies ergo pereat dum floreat Hallus,
    Ingenii cuius tot modo scripta uigent.

⟦ Herevnto in the ende is also adioyned a
Table, wherby any thyng therin may
redyly be founde.

VNTO THE FAITHFUL

preacher of Goddes sacred Truthe and feruent fauarer of the most Catholike and right religion
master Thomas Cole doctor of diuinitie, and arch
deacon of Essex, I.H. wysheth his hartes de- 5
syre and most happy successe in all hys most
vertuous affayres.

AS dayly in most men we see,
That bokes set foorth of ought:
Whether it be to teach good things 10
Or blame that whych is nought.

They dedicate theyr workes to suche,
Of whome they haue before:
Receaued some great benefyte,
Or worldly profyte store. 15

But fewe I see dooe in theyr workes,
As semeth best recyte:
The benefytes of suche as taught,
Them vertues ways aryght.

But yf it be a thyng as due, 20
Or more then other are:
To render frutes of vertue where,
As fyrst she dyd prepare,

To plant and graffe, such fruitfull trees,
As worthy frutes should beare: 25
Then may I folow thys intent,
Without all dread or feare.

My yong, my frayle, and haltyng age,
Fyrst cured was by you:
Your godly lyfe, ioynde wyth your wordes, 30
Inducyng to vertue.

In

3

In youthfull state, ye made me stoppe,
And streyght wayes made me olde;
Delyueryng me from dangers great,
Yea many thousand folde.   5

The rage of yong and wanton dayes,
You made me soone to hate:
And excellently made me see,
The diffrence of estate.

Betwene the ways that synfull men,   10
Delyght in styll to dwell:
And perfect workes of vertue pure
Whyche dothe in grace excell.

Your age also, whych dyd wyth myne,
Euen very nere agree: 15
Was not the least cause as I iudge,
Your vertues wrought in me.

Your frendly louyng heart to me,
Whych God dyd ordeyne so,
I moued am by these I say,   20
And other causes mo,

The *Court of Vertue* to commyt,
And dedicate to you:
Whose blessed rules as semeth me,
You euer dyd ensue.   25

In whyche I shall not nede to aske,
I know your good defence:
To take her part wyth all your powre,
And lerned dilygence.

For all your tyme, your whole delyght,   30
Hath ben to serue hyr grace:
Procuryng also many mo,
To folowe that same race.

In

4

In learned sermons preached here
In good kyng Edwardes tyme:
Wherin ye taught religion true,
Wyth blamyng synne and cryme.   5

Ye vsed there, the net of grace,
And playde good Peters part,
And on the ryght syde cast it foorth,
In true and perfect rate.

In suche wyse haue you done your part,   10
Settyng apart all feare:
That vertues God hath caused you,
Rule in hys Churche to beare.

Both truthe to teache and to correct,
With condigne punyshement: 15
All suche as to resyst the truthe,
Or mayntayne lyes are bent.

For whyche theternall God be praysde,
Who only hath you made,
And chosen you to worke hys wyll,   20
In thys moste godly trade.

And I beseche hys maiestie,
That from dame vertues lyne,
Nor from hys pure and perfect giftes
Ye neuer doo declyne.   25

But that the enemies of the truth,
As in tymes past may styll
Constreygned be to prayse your lyfe,
Though sore agaynst theyr wyll.

And nowe agayne vnto my sute,   30
And moste humble request,
Thys poore gyfte in good part to take
And iudge therof the beste.

                                    Here

5

THE PROLOGUE

AMIDS the twynnes when Phebus bright,
Fayre Cithera, and Ioue benigne,
Last ouer went by his course ryght,
That he with them had conioyning: 5
Commodiously mitigating,
Both Mars and Saturns malice grette,
Whiche in the Crabbe but lately mette.

   Lykewyse Lucina, then hir decte,
With eche planet diligently,   10
Hir selfe to ioyne with lyke aspecte,
Begynnyng first with Mercury:
To Iupiter consequently,
With Sol and Cithera in haste,
With Saturne then, and Mars at laste.   15

   Almightie God that all hath wroughte,
Thus through their course moste naturall,
Within three signes together brought,
These sterres that erratykes men call:
In these three were these planets all,   20
The Crab, the Twyns, the horned Bull,
Of wonders thus his workes are full.

   At this tyme as for my solase,
To banyshe pensyue heuynesse:
I went abrode the tyme to passe,   25
When thought my soule did sore oppresse:
Callyng my muses to relese
My soule, whiche dyd in sorowe smarte,
Who aye were wonte to ease my harte.

   The Muses nyne I meane whiche teache,   30
And Christen poets illuminate,

Whether with pen or mouth they preache,
In vertuous and moste godly rate:
Of grace and knowledge they the gate
Doe open in moste gentle wyse, 5
To all that goodnes exercise.

    The fyrste of these is vertue fayre,
Whiche some men doe Arete call.
The seconde faith whiche doth repayre,
To sauing health as principall. 10
The third place lady hope haue shall.
The fourth is loue: and wysdome fyue,
Which doe with grace ryght well reuyue.

    Dame temperance the sixt muse is.
The seuenth is dame pacience. 15
The eight a lady full of blis.
Is constancie in good pretence.
The nynthe of good experience,
Is mekenes, or humilitie,
The purchasers of Gads mercie. 20

    To these as I before haue sayde,
I made my playnte still as I went,
Desyring them of helpe and ayde,
Els am I all in peeces rent:
For ignorance moste pestilent, 25
With hir sonne error me assayle,
And would against my soule preuayle.

    At lest (quod I) dere helpes alas,
Let come Arete, and dame Spes:
Brynging with them dame Charitas, 30
That they my harte may bryng to ease.

                 And

And take from me my great disease:
This ougly griefe vyle ignorance,
And in hir stede knowledge aduance.

   At last I sate downe on a grene,   5
Vnto a banke lenyng my backe:
But Phebus beames so whot did shyne,
That it constreined me to take,
The shade vnder the freshe grene brake.
Not farre from me then streight I spyde,   10
A groue whiche was there harde besyde:

   Where as eche byrde, with ẏ swete noyse
That nature gaue them to endure,
Began my harte for to reioyse,
Their notes my thought were so demure: 15
Whiche in short space did me procure,
My thoughtfull harte for to apalle,
That I into a sleape gan falle.

But in this slumber as I laye,
My spirit receyude no quiet rest.   20
Wherfore I wakte agayne streightwaye,
So sore encombred was my brest:
Whiche sought therof to be relest.
Thus on my muses gan I craue,
Take pitie on your simple slaue.   25

   But then afreshe I herde agayne,
The byrdes that sang so swete a note,
To whom I sayde with glad harte fayne,
Now Christe his blessing on your throte:
And to my mynde it came I wote,   30

            B2   With

With laude and prayse for to aduance,
In them the Lordes hyghe ordinance.

O God (quod I) omnipotente,
We render the with hartes so pure, 5
All laude and prayse with good intente,
Thy handy workes doe me allure,
That my harte can ryght well indure,
For euer in this place to dwell.
And straight againe on sleape I fell. 10

But sure I had not rested long,
Yer that into a dreame I fell.
I sawe my thought the flowres among
Fayre ladies three, whiche dyd excell
The prayse that any tongue can tell, 15
Aprochyng towardes me full faste,
For soth I was right sore agaste.

Me thought they compaste me about,
Standing as in a syrcle trayne,
The midlemoste without all doubte, 20
Dyd farre excelle the other twayne,
Them to beholde my harte was fayne :
Forsothe it was a semely syghte,
My harte therin dyd muche delyghte.

As I dyd earnestly beholde, 25
These ladyes three that weare so bryght.
From care my harte began vnfolde :
For I receiued perfecte syghte,
That madame hope so full of myght,
Was one of that same ladyes three, 30
That so about had compast me.

Of

Of whom I had the knowledge founde,
By readyng of the worde of God.
As I behelde hyr in that stounde,
Hyr head at me she gan to nod.   5
Then from my harte the heauy lode,
Consumde away, with all my thought:
For hope was come whom I had sought.

Then vp to hyr my handes I caste,
And kneled downe vpon the grounde: 10
Welcome (quod I) my hartes repaste,
That I haue sought, now haue I founde,
The healer vp of this my wounde,
That iustice hath so fiersly made,
With thought, that sharpe and cuttyng blade.   15

She tooke me then in hyr armes twayne,
And thus to me she sweetly sayde.
Be strong (quod she) stande vp agayne,
Oh man why shouldste thou be afrayde,
For God hath made me for thyne ayde: 20
To thee we are sent from aboue,
Both vertue, hope, and also loue.

To loue then dyd I turne my face,
And vnto hyr I bowde my knee.
And gently she did me embrace,   25
Be of good chere O man (quod she:)
For here is also come to thee,
(According to thy prayer true)
Arete or lady vertue.

When I had heard howe they had sayde,   30
That lady vertue was in place,

My harte forsothe was sore dismayde,
And colour rose streyght in my face:
And downe I fell before hir grace,
Desyryng hir beneuolence,   5
To pardon my rude negligence.

    That lady then did me beholde,
And stepte and caught me by the hande.
Be not dismayde (quod she) be bolde,
And vp vpryght before me stande: 10
For I doe the to vnderstande,
That I am come downe from aboue,
And brought with me both hope and loue.

    To hope and loue then dyd she call,
And thus began her tale to tell.   15
Marke well (sayd she,) for shewe I shal,
How men from them do me expell,
And against their lorde God rebell:
Estemyng me but of small pryce,
And wholy geue them selues to vyce.   20

    The lorde did ordeyne me for man,
That I should richely hym endue.
Why doe they thus forsake me than,
And synne and vyce so muche ensue?
Forsoth, because they be vntrue,   25
Regardyng their owne wyt and wyll,
And wyll not harke gods worde vntyll.

    Gods worde, no no, alas therfore,
Ther is no thyng I dare well saye,
That worldly men doe more abhorre,   30
He that hath wyt perceyue it may:

                       Their

Their outwarde workes doe them bewraye,
For when gods worde byds them amende,
With reason they their vyce defende.

And to be briefe nowe eche estate,   5
Doth seke all meanes vyce to maynteyne :
And are with me at great debate,
So that I doe not ryghtly reigne.
At me the most part haue disdeyne :
All saue a fewe doe me resiste,   10
Whiche fewe are the electe of Christe.

And thou O man marke what I saye,
To the I wyll my mynde declare :
That thou mayst nowe perceyue the waye,
Of worldly men, and howe they fare :   15
That afterwarde thou mayest prepare
Thy selfe to doe and worke my wyll,
In that whiche I saye the vntyll.

Their pryde they name nowe cleanlynes,
And auarice is polycie :   20
So doe they name wrath manlynes,
And loue they call vyle lecherie,
Namyng enuie good memorie.
They call glutony fare honeste
And slouth they call naturall reste.   25

Extortion lawfull gettyng,
Idolatrie catholyke fayth,
Vsury is wytty wynning,
Vyce is vertue as eche man sayeth :
But in the truthe who nowe hym stayeth?   30
Rebellyon is common welth,
And manly shifte, robrie and stelth.

B4   Oppression

Oppression is good gouernance,
Cruelnes is seueritie,
The prodigall their dedes aduance,
And call it lyberalytie.　　　　　　　　　5
And Sodoms synne is chastitie,
Among those whiche compte mariage synne,
Whose wickednes wyll neuer blynne.

Some lyue in wylfull pouertie,
And beggars haue the proudest harte.　　10
Thus wade they in hipocrisie,
And idlenes for the moste parte,
Whiche causeth vertue to departe:
For idlenes the mother is,
Of all mischiefe and thinges amys.　　　15

It is a thyng ay incident,
That eche man hath felicitie,
On some one thyng the mynde is bente,
In wysdomes schole, or in folye:
And doe their myndes wholy aplye,　　　20
That they may it attayne and gette,
Wheron theyr harte is fyxte and sette.

The couetous delyghte in goulde,
The lechour in his fleshly luste.
The proude would haue all men beholde,　25
Their painted shethe of dounge and duste:
The slothfull sleape, and slomber muste,
The wrathfull and the enuious noye:
Whose whole delyghte is to destroye.

The gluttons loue their panche to fyll,　30
The dronkards doe delyghte in drynke:

　　　　　　　　　　　　　　　And

And eche of these to haue theyr wyll,
No coste nor charge to great they thynke:
Thus in a fansie all men synke,
And eche mans care is to aspyre,   5
Vnto his luste and hartes desyre.

 Some studie in Astronomie,
Delyghting to beholde the sterres,
Some in musyke and harmonie,
And cosmographie some preferres.   10
Some in fygures, some in numbers.
Some doe delyghte philosophie,
To knowe on earth eche herbe and tree.

 The fowlers haue their whole delyghte,
To deuyse engyns byrdes to take: 15
Suche as in fyshing haue a syght,
They angles and their nettes wyll make,
And take great payne for fansies sake.
The faulkners hauke is his pleasure,
The hunter wyll good houndes procure.   20

 In all thynges either good or yll,
That man doth folowe or embrace,
Feliticie they haue and wyll:
Their hartes desyre for to purchace.
Then happy are they whiche by grace,   25
Loue vertues supernaturall,
Whiche bryghtly shyneth aboue all.

 Ye happy are those men I saye,
That haue in vertue their delyghte:
For in their sorowe they wyll praye,   30
For helpe and ayde to God almyghte,

And in their myrth their fayth moste ryght,
Doth cause them holy psalmes to synge,
And spirituall songes to his praysyng.

As vyce doth cause delyght in synne,   5
To folowe all iniquitie,
And alwaye seketh waies to wynne,
Mens souls in wretched vylaynie:
So vertue in the contrarie,
Doth by all meanes hir selfe behaue,   10
The soule of man to blesse and saue.

O then you that my seruantes be,
In me haue all your exercise.
And as ye doe delyght in me,
So looke that ye doe enterpryse,   15
All good thynges vertuous and wyse:
That by your badge it may be sene,
That I am your lady and quene.

Suche as in carnall loue reioyce,
Trim songes of loue they wyll compile,   20
And synfully with tune and voyce
They syng their songes in pleasant stile,
To Venus that same strompet vyle:
And make of hir a goddes dere,
In lecherie that had no pere.   25

A booke also of songes they haue,
And Venus court they doe it name.
No fylthy mynde a songe can craue,
But therin he may finde the same:
And in suche songes is all their game.   30

                                        Wherof

Wherof ryght dyuers bookes be made,
To nuryshe that moste fylthy trade.

I will that my seruantes therfore
Shall be as apte me for to serue,   5
In prayse of God sinne to abhorre
And from me Vertue not to swerue.
That they may godly fame deserue,
Of good men here, and after this
To reigne with God in heauen blys.   10

As prayer in sadnes is mete :
In myrthe so godly songes to synge,
For Christen men lo this is fytte.
I charge thee therfore with this thynge :
That thou thyne exercise doe brynge,   15
To make a boke of songes holy,
Godly and wyse, blamyng foly.

To whiche boke godly men may adde,
(From tyme to tyme as they see cause,)
Ryght sober songes godly and sadde,   20
Compyled of gods holy lawes :
Of vertue and wyse olde sayd sawes,
That may to goodnes men procure,
Whyle here their lyfe dayes doe indure.

As thou wilt therfore at thy nede,   25
Haue hope and loue and also me,
So thou accomplishe this with spede :
My systers twayne therto agree.
And then they warned me all three,
That in this thyng I should not staye,   30
But make that booke without delaye.

My

The Prologue

My cunnyng small though then I knewe,
In eche degree my wytte full weake:
Though lacke of learnyng eke I rue,
Yet of excuse I durst not speake:
But granted my poore head to breake,
About suche exercyse, as she
So streyghtly had commaunded me.

5

At that instant they dyd me kys,
And frendly did from me departe,
To heauen they went all Iwys,
And lefte me with an heuy harte:
So their departure made me smarte.
And in that thought I waked thore,
Merueyling at my dreame full sore.

10

15

In songes therfore sythe I must wade,
Accordyng as my dreame me toulde,
I wyll delyght to treade the trade
That lady vertue sayde I should:
As blynde bayard none is so boulde,
And fyrste for lady vertues sake,
A song in hyr prayse wyll I make.

20

And then in mo procede I wyll,
As God shall geue me of his grace.
My wyt is rude, and small my skyll,
To stande and supplie suche a place.
Yet must I nedes walke in the trace,
That vertue did assigne me in,
Therfore in hyr prayse I beginne.

25

The

30

THE COURTE OF VERTUE

⟦ THE PRAYSE OF VERTUE

Al men that wyll walke in Gods de-uine wayes, To ver - tue they must geue ho -nor and prayse: for ver - tue is she by whom they possesse, All good fame and prayse that lcue god - ly - nes.

5

THERE neuer was man that wan godly fame,
But doubtles dame vertue was cause of the same.
Though Abram by fayth, was only made iuste,
By vertue that faythe was knowne and discuste.

Ye Isaac and Iacob, were compted lyke wyse,   10
Both faythfull and iuste in their exercise.
The patriarkes all from Adam to Christe,
With prophetes and kynges, that synne dyd resiste.

By

By vertue the praise of faith did obteyne :
Whiche yet to this daie, doth dure & remaine.
Ye Christ by the vertue, that in him was sene,
Aboue all the holy, that holiest haue bene,　　　　5

To be true Mesias, his flock did him know :
Whiche to this daye doth his foes ouerthrowe.
And he his disciples then charged eche one,
To folowe the steps that he so had gone.

Likewyse his Apostles, that since his tyme was,　　10
The martyrs and sainctes, to whom he gaue grace,
Their light did so shine, before the world here :
That by their true vertue, well dyd appere,

That they were true seruātes, of Christ their good lord,
Whom truly their liues, did preache and recorde.　　15
Let vertue therfore be had in all pryse,
Whiche styll to goodnes, doth good men entyse.

And well doth rewarde, all suche as hir serue,
And kepeth nought back, that they doe deserue :
But with goodnes styll, doth rychly augmente,　　20
All suche as vnto hir seruice be bent.

And neuer doth leue them, ne yet forsake,
Till ended be all, that they vndertake.
She neuer doth sease, to spurre them forwarde,
Tyll they be in blysse of heuens rewarde.　　25

Whiche is the whole thyng they seke for and sue,
That serue in the court of Lady vertue.
And styll for hir sake, doe suffer and byde,
The frumps and the mocks, of suche as deryde.

　　　　　　　　　　　　　　　Ye　　30

Ye hatred and scorne, and all kynde of spyghte,
Of suche as in vyce and synne doe delyght.
But vertue doth teache, to suffer this rage,
That we may styll passe on in our pylgrimage.   5

Considering that we but strangers are here,
And wander styll towarde our countrey dere.
And make ourselues lyght, from burden and lode,
Sythe in this vayne worlde, is no sure abode.

No meruaile though then the worlde doth them hate,   10
And euer be styll with them at debate:
For Christ vnto his hath made it well knowne,
The worlde shall aye loue and fauour his owne.

And those from the worlde and sinne that remoue,
It is not possible, the worlde should them loue.   15
The cause as sayeth Christe, of all this whole stryfe:
Is that from the worlde they differ in lyfe.

For as in this worlde no mans lyfe is sure,
The vertuous lyfe shall eternally dure.
Though here they be murdred and (sene for to die)   20
Of suche as all vertue and goodnes denye.

Then howe can we counte them short tyme to lyue,
To whom lady vertue rewarde doth gyue.
Whom as sayth Gelasius, ought styll to be,
From teror and dread, and wrath euer free.   25

Her consolation where she doth bestowe,
In ryche or in poore, in hyghe or in lowe,
From bondage of sinne she doth them free make:
Lo thus are her seruantes safe for hyr sake.

                                                    Among   30

of Vertue

Among the good rootes that depely besette,
Vertue sayeth Tullie, the chiefe prayse doth gette:
The whiche by no kynde of vyolence may
Be hurte or destroyde, by nyght or by daye.　　　　5

From wanton desyres her seruantes flee all.
And folowe styll iustice, as sayeth saint Paule:
Faith loue and vnitie well doth accorde,
In them whiche with cleane hartes honor the Lorde.

Lactantius also would all men remember,　　　　10
That they the true honor to vertue doe render.
With sensing or prayer she honor hath none,
Nor yet with an Image, of woodde or of stone:

But only with good wyll and purpose true,
This honor to vertue, alwayse is due:　　　　15
For he that in Christes fayth doth not remayne,
In no wyse to vertue may apertayne.

Vertue refreyneth wrath without measure,
And also absteyneth from carnall pleasure:
The frutes of the spiritie, as true godly loue,　　　　20
Pacience, and peace, and ioy from aboue,

Bounteousnes, goodnes, and longe sufferance,
Gentlenes, fayth, and modest temperance,
Sobernes, continence, and chastitie:
All these in vertues courte officers be.　　　　25

Therfore the quene vertue, it may well beseme,
To were a moste hyghe and ryche diademe.

　　　　　　　　　　The

⟦ THE PRAYSE OF FAITHE
Hebre. 11

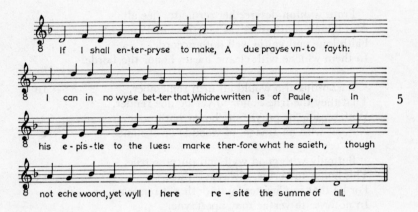

If I shall en-ter-pryse to make, A due prayse vn-to fayth:

I can in no wyse bet-ter that, Whiche written is of Paule, In   5

his e-pis-tle to the Iues: marke ther-fore what he saieth, though

not eche woord, yet wyll I here re-site the summe of all.

C   Faythe

Faythe is a perfect confidence,
Of thynges that hoped are,
And a most constant certeintie,
Of thynges whiche are not sene.   5
For therby did the fathers olde,
(As scripture doth declare,)
Obteyne a iust and good reporte,
That long tyme since hath bene.

And we through faythe doe vnderstande,   10
God dyd the worlde ordeyne,
By Christe his sonne the blessed worde,
That no beginnyng had.
By it also howe thynges were wrought,
We doe knowledge obteyne: 15
Thynges that are sene by thinges not sene,
Were ordeyned and made.

By fayth also (as we doe reade,)
The ryghteous man Abell,
Dyd offer vp a sacrifice,   20
More plentyfull then Cayne:
And therby had a wytnes true,
(As holy wryte doth tell,)
That he was iust: Though he be dead,
His fame doth styll remayne.   25

By fayth Enoch, translated was,
That death he should not see,
And was not founde: for god therfore
Had taken hym awaye.
Before whiche tyme he wan the name,   30
A ryghteous man to be,

Be-

Because he dyd the wyll of god,
And pleasde hym nyght and daye.

But sure without a lyuly fayth,
It can be in no wyse,   5
That any man by any meane,
The lyuyng god should please :
For all that come to god beleue,
(And their fayth exercyse,)
That he rewardeth them that seke   10
Hym, with eternall ease.

By fayth Noe (beyng warnde of god,)
Vnsene thynges dyd eschue,
Preparde an arke, and saude his folke,
As holy scripture sayth.   15
Wherby he dyd condemne the worlde,
That synne dyd styll insue :
And became heyre of ryghteousnes,
Accordyng vnto fayth.

By fayth our father Abraham,   20
When he first called was,
To goe into a place most strange,
Dyd by and by obeye.
Whiche place though he inherite should,
As after came to pas :   25
When he went forth he knewe it not,
Nor no part of the waye.

By fayth into the promyste lande,
I saye he dyd remoue,
A strange countrey where he dyd long,   30
In tabernacles dwell :

C2   And

And so dyd Isaac and Iacob,
Heyres with him from aboue.
All these dyd for a citie looke,
Which God had buylded well.　　　　　　　5

　Through fayth Sara receiued strength,
When she was nowe past age,
To conceyue and bryng forth a sonne,
That perfect was and pure:
Because she iudgde the promyser　　　　10
Both faythfull, true, and sage.
Lo thus by fayth there sprang great health,
Where thought was no recure.

　And therfore sprang there forth of one,
That dead was to esteme,　　　　　　　15
As many folke in multitude,
As are starres in the skye:
And as the sand on the sea shore,
Hir ofspryng then did seme,
The whiche without number to be,　　　20
No creature can deny.

　These dyed in fayth, yet the promys
None of them dyd receyue:
But seyng it as afarre of,
They dyd right well beleue,　　　　　　25
That as many as so it sawe,
And to the same dyd cleaue,
Salutyng it by liuly fayth,
None euell should them greue.

　These faythfull men the fathers olde,　30
As truthe was did confesse,

　　　　　　　　　　That

That they strangers and pilgrymes weare,
Vpon this earthly vale.
For they that see suche thynges before,
Of truth declare no lesse,   5
But that they doe a countrey seke,
Ryght hygh aboue this dale.

   Also if they had mynded once,
The countrey whence they came,
They had leysour to turne agayne,   10
To that whiche they dyd loue:
But now it shewes they dyd desyre,
A thyng of better fame,
That is to saye a heauenly soyle,
With God the lorde aboue.   15

   Wherfore the lyuing God hym selfe,
Estemeth it no shame,
To be called the God of these,
And suche lyke godly men:
For he a citie excellent,   20
Hath builded for the same,
And thynketh nothing ill bestowde,
That may well pleasure them.

   Who so the texte wyll farther reade,
To folowe there shall fynde,   25
That Isac, Iacob, and Ioseph,
And Moses did the lyke:
By fayth how the redde sea went back,
Contrary to his kynde:
As on drye lande howe Israell   30
Dyd passe through that drye dyke.

C3   The

The Egiptians when they the lyke
Would seme to enterpryse,
They lackyng fayth weare drowned all,
As for their iust rewarde.   5
By fayth the walles of Ierico,
Did falle downe in lyke wyse,
No force or engyn of the warres,
Against it once preparde.

The harlot Rahab in lyke wyse,   10
Howe she dyd saue hir lyfe,
And perisht not with them that dyd
Resist the wyll of god :
When she the spies receaued well,
In peace without all stryfe :   15
For she beleude, that god would plage,
That contrey with his rodde.

What should be sayde of Gedeon,
Of Barach, and Samson :
Iephte, Dauid, and Samuell,   20
And eke the prophetes all,
Who dyd by fayth great realmes subdue
And myghty kyngdomes wonne :
They turnde their enemies to flyght,
And gaue their foes a fall.   25

By fayth some stopt the lyons mouthes,
Some quencht the rage of fyre :
By fayth some wrought out rightousnes,
Some promyse dyd obteyne.
Some scapte the sworde, some were made strong,   30
Whom weaknes erste dyd tyre :

                                                        And

And women dyd their dead receyue,
To perfect lyfe agayne.

   Some racked weare, and would not voyde
The danger of that wo,   5
Knowyng that they should ryse agayne,
Possessing better ioye.
With mockes and scornes and prisonment,
Lo some were tryed so :
Some were stoned, some were tempted,   10
Thus did the worlde them noye.

   Some hewed were asonder quyghte,
Some with the sworde were slayne :
Some in the skynnes of shepe and gotes
Disdeyned not to go,   15
In trouble and necessitie,
They were content to reigne
In mountaynes, desertes, and in dennes,
By fayth this could they doe.

   These, was the worlde not worthy of,   20
Yet dyd it them despyse.
Though they did all (through lyuly fayth)
Obteyne a good reporte :
Yet dyd they not that tyme receyue,
That God dyd them promyse :   25
That we with them, and they with vs,
Myght ioynctly haue comforte.

   For Christe that holy promyse was,
The frute of all our fayth :
Without whom none can saued be,   30
No neither we nor they,

                 C4   For

For in hym all fulfilled is,
That holy scripture sayth:
Ye Christ is he in whom both we
And they our fayth doe staye.   5

    For which all honor laude & prayse
To God ascribed be,
To the father, and to the sonne,
And to the holy spyrite:
In vnitie, and trinitie,   10
One God and persons three,
As hath ben, is and shalbe styll,
For euer so be it.

⟦ THE PRAYSE OF HOPE, OUT OF MANY PLACES
              OF SCRIPTURE   15

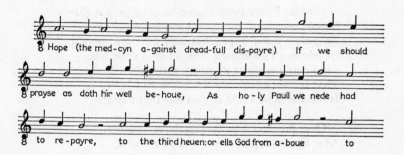

Hope (the med-cyn a-gainst dread-full dis-payre) If we should

prayse as doth hir well be-houe, As ho-ly Paull we nede had

to re-payre, to the third heuen: or ells God from a-boue to

                                        sound

sound his voyce, to one that he doth loue: as in the ho-ly mount

Moy-ses dyd here, And to E-li-as lyke-wyse did a-pere.

Or as the most blessed Apostles three,
At Olyuet, euen Peter, Iames, and Iohn,   5
Where they the glorie of the Lord dyd see,
Transfigured that holy mount vpon:
Beside which syght, they herde this voyce eche one:
This is myne only sonne and worde so bryghte,
In whom I fixe and set my whole delyght.   10

Who so I saye myght once haue suche a syghte,
Should afterward lacke no knowledge nor skyll,
To prayse dame hope, that lady pure and bryght:
In whom all good men haue of ioye their fyll.
Who could without despayre suffer the ill,   15
That in this worlde we dayly see and byde,
If blessed hope stode not on our ryght syde?

Our spirituall foes that dayly vs assaulte,
As is the fende, the flesh, and world also,

C5   With   20

With ignorance and error eke so haulte,
Behynde, before, we no where lacke a foe,
So that if hope once banyshte were vs fro,
Alas who could of gods fauour be sure,   5
That daily sethe his owne wayes so vnpure?

What man doth as god hath commanded playne,
That we should doe, or els perysh in hell?
Sith none therfore can there vnto attayne,
(For all doe disobey, synne and rebell: 10
Howe can we thynke in heauen then to dwell,
If blessed hope doe not oure fayth directe,
That we in Christe are vnto blysse electe.

In all the stormes of Sathans cruell rage,
Wherwith he seketh mans soule to destroye,   15
If in our soules good hope dyd not aswage,
The sorowes that doe seke the same to noye,
And comfort them with quietnes and ioye,
Assuryng them that doe their whole good wyll,
That Christ our lorde wyll all our wante fulfyll: 20

Without this hope I saye who could indure,
The boystrous brunte of this moste mortall fyght?
Our enmies are no babes I you assure,
But very strong in respect of our myght:
Wherfore we ought to praye both daye and nyght,   25
To god our lorde, that he woulde graunt vs aye,
That blessed hope with vs continue may.

Howe apte are we from comfort to decaye,
If we hyr helpe had not in our distres.
Sith she in Christe doth cause vs for to staye,   30
And to be bolde not fearyng our weaknes.

                                    Syth

Syth our captayne in his great manlynes,
Is able styll our foes for to withstande,
If we in hym that battell take in hande.

As sayth saynt Paule hope is the geft of god,   5
In whiche we are made safe in all our nede,
And takes away of care the heauy lode,
An armor strong, and spirituall indede,
An helmet sure, wherwith we may procede
Against the powres of darknes and of hell,   10
For heauenly thinges that we may wrestle well.

In it we ought to ioye and to reioyce,
As to the Romanes he doth farther saye:
And Peter also, with a feruent voyce,
Sayth that we ought without all doubt and staye,   15
To yelde a reason of our hope alway.
Hope is the meane that men to God drawe nere,
Without the whiche none faythfull may apere.

Who without hope can truly loue the lorde?
Who without hope can serue god in true feare?   20
Who without hope can cause his lyfe tacorde
To vertues lore, and fylthy synnes forbeare?
Who without hope can praye in true maner?
Who without hope can yelde god laude and prayse?
Who voyde of hope wyll walke in Christen wayes?   25

The blessed martyrs, by the hope and truste,
That they had in the glorious lyfe to come,
Dyd from this worlde withdrawe their mynde & luste:
And gladly suffred cruell martyrdom,
By fyre, by sworde, and briefly all the summe,   30
No kynde of death or tormente dyd despyse,
That wicked worldlynges could for them deuyse.

By

By hearyng scripture true hope doth procede,
And otherwyse can lyghtly not be had,
Confounded shall they neuer be in dede,
Whom perfect hope hath once with ioy made glad: 5
Whiche takes away all doubtfull dred so sad.
Whose hope in Christe therfore doth staye and reste,
We may well call them faithfull folke and bleste.

What so before tyme wrytten is sayeth Paule,
It written was vs to instructe and learne: 10
That we through comforte of the scriptures all,
And pacience: might perfectly deserne
The perfect hope, to hope in God eterne,
Lo thus doth God in scripture vs procure,
Through hope in him of heauen to be sure.   15

We knowe sayeth Paule that tribulacion,
Doth bryng forth pacience, that goodly grace,
And pacience doth render forth anon
Experience, the whiche doth hope purchace:
Whiche blessed hope who so that may imbrace,   20
She neuer wyll confound them with no shame,
But bryngeth forth a lyfe free from all blame.

This pure and perfect hope that we declare
The gift is of the Lorde and at his wyll,
Whiche none can get by worldly wytte nor care: 25
But with this hope god his electe doth fyll,
With whome she doth continue euer styll:
Not by mans wyll, but by gods mercy pure:
This blessed hope with good men doth indure.

The God of hope therfore replenysh vs,   30
With peace and ioye, and with a lyuly fayth,

And

And make vs ryche in hope of Christ Iesus,
And tholy ghoste, whose powre all mistruste stayth,
Whiche is our comfort as the scripture sayth.
This Trinitie be praysed now therfore,　　　　　5
As hath been, is, and shalbe euermore.

⟦ THE PRAYSE OF GODLY LOUE OR CHARITIE
OUT OF

1. Cor. 13. & Iohn. 4

Of Cha-ri-tie or god-ly loue　To make a per-fect prayse,　　　10

This god-ly loue to prayse I saye,　In or-der good and due.

I tooke to me gods word, and wrote What the ho-ly gooste sayes,

In di-uine Iohn and ho—ly Paule: whose wordes are ve-ry true.

Atende

Atende therfore ye Christians dere,
And louers of the Lorde,
Harke and geue eare vnto the truthe,
And blessed worde of lyfe :
And pray to god for perfect loue,
Your lyues therto accorde,
That ye may lyue in christen peace,
Free from all seruyle strife.

By office of a lyuly fayth
What euer we receyue,
Or by the office of our hope,
What so we doe retayne :
By charitie or godly loue,
To gods truthe if we cleaue :
The frute therof we must applie,
To render well agayne.

As faith the firste preferment hath
Our soules to iustifie,
(For by the same we only doe
Receyue our sauyng health :)
So loue of vertues is the chiefe,
Wherby we edefie,
By it we worke the wyll of god,
And seke our neyghbours wealth.

Though I coulde speake sayth Paul with tongues
Of men or angels bryghte,
And had no loue : then were I lyke
Vnto the soundyng bras,
Or lyke the tynklyng simbales sounde,
A short and vayne delyght :

                                        Whiche

5

10

15

20

25

30

Whiche beyng gon, men streight forget
What maner noyse it was.

Ye though that I could prophesie,
And secretes vnderstande,   5
All knowledge, or suche mighty fayth,
As could mountayns remoue,
And set them in the ocean seas,
Or in some other lande:
For all these yet I were nothyng   10
If that I had not loue.

If I dyd all my goodes bestowe
To fede therwith the poore,
Or geue my body to the fyre,
Therin consumde to be,   15
And finally all that I can,
Tyll I could doe no more:
If I be destitute of loue,
It doth not profite me.

Loue suffreth longe, is courteous,   20
And neuer doth enuye,
Loue neuer dealeth frowardly,
Nor venemously swell.
Loue seketh not hyr owne, therby
To deale dishonestly.   25
Loue vnto wrath prouoketh not,
But alwayes thynketh well.

In euels loue doth not reioyce,
Nor ioye in wyckednes,
But alwaye doth reioyce in truthe,   30
And suffreth all thynges well:

Bele-

Beleueth all, and hopeth all,
And doth indure no les.
Thus loue in goodnes doth excede,
All that our tongues can tell.   5

   Though prophesiyng doe faile, & serue
No vse in any case,
And tongues to speake, & knoledge to
As once they shall I saye :
(After this lyfe these haue no vse,)   10
Yet loue shall then in place,
Remayne, with gods elect in ioyes,
And neuer fall awaye.

   Our knowledge is but vnperfecte,
So is oure prophesiyng,   15
When perfectnes doth come in place,
Vnperfectnes must flee :
For when I was a chylde, my talke
Was then chyldysh talkynge :
Myne vnderstandyng in lyke case,   20
All then was chyldyshly.

   And as a chylde also that tyme
I dyd imagin playn :
But then so sone as manhod came,
My chyldishnes was gone.   25
Now see we but as in a glasse
By speache moste darke and vayne :
But then shall we see face to face,
When let there shall be none.

   My knowledge now vnperfect is,   30
Then shall it not be so,

                         Then

Then shall I knowe as I am knowne,
By rule of ryght beliefe.
Faith hope and loue doe nowe abyde
Away they will not goe: 5
And of all those after this lyfe,
Loue shall abyde as chiefe.

  Saynt Iohn diuinly counsels vs
One an other to loue,
For euery one that loues sayeth he,   10
Of God is truly borne.
For loue doth euer suerly come
From God the lorde aboue:
Suche as loue not, doe not knowe god,
But rather doe hym scorne.   15

  In this the loue of god to vs
Doth perfectly apere.
He (but not we) dyd truly loue
And payne for vs did take:
For he into thys worlde did sende   20
His only sonne so dere,
That for our sinnes he myght therby
A full agrement make.

  Wherfore (my louyng brethern dere)
If god so loued vs,   25
That we should one another loue,
We certeynly are bounde:
If we loue one an other then,
Our loue doth playne discusse,
That god in vs doth dwell and reygne,   30
And hath a perfect grounde.

         D   For

For god is loue, and who so doth
In loue abide or dwell,
Dwelleth in god and god in him,
Thus loue in vs is sure: 5
That in the day of iudgement iuste
We should in hope excell.
For in this worlde we are lyke hym,
By loue perfect and pure.

By this we knowe the godly loue,   10
That there in is no feare:
It casteth out all feare and doubte
Wherin is paynfulnes.
Wher timor is the perfect loue
In nowyse can be there,   15
For loue doth alwayes fixe hyr selfe
On peace and gentylnes.

If we loue god, he loude vs fyrst,
Then wherof can we boste?
But who so sayeth he loueth God,   20
And doth his brother hate:
He is a lyer verely,
And none of Christes hoste:
And therby doth prouoke the plage
To lyght vpon his pate.   25

For how can he that loueth not
His brother in this lyfe,
Whom he may with his eyes beholde,
At all tymes when he wyll:
Howe can he with the lyuyng god   30
Be other then at stryfe?

                              Or

39

Or loue him whiche he can not see
By nature or by skyll?

Therfore hath Christ cōmaunded vs,
That he whiche loueth god,   5
By perfect loue as he forbeares
All that god doth abhorre:
That he also his brother loue,
All hate is hym forbod.
All honour prayse and laude to god   10
For this nowe euer more.
    Amen.

⟦ THE PRAYSE OF GODLY WYSDOME
OUT OF THE BOOKE OF WYSDOME, CALLED

Sapientia. cap. vi.   15

The worth-y wyse kyng Sa-lo-mon   in wys-doms ex-er-cyse,

The god-ly wys-dome doth commende,   And praise hir on this wise.

D2   wisdom

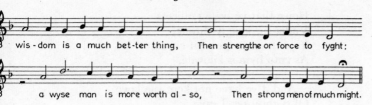

wis-dom is a much bet-ter thing,   Then strengthe or force to fyght:

a wyse man is more worth al-so,   Then strong men of much might.

This wysdome O ye myghtie kynges
Se that ye conne and learne,   5
To you sith iudgement on this earth
Is geuen to decerne.
Geue eare to hyr I saye all you,
That rule the multytude,
Whiche in much people haue delight,   10
And all thynges should conclude.

The god that gaue you powre & strēgth
That lorde I saye most hye,
Shall serch out all that ye inuente,
And your workes truly trye.   15

                              Howe

Howe that ye beyng officers
Vnder his kyngly throne,
Ye did not iudgement execute
As vnto hym is knowne.   5

   And if ye haue not kept the lawe
Of ryghtiusnes I saye,
Nor haue not done his blessed wyll
By walkyng in his waye:
Full horribly and that ryght sone   10
To you he shall apere,
And right hard iudgement shal they haue
By powre that gouerne here.

   His mercy sure he wyll extende
Vnto the innocent,   15
But suche as beare authoritie,
Shall haue sore punyshment,
For god whiche is the lorde of all,
By iudgement iust and ryght
Shall stande in awe of no mans powre,   20
Though he be of great myght.

   For he made both the great and small,
And cares for them alyke:
But they that be of greatest powre
The more he wyll them stryke.   25
Ye kynges eche one take hede therfore,
Se that ye ponder this,
And guyde your fete by wisdoms scole
That ye goe not amysse.

   All suche as obserue ryghteousnes,   30
Shall iudged be therby,

D3   Suche

Suche ryghteousnes who so wyll learne
Shall answere readily.
On wisdomes lore I saye therfore
Set all your loue and luste: 5
To nourture so ye shall atayne,
In season due and iuste.

   For wysdome is a noble thyng,
Whiche wyll not flete nor moue,
And wyll be sene full easily   10
Of all that doe hyr loue:
Suche as vnfaynedly hir seke,
She wyll preuent them so,
That they shall haue hyr in their syghte,
In eche place where they goe.   15

   Who so wyll wake to hir betyme
Shall haue no great traueyle,
For at his dore he shall hir finde,
She wyll him neuer fayle.
Ryght perfectly they vnderstand   20
That doe thinke hir vpon,
And they that watche for hir shalbe
Ryght safe and that anon.

   For she alwayse doth goe about
And seketh euery where,   25
For suche as for hir schole be mete,
And doe god loue and feare:
Before their eyes ryght chierfully
Hyr selfe she doth forth showe,
And meteth them dilygently,   30
Because they should hir knowe.

             The

The faythfull and the iust desire
Of reformation,
Is the beginning and the grounde
That wysdome buildeth on. 5
The busye care for wysdoms lore
Is loue and pure prudence,
And loue doth also kepe the lawes,
And that with dilygence.

To kepe the lawes is perfectnes, 10
And rightly doth accorde.
An vncorrupt lyfe maketh man
Familiar with the lorde.
Se that your ioye in royall seates
And scepters be not sette, 15
Ye kynges that doe the people rule,
By myghty powre and great.

But set on wysdom your delyght,
All folysh thinges abhorre:
That ye may reigne in glory great 20
With god for euer more.
O loue the lyght, all ye that rule
The congregation:
And I wyll make of wisdom nowe
A declaration. 25

What wisdome is, howe she came vp,
I will you tell this tyde,
The misteries of god the lorde,
From you I wyll not hyde:
But I wyll seke hir out in dede, 30
That all men shall it se

D4   Ye

Ye from the first oryginall
Of hyr natiuitie.

And bryng the knowledge of hyr lyght,
And shewe you all the grounde.   5
And as for keping backe the truthe,
In me shall not be founde:
Ne yet wyll I haue ought to doe
With enuy nor disdayne.
For why suche men in no wyse may   10
To wysdome aperteyne.

Where many wyse men haue abode
The worlde may ioyfull be:
And where as kynges by wysdome rule,
Their realmes haue equitie.   15
O aprehende hir nurtour then,
Let wysdom be your foode:
And at my wordes your councell take
For it shall doe you good.

I am a mortall man my selfe   20
After the common trade,
And am of that same very kynde,
With hym that first was made:
And formed in my mothers wombe
In fleshe there was I wrought,   25
And tenne moneths had my nutryment
Of bloud that there was brought.

Where through the fruitfull seede of man
I had my substance thus,
In whiche the apetite of sleape,   30
Is moste commodious.

                                              When

When I was borne I tooke lyke ayre,
As doe all others lo :
I fell on earth whyche was my kynde
In wepyng and in wo.   5

    I wraped was in swadlyng clothes,
And brought vp with great care :
For why no kyng can in their byrth
Haue other kynde of fare.
For all men in this wretched worlde   10
As well the kyng as slaue,
In entrance, and in goyng forth,
No kinde of difference haue.

    Considryng in my mynde howe that
The most rude multitude   15
Dyd nothyng differ from my byrth,
Nor death whiche doth conclude,
I me bethought therfore howe I
Myght in my beyng here,
Aboue the kynde of common men   20
Ryght excellent apere.

    For wysdom pure to vnderstande
Therfore was my desyre,
The spirite of wysdom came to me
As my harte dyd requyre,   25
By whom I set more pryce and ioye
Then by great kyngdoms fayre :
The royall seates or ryches great
With hyr shall not compare.

                 D5   And   30

And precious stones I neuer did
Compare to hir I saie,
For gould is grauell in hyr sight,
And syluer is but claye.
Wealth and beautie I wayed not,   5
But toke hyr for my light:
The beames of wysdome none can quĕch
That shyneth aye so bryghte.

By hir all thinges I did possesse,   10
All good thinges came to me,
The ryches without number is
That in hir handes styll be.
But yet in childyshe ignorance
I could not make dyscourse,   15
Of all good thinges howe wysdome is
The mother and the nource.

But nowe sithe I vnfeynedly
Haue learned what she is,
Partakers other men to make   20
Of hyr I will not mys.
Hyr ryches and hir treasure great
From you I wyll not hide:
Whiche passeth all infinitly
That is in this worlde wyde.   25

Whiche who so vse, they ioye with god
In friendship and great loue:
And in his syght excepted are,
Through wysdomes giftes aboue.
God hath me graunted wisdomes talke   30
In forme conuenient,

                                        To

To handle all whiche he to me
Hath graciously lent.

For he it is that to wysdome
Doth leade and introduce,   5
And teacheth howe that in hir kynde
Men shall hir ryghtly vse.
In hym are we, and all our wordes,
Our wysdome, and our skyll:
Our knowledge, and our science all,   10
Our workes, and all our wyll.

For vnto me he geuen hath,
The knowledge and the trade
Of all those thynges, so that I knowe
Howe that the worlde was made: 15
And by his wisdome hath me taught
Astronomy to knowe,
The elementes, with all their powrs,
And wonders whiche they showe.

Howe tymes doe both begin and ende,   20
The mydste of tymes I see:
Howe tymes alter and doe succede
Eche one in his degree.
I knowe the order and the ende
And course of euery yere,   25
The dispositions of the starres
To me doe well appere.

In naturall philosophie
I haue the perfect arte,
I knowe the nature of eche beaste   30
One from other aparte:

How

How some be gentill in their kynde,
Howe some in fury rage:
I knowe the cause, and howe one may
By wysdome them aswage.   5

    I knowe the wyndes of euery coaste,
Theyr natures hotte or colde:
And by that arte send shyps with sayles
To Ophir for muche goulde,
What mans imagination is   10
Some wyse some fonde and vayne:
By Adams lyne, and wysdoms lore,
The difference sheweth playne.

    I knowe the natures and degrees
Of eche plante in his kynde,   15
All herbes, & rootes that growe on earth
Their vertue I can fynde.
And howe they differ in degre
In qualitie and powre:
All secrete and vnsought knowledge,   20
Doth spryng in wysdoms flowre.

    Whiche he hath geuen vnto me
That all this worlde hath made,
He taught me howe to vse this flowre
That dures and doth not fade.   25
In hyr is spirite to vnderstande
In holy exercyse,
In knowledge great she doth abounde,
And all thynges that are wyse.

    I saye that with almyghty God   30
All only she is one,

Sub-

Subtyll and full of gentylnes,
And gracious alone.
She is courteous and discrete
Quycke, vndefilde, and playne: 5
Swete, and doth loue all that is good,
Reiectyng that is vayne.

She is sharpe, yet forbideth not
To doe ryghtly and well:
Kynde, sure, and free, and to be briefe   10
In vertue doth excell.
In althynges she is circumspecte
Wherof she taketh cure:
All knowyng spirites she doth receyue,
That are both cleane and pure.   15

For wysdom doth in nymblenes
All other thynges excell,
And therby through all thynges to pas
She doth atayne full well.
For of the lyuyng god she is   20
The breath of powre doubtlesse,
The cleanes of almyghty god
Therby she doth expresse.

Therfore can no defyled thyng
Come once within hyr syght,   25
For she the very bryghtnes is
Of euerlastyng lyght.
She is the myrror vndefylde
Wherin all good men see,
The Image of almyghty god   30
In his great maiestie.

                                    And

And for so muche as she is one,
All thynges are hyrs as due:
And beyng stedfast in hyr selfe,
She doth all thinges renewe.   5
Among the multitude of folke
She doth hir selfe conuaye,
And entreth into holy soules
In them to byde and staye.

She maketh god prophetes and frends,   10
The truthe to preache and tell:
For god doth loue none but suche men,
With whom wysdome doth dwell.
The sonne and starres may not compare
With hir in lyght I saye: 15
For why hyr lyght doth farre excede
The brightnes of the daye.

For be the daye neuer so bryght,
Yet night approcheth faste,
To quenche the beautie of the same   20
And puttes it out in haste:
But wisdome can not be subdude
I saye by wickednes,
Nor in hir sight to blemyshe hyr,
Can byde no folyshnes.   25

[*An example of a contemplatiue*
   minde in the seruice of God, out of the
   xxv. Psalme.

THE noble king Dauid by name,
Hauing the spirite of truthe,   30

Who

51

Who euer truly serued God,
Euen from his very youth:

  He knowyng that by humblenes
He sonest should aspyre,   5
To haue his prayer heard of God,
And obteine his desyre,

  Disdeined not vpon his knees
Hym selfe to prostrate lowe,
For sithe the harte must humble be,   10
Let outwarde members knowe

  That they shal not them selues refrain,
Their dutie to expresse:
My knees therfore shall doe their due,
So shall my handes no lesse.   15

  Myne eyes shall vpwarde also tourne
The heauens to beholde,
With stretched handes and bowed knees
My prayer to vnfoulde.

  My voyce I wyll not silent kepe,   20
But wyll expresse with tongue,
The meaning of a faythfull harte,
And sing it in a song.

  Debating with him selfe this thing,
Directing all aryght: 25
In this wyse he began to sing
To god with all his myght.

Ad te

of Vertue

Ad te dominum leuaui

TO the oh lorde I lyfte my soule,
My god I truste in thee:
O suffer not myne enemies   5
To tryumphe ouer me.

   Ne yet let such as in thee truste,
Rebuke or shame susteyne:
But rather confounde scornefull men,
That spitefully dysdeyne.   10

   To the I praye my kyng and god,
O shewe to me thy wayse:
And teach thy pathes O lord to me
Thy name that I may prayse.

   O lorde leade me to speake thy truthe,   15
And learne me to be iuste:
Myne only god and sauyng health,
All daye in thee I truste.

   Forget not lorde but call to minde
Thy tender mercy pure,   20
Let not thy louyng kyndnes slacke
That euer hath ben sure.

   Forget my sinnes, remember not
The fraylnes of my youthe:
For thy goodnes and mercy lorde,   25
Thynke vpon me with ruthe.

   O ryghteous lorde with frendlynes,
Wytsafe to shewe thy myght:

                            Wherby

Wherby thou shalt the sinners teache
To walke thy waye a ryght.

The simple thou doest teache & guyde
Thy perfect wayes to knowe,   5
And thou doste suche instructe aright
As humble be and lowe.

Thy wayes O lorde are mercifull,
Thy faythfulnes is bent,
To all that kepe thy couenant,   10
And faythfull testament.

For thy names sake therfore O lorde
Be mercifull to me,
And to my synnes that are so great
And myne iniquitie.   15

Who so therfore doth feare the lorde,
He wyll hym shewe I saye:
His hyghe and his diuine preceptes,
His pure and chosen waye.

His soule shall euer be at ease   20
His wayes shal prosper well:
His sede also shall styll possesse
The lande, therin to dwell.

The lorde his secretes dothe shew forth
To suche as feare him styll,   25
Declaring them his testament,
His couenant and will.

                E   O lorde

O lorde my god to the therfore,
I wyll myne eyes dyrecte,
And praye to thee tyll thou haste losde
My fete out of the nette.   5

O turne thee vnto me therfore
Now for thy mercies sake,
Consider lorde my mysery
Howe I am desolate.

The sorowes of my harte are great,   10
Ryght sore they doe me greue:
O ryd me from these troubles all,
For in thee I beleue.

O loke on myne aduersitie,
And my great mysery: 15
Forgeue me all my sinnes also
Where I offended thee.

Consider how myne enemies
Are many and peruearte,
That towardes me maliciously   20
Are bent with hatefull hearte.

Oh preserue thou my soule therfore
Within thy kepyng iust:
And let me not confounded be,
For in thee doe I truste.   25

Let iust dealyng and innocent,
O god styll with me dwell:
And from all vyle aduersitie
Delyuer Israell.

                                              An   30

55

⟦ *An example how that we should*
   alwayes be thankefull vnto almighty God for his benefites, out of the
   xxxiiii. psalme of Dauid.   5

AS in our streightes of nede
We all are glad and fayne,
Some comfort at the handes of god
By prayer to obtayne.

   So when we haue receud   10
Of god our whole desyre,
That we should therfore thankfull be,
Good reason doth require.

   For who so benefites
At mortall men receaue,   15
If afterwarde the geuer dothe
Ingratitude perceaue:

   The same will streyght withdrawe
His liberalitie,
From suche a stubberne blocke hed beaste,   20
As can not frendshyp see.

   If vyle ingratitude
To men be suche a cryme,
That it wyll frendly loue kepe backe,
Against an other tyme: 25

   What beastly dogges are they?
Howe can we call them lesse?
That for great kyndnes of the lorde,
Doe paye vnthankfulnesse?

                    E2   Whiche   30

56

Whiche asketh nought of vs
But honour laude and prayse,
For all the good he doth bestowe
On vs a thousand wayes.   5

Wherfore that noble kyng,
And prophet of the lorde
Dauid, who dyd after Gods harte
Agree and well accorde,

Gods glorie doth expresse,   10
In doyng of his due :
And for the benefites of God
His harte declareth true :

Not only in hym selfe
To flee ingratitude,   15
But other also to instructe
That are vnlernde and rude.

In darke obliuion
Gods goodnes for to hyde,
Or to forget his benefites   20
Dyd neuer hym betyde.

His harpe he toke in hande,
And thus began to synge :
That with gods honour laude and prayse,
All Israell dyd rynge.   25

Benedicam dominum

I WYLL vnto the lorde
Be geuing thankes alwayes,

My

My mouth and tungue shall euer be
A speakyng of his prayse.

    My soule shall make hyr boste,
In God the lorde of myght,   5
That poore oppressed men may here
The same, them to delighte.

    Together let vs nowe
In honor doe our partes,
His name to prayse and magnifie,   10
With meke and humble hartes.

    For when I him besought,
He heard my prayer so,
That he did streyght delyuer me,
From all my care and wo.   15

    Receaue therfore the lyght
And to hym drawe you nere:
And so without all shamefastnes
Your faces shall appere.

    For I poore man made once   20
To him my playnte and mone:
He heard me crye, and dyd me ryd,
From troubles euery one.

    His angell pytched hath
His tente about his shepe,   25
I meane all suche as feare the lorde,
In saftie them to kepe.

    His frendshyp proue and see,
And take therof a taste:

             E3   For   30

For they that truste in hym are sure
Most happy at the laste.

O feare the lorde all ye
His saynctes of him electe: 5
For such as feare him lacke nothyng,
He doth them well protecte.

The lyons ofte doe lacke
And hunger for their foode:
But they which seke the lord, shal wante   10
Nothyng the whiche is good.

Ye children all I saye
Come harken to my voyce:
I wyll you teache to feare the lorde,
And in him to reioyce.   15

If thou to lyue in ioye
And see good dayes be fayne,
Thy lyppes & tongue from guyle & wrõg
See that thou doe refrayne.

Se that thou doe none ill,   20
In goodnes neuer cease:
But se thou seke and folowe faste
On quietnes and peace.

The lorde doth fixe his eyes
On iust men louingly,   25
And to their prayers openly
He doth his eares applye.

Con-

Contrariwyse the Lord
Doth bende his countenance,
Of from the earth ill men to moue
And their rememberance.   5

But to the iuste the lorde
Doth so inclyne his eare,
That when they praye he wyll them ryd
From all trouble and feare.

The Lorde is nyghe to suche   10
As are in harte contrite,
And he wyll saue suche as be meke,
And of an humble sprite.

Though iust mens troubles be
Both manifolde and great,   15
The lord from care wyl make them free,
When they doe him intreate.

Their bones he wyll defende,
And kepe so free from cryme:
That not so muche as one of them   20
Shall breake at any tyme.

Misfortune or ill happe,
The wicked men shall kyll,
And suche as doe the iust men hate,
Shall peryshe in their ill.   25

The Lorde will saue the soules
Of all that doe hym serue,
And all that put their trust in hym
Shall not in peryll swerue.

E4   *An*   30

⟦ *An example that God heareth all*
such prayers as are made with a faithfull harte, out of the. liiii. Psalme.

EVERY good phisicien,   5
That doth a medcyne proue
To take effecte in curyng well,
Is striken streyght with loue,

  Not only to geue god the prayse
For his vertue and grace: 10
But dothe the same in wryting put,
To comfort all his race.

  That all whiche after folowe hym
In that moste godly arte,
May proue the lyke and prayse the lorde   15
In lyke case for their parte.

  Noble kyng Dauid in suche wyse
Doth godly loue bestowe,
By wryting medcines for the soule,
That other men may knowe.   20

  As if they doubte at any tyme
Howe he dyd health obteyne,
He dyd the same declare abrode
In wryting to remayne:

  That when to others lyke distres   25
Here after may betyde,
With cleane hartes that they may prepare,
And lyke medcines prouide.
                                        But

But I will neuer teache (quod he)
In darke or doubtfull waye,
But suche as I in practice dyd
By perfect proofe assaye: 5

And of my selfe *probatum est*,
Suche medicines I bryng:
And in example to you all
In this wyse wyll I synge.

Deus in nomine tuo.   10

O GOD I call to thee for helpe
In my distresse and nede
For thy names sake, & in thy strē-
Auenge my cause w̓ spede.   (gthe,

For strangers full of tyranny   15
Against me ryse and raue:
Such folyshe folke as feare not God
Doe seke my lyfe to haue.

But lo God is my helpe at nede,
Yea only it is hee,   20
That doth my soule vpholde and saue,
From their iniquitee.

And euell shall the lorde rewarde
Vpon myne enemyes,
And in his truthe destroy them all   25
That vertue doe despyse.

With offrynges of an harte most free,
Now wyll I prayse thy name:

E5   Because

Because O lorde my comfort styll
Consisteth in the same.

    For thou lorde didst delyuer me,
From troubles manyfolde: 5
So that vpon my foes myne eye
Doth his desire beholde.

    For this to geue glory to god
Shall be my hartes delyght,
To the father, and to the sonne,   10
And to the holy sprite:

    As it from the begynnyng was,
And at this time is sure,
And as it shall worlde without ende
Continue and endure.   15

⟦ *An example that the thankefull*
    age gaue prayse to god, for al his bene-
    fites geuen to his creatures, out of the
    lxv. Psalme of Dauid.

I HERDE a preacher once declare,   20
Two partes to be in prayre,
The one to god in all our nede
For succor to repayre,

    And aske of hym with stedfast fayth
All wherof we haue nede: 25
For Christ hath surely promysed,
That therof we shall spede.

                    The

The second part of perfect prayre
Is geyung thankes and prayse,
To God for all his benefites,
That we receyue alwayes.   5

This is the lyuly sacrifice,
The lyuing God to please:
As prayer of the penitent,
His anger doth appease.

And sure (quod he) the very cause   10
That god ofte wyll not here,
Is that men for his benefites
Vnthankfull doe appere.

For when we praye in tyme of nede
For plenty of our foode,   15
Howe can we thinke that God to vs
Will geue ought that is good?

If we in tyme of plentie be
Vnthankfull and ingrate,
To geue him praise and honor both,   20
According to the rate?

Yea I may also farther saye,
This lyuing without awe,
Ingratitude doth cause the lorde
His goodnes to withdrawe.   25

And surely Dauid in this Psalme
Lykewyse doth well declare,
That to prayse God we neuer should
Any tyme cease or spare.

                                              But   30

But for the goodnes whiche god doth
On mortall men bestowe,
In prayse of his most holy name,
Some thankfull psalme to showe.　　　　　5

Howe men shall with a faythfull harte
Gods holy name agnise,
He doth instruct all Christen men
By synging in this wyse.

Te decet hymnus deus in Sion.　　　　　10

TO the O God in Sion still
Great prayses are in store:
To the also they vowe and kepe
Their promyse euer more.

My prayer lorde sithe thou dost heare,　　　　　15
And art my whole comfort:
All fleshe to the for succour shall
In their due tyme resorte.

My mysdedes and my wickednes
Against me doth preuayle,　　　　　20
Oh to my sinnes be mercifull,
That thus doe me asayle.

For thei are blest whom thou dost chose,
And in thy house retayne:
Or doste elect, within thy court　　　　　25
To dwell and to remayne.

For

For he shall leade a plesant lyfe
Within thy holy place:
Thy temple shall hym satisfie
With goodnes and with grace.   5

For wonders great thou doest declare
In truthe to teache vs ryght:
O god of our saluation
In the is our delyghte.

Of all thynges how thou arte the hope   10
It can not be discuste:
All that on earth or sea remayne,
In the doe hope and truste.

Thou gyrded haste thy selfe also,
With myghty strength and powre,   15
And hast the myghty mountaynes sette
As they stande at this howre.

Thou of the sea stillest the waues,
Their roryng and their rage,
The madnes of the multitude   20
Thou also canst aswage.

The outmoste dwellers on this earth,
Thy signes doe see and feare:
By the mornyng and euenyng starres,
Thy prayses doe appeare.   25

The earth eke howe thou visitest
With good it for to blesse,
And bryngest plentie on the same,
We knowledge and confesse.

For   30

For the ryuer of god doth flowe
So full of water pure,
That on the earth plentie of corne
For man he doth procure. 5

The sorowes he doth water so
That clotts doe breake in pece,
Swete drops of rayne doth soften them,
And cause ful great increce.

The yere thus doth he crowne & blesse 10
With plentie and goodnes,
The clowdes do drop great fatnes down
Ingendring plentiousnes.

The dwellinges in the wyldernes
Are fat in lyke maner: 15
The little hilles on euery syde
Doe plesantly appere.

The fouldes with shepe, ẙ vales with corne,
So ratefie this thing:
That in thy prayse for very ioye, 20
All people laughe and synge.

⟦ *An example howe happye and*
blessed they are that faythfully feare
god, out of the Cxii. Psalme.

SVCHE good historiographers 25
As wryte the dedes of men,
Of kynges & lordes, some good some ill,
That reigned nowe and then:

As

As they doe wryte of euell men
In rebuke and disprayse,
That lyuing men may lerne to flee
And voyde suche wicked wayes.   5

So doe they prayse and muche cōmend
Suche men as lyued well,
The worthy and the noble actes
Wherein they did excell.

That others they myght so prouoke   10
To folowe in lyke wyse,
To wynne the spurres of godly fame
By vertues exercise.

So Dauid to prouoke all men
To godlynes and grace,   15
Doth vse the lyke, that all men may
The feare of god imbrace.

In fayth howe that the feare of god
All goodnes styll dothe bryng,
He vsed in an holy Psalme   20
In this wyse for to syng.

Beatus vir qui timet.

THE man is blest and happy which
Doth feare the Lorde aryght,
And to kepe his cōmaūdementes,   25
Dothe set his whole delyght.

                                        His

His streene or sede vpon the earth
With myght shall be increste,
Thus shall the kynde of faythfull men
Eternally be bleste. 5

For ryches ioye and plentie great
His house shall wynne and gayne,
His iust dealyng and ryghteousnes
For euer shall remayne.

For to the godly in darknes 10
Great lyght there doth aryse:
Whiche sheweth loue and mercy both
In vertuous exercyse.

A good man sure is mercifull
And lendeth where is nede, 15
And doth discretly waye his wordes
Before they doe procede.

And suche a man for no distres
From god wyll moue or flee:
Wherfore his ryghteousnes shall haue 20
Eternall memorie.

Of ill tydynges or heauy newes,
Suche one is not afrayde:
His hearte doth stande faste and beleue,
The lorde to be his ayde. 25

His harte I saye is stablyshed,
And wyll not shrynke, vntyll
That he vpon his enemies
Hath his desire and wyll.

He 30

He from his store abundantlye
Disperseth to the poore:
For righteousnes are all his workes
And doynges euer more.   5

   With honor shall his horne or strengthe
Exalted be on hye:
Whiche when the vngodly beholde,
They wyll the same enuye,

   Which in their hate shal gnash their teeth   10
And so consume away:
Thus in their owne luste wycked folke
Shall peryshe and decaye.

⟦ *An example of the prayse of God,*
   for his omnipotencie, out of the. Cxiii.   15
   Psalme.

KYNG Dauid knowyng well,
Howe vertue dyd excell
All other worldly thyng:
Did chiefly in Gods feare,   20
All wyckednes forbeare,
That may gods anger brynge.

   For god is of suche powre,
That nothyng at no howre
Can hym withstande or byde: 25
For he may worke his wyll
All mortall men vytyll,
At euery tyme and tyde.

             F   Ther-

Therfore we are al bownde,
That dwell in this worlde rounde,
To prayse the lyuing lorde:
And in that lorde of myght   5
To set our whole delight,
And in his holy worde.

Wherfore this noble kyng
Studied aboue all thyng
His dutie to walke in,   10
To syng Gods laude and prayse,
He maketh no delayes,
But thus he doth begynne.

Laudate pueri dominum.

YE seruantes prayse the lorde,   15
And with hartye accorde
Se that ye doe the same:
Loke that ye render store
Of prayses euer more,
Vnto his blessed name.   20

His name that we should prayse,
He is worthy alwayse,
Euen from the rysing tyme
Of the sonne fayre and bryght:
Vntyll it be in sight,   25
That downe he doth inclyne.

The lorde is hie of myght,
There is no kynde of wyght,

That

That can with hym compare:
His gloris certainly
Aboue the heauens hye
Remayne and euer are.   5

   Who is lyke vnto him,
Or wyll presume to clymme
Where he so hygh doth dwell?
Yet is this lorde so meke,
To beholde and take kepe   10
Of earth and heauen well:

   Whoe doth the symple take
Out of the myery lake,
To set them vp agayne:
He takes out of the dust   15
All that in him doe truste,
To ryd them from their paine.

   So that he may them sette
Among the prynces great,
By his great powre and myght: 20
The prynces all among,
Whiche gouerne doe the thronge
Of people daye and nyght.

   He doth redeme also
The woman from hir wo,   25
That barayne long hath bene:
A mother full of blys
Of children nowe she is,
Hir housholde may be sene.

F2   *An*   30

⟦ *An example how Dauid praysed*
God, for his delyueryng of Israell, by
great miracles, out of Egypt. Out of
the. C.xiiii. Psalme.   5

WHOSO in *Exodus* wyll reade,
Shall see what wonders god there wrought:
From Egypt when as he dyd leade
His people, and from thence them brought.

What myracles by Moses hande,   10
To Pharao was expressed playne:
That he therby myght vnderstande,
No more gods people to restrayne.

And how God by his mighty powre
And stretched arme did bryng them thence: 15
And howe the red sea dyd deuoure
Kyng Pharao for his recompence.

And howe God did in wyldernes,
Prouyde his people drynke and meate:
So that they lackte in their distres,   20
No kynde of thynge to drynke or eate.

Whiche Dauid bearyng well in mynde
Did with a Psalme geue god the prayse:
And doth therto all good men bynde,
With godly harte lo thus he sayes.   25

In exitu

In exitu Israel de Egypto.

FROM Egipte lande when Israell,
(where they lõg tyme weare thraule & bonde)
From among people strange and fell,   5
When Iuda gan to scape the honde:

This Iuda then I saye was made
His holy people and his flocke,
And Israell was in lyke trade
Becomde his lordship all the stocke.   10

Whiche when the ragyng sea behelde,
It fled as one should it desire:
And Iordan in lyke case dyd yelde,
And backwarde did turne, and retyre.

The mountaynes at the sight of this,   15
Could not be styll but skipte lyke rammes:
The little hylles eke would not mis,
But leaped lyke the playing lammes.

If one myght aske what ayled thee
Thou sea, that thou dydest so forbeare?   20
And Iordan what cause myght there be,
That draue the backe in suche a feare?

Ye myghty mountaynes in lyke case,
Why skipped you lyke rammes I saye?
Ye little hilles, why from your place   25
Gan ye to leape as lammes doe playe?

All the whole earth it shall behoue,
When Iacobs God shall be present,

F 3   To

To tremble shake and muche to moue,
And in his sight hym reuerent.

  For at his wyll he turned tho
The hard rocke in to water clere,   5
Conuertyng harde flynte stones also
To springyng welles as dyd appere.

⟦ *An example of praier against ido-*
latrous tyrātes, that set vp false worship, in the reproche of Gods true worshyp.   10
Out of the. Cxv. Psalme.

IF vnto vs poore mortall men
No prayse is due of very ryght,
Howe are they mockte and blynded then,
How farre are they from perfect sight?   15

  That to a stocke or dead Image
Wil geue such laude as god should haue?
How vayne is he, howe doth he rage
That doth Gods glorie so depraue?

  The whiche sinne and most vyle offēce,   20
Dauid did so abhorre and hate,
That he a Psalme in Gods defence
Compiled hath: that eche estate

  May vunderstande howe farre awrye
They wandred be from righteousnes,   25
The lyuing God that doe denye,
By an Image or false lykenes.

                And

And therefore doth all men exhorte
To feare the lorde and in hym truste:
Whiche is a true and sure comforte
To all that in his hope are iust.   5

His harpe in hande he therefore tooke,
And on his knees this noble kyng
(As it is in the Psalter booke)
This holy Psalme began to synge.

Non nobis Domine.   10

NOT vnto vs lord, not to vs
But to thy holy name alwayse,
For thy mercy & truthe done thus,
Ascribed be all laude and prayse.

These heathen folke that faythles be,   15
Why should they saye to vs in spighte?
Where is their God let vs hym see,
In whom these Christians haue delyghte.

For their false Gods their chiefe & best,
Are nothyng but syluer and goulde: 20
The handes of men both most and lest,
Haue forged them out of the moulde.

Yet haue they for their idols made
Mouthes, wher͗ they can speak nothing
And eyes also wherof the trade,   25
Is to be blynde from all seyng.

Suche eares also in them are wrought
As heare nothyng that one can tell:

                         F4   And

76

And noses whiche are likewyse nought,
For they with them can nothyng smell.

Vayne handes haue they and fete also,
For with their handes they handle not: 5
Nor with their feete they can not goe,
Nor sounde no voyce out of their throte.

Wherfore suche as doe Idols make,
Doe their owne workes resemble iust,
And they also that doe them take   10
For Gods, or haue in them their truste.

Let Israell then in the lorde
Set all their truste and confidence:
And Araons house therto accorde
For he is their most sure defence.   15

All ye that feare the lorde aright,
Truste in hym well be not afrayde:
For he will surely shewe his myght
To succoure you and be your ayde.

The lorde will not forget doubtles,   20
But haue vs in his mynde full well,
The ryghteous houses he wyll bles
Of Araon and of Israell.

Ye that doe feare the lorde therfore,
Are blessed both the great and small: 25
The lorde increase you more and more,
Both you and eke your children all.

For

For sithe ye are his chosen sorte,
And haue the lord whole in your thought,
He wyll you blesse with great comforte,
Both heauē & earth that made of nought.　　5

The heauens and the firmament
Are his and at his holy wyll:
But the rounde earth he hath forth lente
The sonnes of mortall men vntyll.

The dead O lorde that are gone hence　　10
Can not in graue expresse thy wayes:
Nor suche as downe are in sylence,
Can honor thee or geue the prayse.

But we O lorde that be alyue
Thy prayse wyll spreade and ramifye,　　15
And in our hartes due thankes contryue
Vnto thy name eternally.

An example of prayer from a re-
pentant harte out of the. Cxxx. psalm.

SYTHE in this worlde all men doe fall　　20
And none from sinne is free and clere:
It doth behoue we study all,
In humblenes for to appere.

For in this lyfe we dayly see,
By stoutnes none can wynne nor gayne,　　25
But rather it in eche degree
Doth purchase woe and cruell payne.

F5　　　Who

Who is so fonde if he offende,
To stande hym selfe to iustifie?
And rather doth not knele and bende
Tyll he haue pardon and mercy?   5

The noble prynce Dauid therefore,
Knowyng the frutes of humblenes:
Did frō his harte powre forth great store,
Of teares and contrite gentilnes.

Because he would all men should lerne   10
The lyke to doe in their great nede:
He sheweth howe his harte did yerne,
Tyll he had felte mercy in dede.

Him selfe prostrating in due wyse
For sorowe of his greuous sinne,   15
In prayer was his exercise:
Thus doth his humble sute begynne.

De profundis clamaui.

FROM care of harte that caue so depe,
So hath my soule my sinnes abhorde: 20
Repentantly I humbly crepe,
And call to thee for helpe O lorde.

O lorde witsafe my voyce to here,
I thee beseche to bowe thyne eares.
Suffer my prayer to appere,   25
Pourde forth to thee w̃ piteous teares.

For if thou wylt for euermore
Our wyckednes laye by thy syde,

                              Or

79

Or kepe a note of them in store:
Oh lorde who then mayest abide.

Thy mercy lorde then make vs taste,
Whiche is to thee most naturall: 5
That graciously forgeue thou mayste,
And rayse them whiche by frailtie fall.

This made me on the lorde to wayte,
My soule also on hym to byde:
His promise is without deceyte,   10
And from his worde he wyll not slyde.

My soule hath more earnest delyghte
Vpon the lorde to watche and staye,
Then watchmen, whiche wake al y̆ night
And long ryght sore tyll it be daye.   15

Let Israell the Lordes electe,
(The iust that godly be and wyse,)
Haue to the lorde their whole respecte:
For mercy is his exercyse.

This Israell I saye he shall,   20
All wickednes from them expell,
From sinnes he shall redeme them all,
Though thei be more then tongue can tel.

Glory be to our god aboue,
The father whiche of myght is moste,   25
And to the sonne as doth behoue,
And also to the holy ghoste:

As

As it from the beginning was,
And yet doth to this tyme extende,
And shall be still as tyme shall pas
For euer more worlde without ende.   5

⟦ *An example that as wel penitent*
prayer, as ioyfull thankes and prayse,
haue their due tyme and place, out of
the. Cxxxvii. Psalme.

AS eche thinge hath his due tyme here,   10
On this earth where we goe:
So is ther tyme for ioye and glee,
And eke for care and woe.

    For as we ioye in tyme of welth,
Praysing the lorde therfore: 15
So in the tyme of pensyunes,
Of myrth we make no store.

    In one subiecte two contraries
Can neuer well agree:
Both myrth and wo at once in one   20
A strange thyng were to see.

    It would be thought a great madnes,
In ioye to wayle and wrynge:
Neither can it be coumpted les
In sorowe for to synge.   25

    As when the Iewes in Babylon
Where they were captiue all,

                        Com-

Commaunded were to playe and synge,
Of suche as made them thrall.

Which vaine request of their great foes,
These miserable Iewes   5
Would not accomplyshe in no wyse,
But did the same refuse.

They hangde asyde their instrumentes
And laide their songes awaye,
And knewe it was not tyme to synge: 10
But rather for to praye,

That god would them delyuer once,
From that their bondage vyle:
Wherin they had bene punyshed
A long and wery whyle.   15

But after thre score and tenne yeres,
When God them home had broughte,
With holy psalmes to prayse his name,
They diligently sought.

And in remembrance of the wo,   20
And bondage, where they were,
And ioye of their deliuerance,
They songe as ye shall here.

Super flumina Babilonis.

ONCE as we by the ryuers sate   25
That runne in Babylon,

                                        With

With bytter teares waylyng our wo,
When we thought on Sion:

  We layde a syde our thankfull tunes,
Of honour laude and prayse,   5
And hung our harpes on wylow trees,
That grew there in those dayes.

  Therfore our foes whiche to that land
As captiues did vs bryng,
(The more our sorowes to augmente,)   10
Required vs to sing.

  Cōmaunding vs with spightful scorne
And great derision:
Sing vs (quod they) some hebrue songs
Of your blessed Sion.   15

  As though it were conuenient
Contrary to gods wyll,
Suche vayne preceptes of wycked men,
To folowe or fulfyll.

  In suche a lande gods laude to singe   20
With songes of his swete worde:
Where Images the honor haue
That due is to the lorde.

  If euer we Ierusalem
So from our myndes consume: 25
We wysh our right handes might forget
Our harpes to touche in tune.

                  And

And that our tongues within our mouth
May cleue we are content,
When we should vtter any thyng,
That mynde may vs inuente: 5

Thy prayses oh Ierusalem
If we preferre not styll,
Before the moste or greatest ioye
That hap may vs vntyll.

These Edomytes our enemyes   10
Oh lorde remember them,
Their wyckednes when they destroyde
Thyne owne Ierusalem.

Among them selues thus gan they say,
Our citie to confounde: 15
Destroye and sacke it, down with it,
And rase it to the grounde,

And thou O daughter Babylon,
(Well worthy of no les)
Thy mirthe shall turne to misery,   20
And thy ioye to distres.

And he shall be a happy man
That with suche lyke agayne
Shall the rewarde, as thou didst vs,
With great reprofe and payne.   25

Ye blessed shall he be in dede
That shall rewarde the once,
In takyng of thy suckyng babes
And dashe them to the stones.

                                    An   30

⟦ *An example of Gods prayse, for*
his great care ouer his elect, in disa-
pointing their enemies & delyueringe
them. out of the. Cxl. Psalme.   5

WHAT can the mortall man
Inuente deuyse or skan,
Against the wyll of god?
Or howe can we withstande,
Of god the heuy hande,   10
His myghty plague and rod?

    What nede we then to care,
What wicked men prepare,
With crafte vs to destroye?
Sythe god the Lorde of all,   15
Can bryng vs out of thrall,
And turne our care to ioye?

    The noble kyng Dauid
The lyke thyng hath proued,
That who so feare the lorde,   20
There shall no wyght preuayle
Though they doe vs assayle:
With workes of god abhorde.

    For in his tyme of nede
He prayed with all spede,   25
To god for helpe and ayde:
As it doth folowe here,
And ryght well doth appere,
What he therein hath sayde.

                              Eripe   30

Eripe me domine.

DELIUER me O Lorde
Accordyng to thy worde,
Lorde let me not be shent.
On me some pitie haue,
From subtyle wayghtes me saue,
Of enmies violent.   5

In heart they thynke myschiefe,
And seke to doe me griefe
Their tongues they whet so sharpe   10
As aders venym vyle:
That they may vs beguyle,
Full wycked wyles they warpe.

Kepe me O lorde therfore,   15
From enmies euer more,
Whiche wicked be and ill:
Thy helpe let me not wante,
For they would me supplante
From doyng of thy wyll.   20

These proude men they haue sette
For me a pryuy nette,
Where I should out and in:
Yea and in my pathwaye
My soule for to betraye,   25
They laye bothe snare and gyn.

Lorde therfore haue I sayde
Thou art myne only ayde,
Lorde here my depe desyre:
O Lorde thou art my welth,   30

G   O God

O God my sauing health,
Graunt me that I require.

 Let not these men vnpure
On me take their pleasure,   5
Destroye their ill intente:
They are so proude and haulte,
That they them selues exalte,
Therfore let them be shente.

 I meane suche men as be   10
Of their great subtiltie,
At no tyme vnpreparde:
Lorde in their owne deceyte,
Wherwith they layde suche weyte.
Let their owne fete be snarde.   15

 Let coles of fyre fall downe,
And cast them on their crowne,
And throwe them into hell
From whence howe for to ryse
There is no tongue so wyse,   20
That can them rede or tell.

 Let nothyng prosper well
On earth where suche men dwell,
Reproue their ryche renowne:
To mischiefe they be wunte.   25
With plages therfore them hunte
And hedlong throw them downe.

 I knowe the lorde will wounde,
And vtterly confounde,
All men to pryde adicte: 30

     And

And wyll auenge in dede
The poore that stande in nede,
And are thus sore afflicte.

The ryghteous verely   5
Shall prayse and magnifie
Thy holy name therfore:
The heartes of pure pretence,
Shall dwell in thy presence,
Good lorde for euer more.   10

⟦ *An example howe to prayse God*
for his almyghty powre, and gentylnes. Out of the. Cxlv. Psalme.

AS he that would set forth to men,
The prayse of some good kyng,   15
To cause his subiectes hym to loue:
And obey in all thynge,

Doth shew to them his great goodnes,
His powre and all his myghte
That therby he may cause all folke,   20
In him to haue delyght:

And also that his enemies
The more may stande in feare,
And where perhaps they would rebell
To cause them to forbeare: 25

So Dauid doth gods glory shewe,
And powre omnipotente,
To make harde hartes that feare not God,
To soften and relente.

G2   That   30

88

That they myght come in vnitie
Of God and of his lawe,
And leaueth no good meanes vnsought,
Them to intyse and drawe.   5

    That vniformely mortall men,
Whiche in this worlde doe dwell:
Myght all agree praysinge the lorde,
And in vertue excell.

    Whiche if ye staye or stande in doubte   10
Howe to begynne this game,
Take here a Psalme, which will instruct
And leade you in the same:

Exaltabo te deus.

O GOD that arte myne only kyng,   15
I wyll thee magnify:
And so set forth thy laude & praise
To dure eternally.

    From daye to daye euen euery daye,
Great thankes I wyll thee gyue,   20
And prayse thy name for euer more,
Whyle I haue tyme to lyue.

    Great is the Lorde and meruaylous,
And worthy of all prayse:
There is no ende of his greatnes,   25
Or magnificent wayes.

From

From tyme to tyme for euer more
Eche generation
To others shall thy powre declare,
And thy workes eury one.   5

And as for me myne only talke
Shall worshyp styll thy name,
Thy glory and thy wondrous workes,
And prayse the for the same.

Men of thy workes so meruaylous   10
To speake shall haue delyght:
And alwayes shall be talkyng of
Thy greatnes and thy myght.

Of thyne abundant kyndnes we
Wyll kepe memoriall,   15
And syng of thy great ryghteousnes
From henceforth all men shall.

For thou O lorde art gracious
Yea mercifull and meke,
Long suffring and of great goodnes   20
To them that doe hym seke.

To eury man lyberally,
The lorde doth shewe his loue,
And ouer all his goodly workes,
His mercy styll doth moue.   25

And they expresse thy glory great,
Thy kyngdome and thy powre:
To men that all these myght be knowne
At eury tyme and houre.

G3   Thy   30

90

Thy kyngdom euerlastingly
A kyngdome is ryght sure,
Thy lordshyp shall from age to age
Eternaly endure.   5

For in his dedes he faithfull is,
(What so he take in hande)
His workes be all holy and iuste,
Both vpon sea and lande.

The lorde vpholdeth all that are   10
In danger for to fall,
Them that be downe he lyfteth vp
When they on hym doe call.

The eyes of all on thee O lorde
Doe wayte and put their trust,   15
And thou dost geue to them their meate
In season due and iuste.

Thou openest thy holy hande,
Thy powre and thy good wyll,
All lyuing thynges plentifully,   20
Therwith that thou mayst fyll.

The lorde is righteous in his wayes,
His workes be holy all:
And he is nyghe to faithfull men,
When they on him doe call: 25

Suche as feare him, he will fulfyll
To them their whole desire.
He will them here and helpe also
When they doe hym require.

                                          All   30

All suche as loue and feare the Lorde,
Them styll preserueth he:
And he wyll scatter all abroade
Suche as vngodly be.   5

My mouth shall speake & prayse ẙ lorde
And that abundantly,
Let all fleshe thanke his holy name
With laude eternally.

[*The nynth chapiter of Ecclesia-*   10
sticus: or booke of Iesus the sonne of
Sirach.

The argument

Of   ie-lou-sie who so wyll heare,   vn - to my tune harke and drawe nere,

G4   howe   15

howe ye shall of the har-lottes vyle esch [ew] the sleyght the fraude and guile.

What mischiefe and what hurte they doe
To suche as harken them vnto,
Howe vayne and vyle adultrie is 5
Howe fonde they are that walke amys.

Howe we shoulde kepe, an olde frend true
And neuer change hym for no newe,
Howe for to leade a godly lyfe,
In holynes without all stryfe. 10

How that a kyng by wysdomes lore
Should rule and gouerne euermore,
Howe eche man should in his degree
Se that his worke well vsed be.

And howe the folysh talkatyue 15
Are the moste wicked folke on lyue,
To Iesus Sirach geue good eare
Whiche telles his tale in this maner.

Ecclesiast. Cap. ix.

BE not ouer thy wyfe Ielouse, 20
But without strife kepe wel thy house:
Lest that she shewe some point of ill,
Or wycked sleight the for to spyll.

Nor

93

Nor tangle not thy powre nor lyfe:
With a false whore which maketh strife:
Lest she redounde within thy strength,
And so confounde thy soule at length.   5

Beholde not women vayne & nought:
Whiche vpon men set all their thought:
On suche I saye set not thy care,
Lest they betray thee in their snare.

Abstayne and flee hir wicked waye,   10
That loues to geste scoffe daunce & playe,
To hir consent not in no wyse,
Though she the tempte and ofte entyse.

Loke not to longe vpon a mayde
Least with hir forme thou be dismayde.   15
Muche lesse on harlotes then haue mynde
Nor on women of suche ill kynde:

Least thou decaye before thyne age,
And so consume thyne heritage.
In townes and cities doe not gase,   20
As one whose wittes were in amase:

Nor wander not in euery strete,
Least with ill men perhappes thou mete.
Chiefly of all turne thy face fro,
The woman gaye whiche worketh wo.   25

Beholde not muche the great bewtie,
Of any one vnknowne to thee:
For in tyme past suche fooles haue bene,
Which with their fonde eyes as I wene,

G5   Did   30

Did so regarde the beuty fayre
Of strangers where they did repayre:
That they decayd through their desire,
Whiche burned lyke the flaming fyre.   5

Wherfore women adulterous,
Should only be regarded thus,
As most vyle dounge durte myre & claye,
That eche man treads on in his waye.

For suche as on them wonder had,   10
Were by their beutie tangled mad.
All wysdom they from them did caste:
So whot of fonde loue was the blast.

Lead thou therfore a godly lyfe:
Couet thou not thy neighbours wyfe.   15
Syt not with hir at any sted:
Lye not with hir vpon a bed.

No talke with hir make thou at wyne:
Least thy heart should to hir inclyne.
Therby makyng thy bloud to fall: 20
And so destroy thy lyfe and all.

Forsake not thou a good olde friende:
For suche a newe is harde to fynde.
For a newe friende is lyke newe wyne:
Whiche is not good tyll it be fyne.   25

But when the wyne is olde and pure,
Then mayst ẙ drynke hym with plesure,
Desyre not the honor therefore,
That synners gayne and kepe in store.

                                        If   30

If thou dydst their destruction knowe,
Whiche will them once all ouerflowe:
To suche honour thou wouldst not haste,
Nor of their vayne welth wysh to taste.   5

Of one thyng more warne thee I will,
Abstain frō such, whose powre may kill.
For if with suche thou makest stryfe,
He may sone take from thee thy lyfe.

Forsee and shurne eche casualtie: 10
So shalt thou scape all ieopardie.
Take good hede of an ill neighbour,
Least with some crafte he thee deuoure.

With wyse men be in company,
So shalt thou gayne great honestie.   15
Let iust men be thy gestes alwayes,
Ioye in gods name and geue hym prayse.

Be courteous gentyll, good and kynde,
Haue gods feare euer in thy mynde.
Let all thy workes and talke be bent,   20
Vpon the lordes commaundemente.

Eche good craftes mā shuld set his wil
His worke to frame by discrete skyll.
Whiche being set before mens eyes,
Shall cause hym to be counted wyse.   25

For eche worke brought to gorgeous end,
Doth cause all men it to commende,
A prynce that rightly gouerne wyll,
Lyke wise of wisdom should haue skyll.

So   30

So well he should wysdom decerne,
That at his talk others myght lerne.
Hym that doth many fonde wordes vse,
A wyse mans parte is to refuse. 5

For suche in towne and in citie.
Doe kyndle stryfe and vylainy,
They neither weye cause, tyme, nor place:
In them is neither wytte nor grace.
They are past shame I saye, therfore 10
Refuse suche men and them abhorre.

⟦ *The maner of true and perfecte*
prayer instituted by our sauiour Iesus Christe, the only sonne of God,
the wisdom of the father, and seconde 15
person in trinitie.

The syxt of mathewe if ye reade ex-am-ple ye may finde.

What

What prai-er is and how to vse the same in per-fect kynde.

For Christ our only mercy seate,
So soundly hath vs taughte,
That in his gospell we may fynde,
Not els where to be sought.   5

When thou doste praye sayth Christe our Lorde
Se that thou doe refuse,
The vayne glory that hippocrites
Doe in their prayers vse.   10

For they wyll in the synagoges,
Their prayers to appere,
In open stretes or in suche place,
As moste men may them here.

For whiche their folysh vaynglorie,   15
That would of men be hearde,
The prayse of men whiche they desyre,
Is only their rewarde.

But at suche tyme as thou wylt praye,
Into thy chamber go,   20
A faythfull and a contrite harte
Prayer must Issue fro.

And when thou hast closed thy dore,
And shut out worldly care,

                                            And   25

And vayn thoughtes of this wretched worlde
Thy prayer then declare.

Vnto thy god and father dere,
Whiche is in secrete still :   5
Seing the bothom of eche harte,
Eche thought, eche worke and wyll.

Whoe will rewarde thee in such wise
That it shall well appere,
That he hath heard thy hartes requeste,   10
Moste lyke a father dere.

But in thy prayer bable not
With many wordes and vayne,
As Heathen men whiche thinke therby
Their purpose to obteyne.   15

It is the harte and not the lyppes
Wherby thou mayste aspyre,
Thy sute to god for to attayne,
And to haue thy desyre:

The harte I saye both cleane and pure   20
Must be the very meane,
For lips doe but prouoke gods wrath
Where hartes be founde vncleane.

For god doth knowe before you speake
Your nede and all your lacke,   25
And wyll you kepe if you be iuste,
That nought shall goe to wracke.

                                    And

And erre thou praye bethynke thy self,
Who did the hurt or greue,
Refrayne thy wrath in continent
And louyngly forgeue.   5

If thou forgeue not other men,
Their trespasses and cryme,
Thinke not that god will thee forgeue,
Thy faultes at any time.

Contrariwyse if thou forgeue,   10
Suche as did the vnryght,
God by his promis wyll thee here
And shewe the mercy bryght.

And where thou hast done any hurte,
It is not worth the whyle   15
To praye before thou make amendes,
And thy selfe reconcyle.

But when thou art prepared thus,
In all pointes as I saye:
With pure harte in moste humble wyse,   20
On this sorte see thou praye.

Pater noster.

O LORDE that art our only god
And father of vs all,
In heauen whiche arte resident,   25
To thee we crie and call.

Thy

Thy holy and thy blessed name,
That we may sanctifie:
Graunt that we may for euer vse
The same reuerently.   5

Oh let thy kyngdom downe descende,
And alwayes vs protecte:
That we may reigne in peace and ioye
Whiche are thyne owne electe.

Thy worthy wyll let it be done   10
Of worldly wretches here:
As it in heauen euer is
Among thy saintes moste dere.

Our daily bread geue vs this daye,
Our bodies to susteyne: 15
And to our soules thy blessed worde,
Thy truthe styll to mainteyne.

Both for the body and the soule,
Relieue vs with thy store:
That we therby may taste thy grace,   20
This daye and euer more.

Our trespasses & our great sinnes,
Redeme and clene forgeue,
As we forgeue and mercy take,
On them that doe vs greue.   25

O lorde into temptation
Aboue our strengthe and powre,
Doe not leade vs at any tyme,
Least Sathan vs deuowre.

                                        But   30

But with thy grace defende vs styll,
Let not thy goodnes cease:
But from all euylles vs defende,
Delyuer and release.   5

For onely to thee doth belonge
The kyngdome very ryght,
The power and gloryous maiestie,
For euer so be it.

[*The abridgement of our Christen*   10
beleefe, written as some suppose into .xii.
Articles, by the .xii. holy apostels of our
sauiour Iesus Chryste.

THE .xii. Apostelles of Iesus our lorde,
After their holy preachyng a long tyme,   15
And settyng forth of goddes most holy worde,
Preaching repentaunce from al synne and cryme
Yet not withstandinge all their dilygence,
Mistaking of goddes worde dyd make offence.

For many heresyes dyd then aryse,   20
And mysbelefe in god our lorde aboue,
By mystakyng, and worldely wyt lyke wise,
Whiche made from true fayth many to remoue.
For carnall reason walketh styll astray,
And vnto fayth dothe alwayes disobay.   25

These holy preachers therfore thinkinge best
In this turmoyle to set order and staye,
Dyd then deuyse bothe vnto most and least,
Of true beleefe a breefe and perfect waye,

Hi   That   30

That all men might, as well the younge as oulde,
Sone lerne the same and in memory houlde.

Syth then the holy ghost hath taught vs thus,
It doth behoue that we dilygently,   5
Do learne the same to knowe and to discusse,
And kepe eche parte therof most faythfully,
Wherefore the summe of it I wyll reherse
As here doth folowe in this kynde of verse.

Credo in deum patrem.   10

I DO beleue with stedfast true intent
In God the father which is of all myght,
Who made heauen earth and al their whole content
The nyght the day the darkenes and the lyght.
And I beleue in Iesus Christ our lorde,   15
Hys onely sonne the euerlastyng worde.

Which of the holy ghost conceyued was,
And of the most pure virgyn Mary borne,
And vnder Ponce Pylat as came to passe
Suffred, and on the crosse was rente and torne.   20
And beyng dead, was buryed in the ende,
And also downe into hell dyd descende.

And the thirde day accordyng to scripture,
He rose from death to perfect lyfe agayne:
And vp to heauen he ascended sure,   25
On god the fathers ryght hande to remayne:
Till at the last he once agayne shall come,
Both quicke and deade to iudge by rightfull dome.

I also beleue in the holy ghoste,

                    And   30

And in the church of chryst catholycall,
And of the sayntes the communion moste,
The forguenes of myne offences all,
And this our fleshe shall ryse agayne at last,   5
And I beleue eternall lyfe to taste.
                              Amen.

⟦ *The songe of prayse and than-*
kesgeuinge of blessed Mary the vyr-
gyn, mother of our lorde and sauiour   10
Iesus Chryst, after the salutation of
the Angell Gabriell, and of Eliza-
beth mother of blessed Iohn baptist.
written. Luke the i. Chapter.

            Magnificat anima mea.   15

MY soule truelye
Shall magnifye
The lorde, and hym honour:
So shall my sprite
Ioy and delyghte   20
In god my sauyour.

   Hys eyes he stayd
On hys handmayde,
In poore and lowe degree,
And kinreds all   25
From henceforth shall
Knowe me blessed to be.

   For he whose myght
Excelleth ryght
Hath exalted my fame: 30

            H.ii.   Doyng

Doyng to me
Great thinges and hye,
And holy is his name.

His mercy sure   5
Doth aye endure,
And doth not wast nor weare :
In kynredes all
Continuall
That do hym loue and feare.   10

He in his powre,
Hath at this howre
His arme put forth at length :
The prowde abowght
Bringeth to nowght,   15
What so their hartes inuenth.

He putteth downe
From their renowme
The mighty and the stronge :
And doth vp set   20
In honour great
The meeke that suffer wronge.

And he doth styll
Both fede and fyll
All those that hunger payne :   25
And doth them good
When without foode
The ryche empty remayne.

He hath in minde
His mercy kynde,   30

His

His folke to helpe and saue:
His seruantes well
Euen Israell,
That for his mercy craue.　　　　　　5

　　As he like wise
Dyd once promyse,
To Abraham before:
Our fathers olde
That fayth dyd holde,　　　　　　10
And their sede euermore.

　　Glory and prayse
And laude alwayes,
Vnto the trynitie:
With one accorde　　　　　　15
Prayse we the lorde
One god and personnes three.

　　As hath ben aye,
And at this daye
Continueth as yet:　　　　　　20
And shall extende
Worlde without ende,
For euer so be it.
　　　　Finis.

⟦ *The songe of prayse and than-*　　25
kes geuinge of holy Zachary, father
of Saynct Iohn baptist, beinge restored to his speche, whiche was taken from him at the vision of the angell, written, Luke the fyrst chap.　　30

　　　　H.iii.　　　*Bene-*

Benedictus dominus deus.

BLESSED nowe be
The almyghtye
Lorde God of Israell,   5
Hys people whych
Visiteth myche
Redemynge them full well.

  A myghtye horne
Of saluation   10
That hath to vs raysed,
Euen in the house
So ryghteous
Of his seruant David,

  As he spake by   15
The mouthes holy
Of hys Prophetes, ech whan,
That ay haue bene
Among vs sene,
Sence the worlde first began.   20

  Which sayde that we
Shoulde saued be,
From our enemyes all:
Who euer that
Hath vs in hate   25
Eyther the greate or small.

  To performe ryghte
Hys mercy bryght,
That he sometyme dyd graunt
Our forefathers.   30

               And

And remembers
Hys holy couenaunt.

Hys othe once sworne
For to performe,
Vnto our father dere: 5
Euen Abraham
That when tyme came
To vs it myght appere.

That from our foes   10
We beynge lose
And cleane delyuered:
We myght serue him
From tyme to tyme
Without all seruyle drede.   15

In holynes
And ryghteousnes
With perfect wayes and pure,
For euermore
Hys face before   20
While our lyfe dayes indure.

And thou O chylde
That art so mylde
Shalt be calld the prophet
Of the most hyest,   25
And hys sonne Chryst
To shewe hys glory great.

The lorde of grace
Before hys face,
Thou chylde shalte go I say: 30

H.iiii.   For

For to prepare
And eke declare
His pure and chosen way.

To geue knowledge   5
Of this the pledge
Of their saluation:
His peoples synne,
That they are in,
The cleane remission.   10

Throughe the mercy
Tender and free,
Of god, wherby the day
Springeth so bright
Euen from the hight,   15
Doth visyte vs alway.

From deathes shadowe,
And darkenes lowe,
Suche as syt to release:
Their feete eche tyde   20
With light to guide,
Into the way of peace.

Glory and prayse
And laude alwayes
Vnto the Trinitie,   25
To the father,
And the sonne dere,
And to the ghost holy.

As hath ben aye,
And at this day,   30

Conti-

Continueth as yet:
And shall be styll
With right good wyll
For euer so be it.   5
      Finis.

[[*The songe of prayse and than-*
kes geuyng of holy Simeon at the
Circumcisyon of our Lorde Iesu
Chryste. Luke. ij.   10

Nunc dimittis.

THY seruaunt nowe
Permyt mayst thowe,
For to depart O lorde
In quiet peace,   15
From strife to cease,
According to thy worde.

Myne eyes, our wealth
Thy sauyng health
Haue sene nowe through thy grace,   20
Of thee preparde
To be declarde,
Before all peoples face.

To be a lyght
Styll shyning bryght,   25
Guyding the gentylles wel:
And for to be
The great glory
Of thy flocke Israell.

        Hv   Let   30

Let eury trybe
Glory ascrybe
Nowe to the deitye.
As hath bene, is,   5
And shall not mysse
To be continually.
        Amen.

⟦ *The x. commaundementes of*
almighty God written, in ij. tables of   10
stone with ẙ finger of God. The first
table conteyning iiij preceptes concerneth our duety towardes God: The
second table conteyning the other vj.
preceptes concerneth our duetye to-   15
wardes our neyghbour. written in
the xx. Chapiter of Exodus, and in
the v. Chapiter Deuteronomium.

            Argument.

The lyuyng God our onely Lorde   20
That all thinges with his word hath made,
And (as the scripture doth recorde)
Doth gouerne all in godly trade,
And knowth how apt man is to stray
And all good thynges to disobay.   25

With hys fynger (for mannes behoue)
In tables twayne of stone dyd wryte
Commaundementes ten, hys heart to moue
From guyle and wrong to truth and right:
In godlynes to guyde hys wayes   30
They folow here note what he sayes.

                        I am

1 I AM thy Lorde and God alone
From Egypt land that brought the ryght,
Beholdyng thy distresse and mone:
From house of bonde I freede thee quight.
Wherefore thou shalte I say to thee   5
None other Goddes haue before mee.

2 Thou shalt no grauen Image make,
Nor picture be it greate or smalle,
Or fygure that thy minde may take,   10
In heauen earth or waters all:
Nor honour them, that shalt not thou,
Nor vnto them ne knele nor bowe.

For I thy God and onely Lorde
A ielouse God am of suche synne,   15
And fathers faultes I haue abhorde
Upon their childern and their kynne:
In kynreds iij. or iiij. or mo
I vysit them that hate me so.

Which iustyce yet doth me not stay   20
From mekenes, mercy, nor from grace:
Which I extende to them alway
My holy lawes that do embrace:
To thousandes though none can deserue,
That I commaunde if they obserue.   25

3 The holy name thou shalt not vse
Of me thy lord and God in vayne,
Vnlawfull othes thou shalt refuse,
Sweare not for false or fylthy gayne:
The Lorde will thee not holde vngylt   30
Hys name in vayne if take thou wilt.

Remember

4 Remember that in any wyse
The Sabaoth day thou sanctifie,
Syx dayes thou shalt thee exercise,
And labour for necessitie: 5
The seuenth day the Sabaoth is
Of god almyght the lorde of blys.

 Therfore this day beare well in minde
No kinde of worke that then thou do,
Vnto whiche lawe thy sonne I bynde, 10
Thy daughter shall it kepe also,
Thy man thy mayde and eke thy beast:
In fyne within thy gate thy geast.

 For in syx dayes the lorde created
Heauen, earthe, sea, and all of noughte, 15
The seuenth day take his rest he dyd:
Wherfore the lorde that all hath wrought,
The Sabaoth day dyd sanctifie,
And blessed it perpetually.

5 Thy father and thy mother dere   20
Se that thou reuerently honour,
Let none ingratitude appere
In thee to them, but them soccour:
So in the lande longe shalt thou lyue,
Whiche thy lorde God to thee shall gyue. 25

6 Thou shalt not kyll note thou it well.
7 Also thou shalt no wedlocke breake.
8 I say also thou shalt not steale.
9 Nor witnes false thou shalt none speake.
Against thy neyghbours, them to wrong: 30
But lyue vprightly them amonge.

       And

And to conclude of this take hede
What my lawes chieflye doe requyre,
Not onely to forbere the dede,
But also from the heartes desyre,   5
Of that thy neighbour doth possesse,
Of any thyng in more or lesse.

10 Particularlye to recite,
Thy neyghbours house couet thou not:
Nor yet hys wyfe, his heartes delyght,   10
Hys man or mayde whych is his lot:
Hys oxe or asse or ought of hys,
Couet thou not, thynke wel on thys.

⟦ *The prayse of God the father*
sonne and holye ghost. wrytten in an   15
holy Hymne, by the worthy fathers
Augustine and Ambrose.

Te Deum laudamus.

O GOD of myghte
As it is ryghte   20
We yelde the laude and prayse,
Wyth one accorde
To be the Lorde
We knoweledge thee alwayse:

The earth throughout   25
And all aboute
Thy worshyppe doth expresse:
Thou doest appere
A father dere
In euerlastyngnesse.   30

To

To thee do call
The Angelles all
And cry wyth a loude dynne:
The heauens hye   5
Eternallye
And all the powres therin.

  Both Cherubin
And Ceraphin
Do in thy prayse reioyce: 10
And thus always
Expresse thy prayse
Wyth an incessant voyce.

  Holye, holye,
Thou art holye,   15
Lorde God of Sabaoth:
Thy maiestye
And thy glorye
Fylles heauen and earth both.

  The gloryous sect   20
Of thyne elect
Apostles euery one:
Thy prayse doth showe,
All in a rowe
And honour thee alone.   25

  The Prophetes all
Do on the call
So goodly in their kynde:
That felowshyppe
Doth not let slyppe   30
To kepe thy prayse in mynde.

                    The

The noble aray
Of martyrs aye
Thy prayse doth styll expresse:
The Church holye   5
Where euer it be
The lyke prayse doth confesse.

Infinitlye
Thy maiestye
O father doth endure: 10
And thy Sonne styll
We honour wyll,
Onely so true and pure.

The holye ghost
Our comforte most,   15
We do confesse to be:
Thou Chryst Iesu,
Mesias true
Art the kynge of glory.

Thou art euer   20
Of the father
The euerlastyng sonne:
Which we confesse
Both more and lesse
That in this worlde do wonne.   25

When for our sake
Thou dyddest take
On thee man to restore:
The wombe so cleene
Of the Virgin   30
Thou dyddest not abhorre.

When

When thou the darte
Of death so sharpe
Dydst vanquishe and depriue:
Thou dydst vnlose   5
Thy blesse, to those
That truelye do beleue.

On the ryghte hande
(We vnderstande)
Of the father so dere,   10
(In glorye greate)
There art thou set
Tyll the last day appere.

Then we beleue
Iudgemente to geue,   15
That thou from thence shalt come,
Most ryghteouslye
Our iudge to be
And iudge vs all and some.

Thy seruauntes pray   20
Thee day by day,
Of thee some helpe to haue:
Whom wyth thy bloude
Precious and good,
Thou dydst redeme and saue.   25

Make them indede
To be numbred
Wyth thy holy sayntes all:
For euermore
Thy face before   30
In glory eternall.

Thy

Thy people saue
Whiche on the craue:
And blesse thyne heritage.
Gouerne them styll,   5
To doe thy wyll,
Euer from age to age.

For we dayly,
Thee magnifie
And worshyp styll thy name   10
And styll intende
Worlde without ende,
To continue the same.

Vouchsafe we praye
O lorde this daye,   15
From sinne vs to defende:
For on thyne ayde
Oure faith is stayde,
And euer doth depend.

Mercy O lorde,   20
Haue mercy Lorde,
Shewe vs thy mercy iuste:
On vs let lyght
Thy mercy bright,
As we in thee doe truste.   25

And synce alway
My truste and staye,
In the lorde is fyxed:
Oh graunt that I
Eternally   30
Be neuer confounded.

I   To

To the father,
And his sonne dere,
And to the holy ghoste,
Glory and prayse   5
Geue we alwayes,
As we are bounden moste.

As was and is,
And shall not mys,
To be eche tyme and when: 10
For euer more
Laude and honor
To our lorde god. Amen.

[*To his friend E. H. at whose*
requeste, the author drue into me-   15
tre, the songe of the three chyldren, whiche were put into the
whot burning ouen, which were
called properly in the hebrue tongue, *Ananias, Asarias, & Misael*:   20
whose names *Nebucadnezer* chā
ged into *Cidrach, Misach*, and
Abednago, in the Chaldey tongue. Written, *Daniel*. iii.

MY louyng friende,   25
Your boune and mynde,
Doth seme to me this tyde,
As Phaeton vayne,
Should once againe
The sonne his chariot guide: 30

Who folyshly
Immediatly

May

May set the world on fire,
Till Ioue almight
Most iust and right
Doe sley him in his Ire.   5

Or one vnwise
Should enterpryse
To make or cause tapere,
From flynt stones dure
Swete fountaynes pure   10
Of waters cristall clere.

Yet for to chuse
Or once refuse,
Your most frendly request,
Is not in me   15
Nor can not be
At any time possest.

Therfore take well
This finall cantell
Of my due and good will,   20
Though momus secte
Then it reiecte,
No force it shall not skyll.

BLESSED be thou
O lorde god nowe   25
The god of our fathers:
For thou always
Arte worthy prayse
And of all great honers.

The name holy   30
Of thy glory,
Worthy to be praysed,
Styll in worldes all
Continuall
Is to be magnified.   35

I 2   Be

Be thou blessed
In euery sted
Of thy temple holy:
Whiche doste vs moue   5
All thynges aboue,
To set vp thy glory.

More then worthy,
Thou arte truly
Of laude and prayse eche daye: 10
Wherfore euer
We wyll preferre
And set the vp for aye.

Blessed alone
In thy hyghe throne   15
Be thou in thy kyngdom:
Thee aboue all
We styll blesse shall,
In worlde of worldes to come.

Blessed be thou   20
That lokest throwe
The depe: and yet doste syt
The Cherubes on,
Worthy alone
Of prayse, deseruing it.   25

The fyrmament
And heauens hente
Thee prayse which arte worthy,
(For thy fauour)
Of all honoure   30
Vnto eternitie.

Bene-

Benedicite omnia opera Domini
domino.

O YE workes all
In generall
Of god the lyuing Lorde,   5
Se that his prayse
Ye shewe alwayes
Set vp and it recorde.

    Ye angels bryghte   10
And heauens lyght
And waters all aboue
The fyrmament:
With one consent
Prayse hym as doth behoue.   15

    The lorde his powres,
Sonne Moone in cours,
Tell and shewe forth his prayse:
And neuer let
Hym vp to set   20
In his due laude alwayes.

    O all ye sterres,
Dewe, and showers,
O all ye wynds of God,
His prayse tell ye,   25
Hym magnifye,
As in his worde he bod.

    Heate and fyer,
Wynter, sommer,
Ye dewes and frostes hore: 30

I 3   Ye

122

Ye frost and coulde,
His prayse be boulde
To set forth euermore.

O Ise and snowe,   5
His prayse forth showe,
Hym laude and magnifye:
Ye nyghtes and dayes,
With the lyke prayse
Laude hym eternally.   10

Lyght and darknes
His prayse expresse,
Lyghtnyng and cloudes I saye:
Let the earth speake
And his prayse breake   15
Forth, for euer and aye.

Mountaines and hilles
With your good wylles,
Herbes, grasse, & al grene things,
Welles, seas, and flood   20
Of hym speake good,
And declare his praysyngs.

Ye whales that lyue
And all that meue,
In floodes and waters clere: 25
All soules of thayre
Lykewyse repayre,
To make his prayse appere.

Bestes and cattell
His prayse forth tell,   30

Ye

Ye chyldren of men pure:
Let Israell
In prayse excell
For euer to endure.   5

   With one accorde
Prayse ye the lorde,
That the lordes seruantes are:
Sprites and soules iust
His prayse syng must   10
Hym set vp and declare.

   Let holy men
Prayse hym eche when,
And humble men of harte,
With good pretence   15
Euer from hence,
From his prayse neuer starte.

   Ananias
Azarias
And *Misaell* prefer   20
His prayses great,
And hym vp set
For euer and euer,

   Whiche hath from hell
Vs saued well,   25
And clene delyuered:
And hath our breath
Kepte safe from death,
And also hath vs ryd

       I4   From   30

From burnyng flame
Amydste the same,
And made the heate retire:
When we dyd craue,   5
He dyd vs saue
In the mydst of the fyre.

Vnto the lorde
Let vs recorde
Both prayse and thankes therfore: 10
His hearte is kynde,
For we doe fynde
His mercy euermore.

O all men ryght
That are contryte,   15
Speake good and prayse the lorde,
For he truly
Is almyghtie,
And of all gods the God.

O geue him prayse   20
With thankes alwayes,
Whose mercy doth extende.
And doth indure
Remayning pure,
Euer worlde without ende.   25

Prayse glorious
Euer let vs
Magnificently moste,
Geue the father,
And the sonne dere   30
And to the holy ghoste.

From

From beginning
Continuyng
And nowe doth perseuer:
And shall doe aye   5
From daye to daye
For euer and euer.

Numeri. xiii.

[[*Sing this as, The dawnyng daye*
beginnes to glare. &c.   10

LET now thy powre be great O lorde,
Lyke as thy lyps dyd once repeate:
And as we fynde it in thy worde,
Thy suffrance long, thy mercy great.

For as thou doste our synnes forgyue   15
And trespasses, when we repent:
So are we sure no man on lyue
From synne is free and innocent.

And of their father the misdede
Thou visitest vpon the childe,   20
His generation and his sede,
In .iiii. degrees therwith defylde.

But nowe oh lorde be gracious
Vnto thy flocke and their offence:
And of thy mercy bounteous   25
Remember not our negligence.

Thy people as thou didst forbeare,
From Egypt into wyldernes,
We the beseche in lyke maner,
That we may taste thy gentylnes.   30

I5   *ii.*

126

of Vertue

ii. Esdras. i.

⟦ *Syng this as O lorde our god we*
.*turne to thee. &c.*

LORDE god that in the heauens hie   5
Doste kepe thy residence:
Thou art a god of terrible
And great magnificence.

  Thou that hast kept thy couenant
And mercy eke in store,   10
For them that loue thee, and obserue
And kepe thy holy lore,

  Oh let thine eares be attendante,
And marke what I doe saye:
And let thyne eyes be vigilant,   15
Beholde me when I praye.

  For I am bent both daye and nyght
To praye before thy face:
That to thy seruant Israell
Thou wilt geue health and grace: 20

  And to forgeue them all their synne,
That they did thee transgresse:
For in the person of them all
Their faultes I doe confesse.

  For I my selfe among them all   25
Doe in the number syt:
My fathers house hath not bene free
But did lyke synne commyt.

               Cor-

Corrupted haue we bene, in that
Thy lawes we haue not kept:
Thy wyll and thy commaundementes
Because we did reiecte.   5

Yet call to mynde thy worde O lord*e*
By Moyses that was sayde,
Thy seraunt whom thou didst commaund
For to proclayme thyne ayde.

The punishment that thou hast made   10
For our transgressions,
Is for to scatter vs a broade
Among the nacions.

But thou hast sayd and promysed
That if we turne agayne,   15
Obseruyng thy commaundementes
And in thy lawes remayne:

That though we scattred were abroade
Neuer so farre about,
Yea in the vtmost partes of all: 20
Thou wouldst yet fynd vs out.

And gather vs from thence agayne,
Into the very place,
That thou vs gaue to dwell therein
Of thy bountie and grace.   25

O heare vs nowe thy seruantes lorde
And people of thy lande,
That were deliuerd by thy powre
And by thy myghty hande.

O lord   30

O lord nowe let thyne eares attende
To marke what we requyre :
For thee to serue and feare thy name,
Is nowe our whole desire.   5

Tobias. xiii.

⟦ *Syng this as The. 6. of Mathew,*
   If ye reade. &c.

O LORDE our God for euer more
Thy greatnes doth extende,   10
Thy powre, thy kyngdom & thy
For euer without end.   (might

For after scurges helth Insues,
And pleasure after payne :
And vnto hell when thou hast brought,   15
Thou bringest out againe.

Wherby thou hast instructed vs
That we may vnderstande,
That there is none by any meanes
That may escape thy hande.   20

Geue thankes therfore vnto the lorde,
Ye children of the iuste,
Before the Heathen let his prayse
Be shewed and discuste.

For therfore hath he scatred you,   25
His wondrous workes to showe,
Among the Heathen, and the folke
That dyd him neuer knowe.

                                    That

That they may knowe and eke confesse
That other there is none
That is a god omnipotent,
But our good God alone.   5

Whiche hath vs made for our misdedes
His chastisment to take:
And wyll vs saue and helpe agayne,
For his owne mercies sake.

Then praye to hym with feare & dread,   10
And ponder well this thing:
And magnifie in all your workes
The euerlastyng kyng.

For I will prayse him in the land
Of my captiuitie: 15
For he dyd shewe the synfull folke
His myghty maiestie.

O turne you vnto God therfore
Ye sinners, and doe ryghte,
Ye may be sure with mercy then   20
That he wyll you requite.

And as for me, so wyll I doe
In soule and with my voyce
For why my god is only he
In whome I wyll reioyce.   25

O prayse the lorde all ye that be
His chosen and electe,
In ioyfull dayes geue hym the thankes
That still doth you protecte.

To-   30

130

Tobias. iii.

[[*Sing this as the forme of perfect pray-*
er beginnyng, The .vi. of Mathewe.

O LORDE god thou art righteous,   5
Thy iudgements all are true:
Thy iust wayes & thy faithfulnes
Doth mercy styll ensue.

  Be myndfull nowe O lorde on me,
And plage not for my sinne.   10
Nor haue no mynde of my misdedes,
Ne of myne elders kynne.

  For we to thy commaundementes
Weare not obedient:
Wherfore among all nacions,   15
Thou hast vs captiue sent.

  And scattred haste vs them among,
That dayly vs deryde:
For dredfull death, & most vyle shame,
Doth euer vs betyde.   20

  In whiche thou hast declard O lorde,
Thy iudgementes great and hye:
We did not as thou didste commaunde,
Nor walkt innocently.

  And therfore now O liuing lorde   25
My prayer shall be styll,
That thou commaunde & deale with me
According to thy wyll.

          Re-

Receaue O lorde my sprite in peace,
To thee I doe it gyue:
For it is more expedient
For me to die then lyue.   5

Iudith. 16.

On tab-rets to the lorde let vs   our thankfull songes be-gin,

V-pon the sim-bals let vs syng   a new songe vn - to hym.

With ioyfull thankes his name to prayse,
And call vpon the same: 10
It is the lorde that warres doth cease,
Yea the lorde is his name.

                                        Whiche

Whiche pitched hath his tentes of strēgth
His people all among:
Vs to delyuer from the handes
Of all our enmies strong.   5

For from the mountaynes of the northe
Came the Assirian,
And many thousandes myght we see,
Within his army than.

His multitude had shut the streames   10
In all our coastes throughout,
And with his horsmen couerd were
The valleys all about.

My markes & boundes he sayd he wold
Consume with burning fyre,   15
To kyll my young men with the sworde
Was also his desyre:

To brayne my suckyng babes, and geue
Myne infantes for a praye.
My maydens and my virgins pure   20
He thought to dryue awaye.

But through the lorde omnipotent
Suche grace we vnderstande,
Of their purpose they are deceud,
Euen by a womans hande.   25

For with the handes of yoūg mē strong
He truly was not slayne:
Nor they that were of Tytan borne
To kyll hym toke no payne.

                            Nor   30

Nor gyant great: but Iudith lo
Daughter of *Merari*.
For with hyr face she scattred them
And with hyr great beutye.   5

Hir wydowes clothes, hir morninge
She gan thē to forbeare: (wede,
And did on suche as she was wonte
On holy dayes to weare.

To helpe the wofull Israelites,   10
Whom ieopardie had hent:
Hir vertuous face she did anoynte,
With oyntment excellent.

And with an houe she trimde hyr heare,
Hir worke thus could she weaue: 15
She ware a lynen stole also,
Thus did She him deceaue.

Hir slypers rauished his eyes,
Hir beutie eke his mynde:
And through his necke his own sworde   20
Suche ende lo did he fynde.   (went

The Persians weare in doubt & feare
At hir audacitie,
The Medes dyd maruell very muche,
Hir bouldnes suche to be.   25

The humble folke reioyced then,
They Ioyde that erste dyd crye:
And they dyd feare that bragd before
And fayne were nowe to flye.

                    K   Our   30

Our womens sonnes then killed them,
Lyke slaues they ran away:
The seruantes of the lorde my God
Thus caused them to straye.   5

A song of prayse vnto the Lorde
To syng I will procure:
Thy glory lorde and strength also
Inuincible and pure.

For eche thing ẙ thy hande hath made   10
Doth serue thee in his kynde:
Thou didst commaūde & straight it was,
Thy worde so strong we fynde.

Thyne holy sprite thou sentest out,
And strayght wayes it was made: 15
For nothyng can resist thy word,
Whiche dures and doth not fade.

For mountaynes they shall moued be
With water from their springes,
And in thy sight harde thinges shal melt,   20
As wexe and liquid thynges.

And yet to them that doe thee feare
Thy mercy doth extende:
From the fyrste tyme to this present,
And euer without ende.   25

Iob. i.

OVT of my mothers wombe
All naked came I loe:

And

And naked shall I turne agayne,
To earth that I came fro.

The Lorde gaue at the fyrst,
As his good plesure was,   5
And at his wyll dyd take agayne,
As it is come to pas.

The lorde his holy name
Be praysed nowe therfore,
As it hath bene, as it is nowe,   10
And shall be euermore.

Prouerb. xxx.

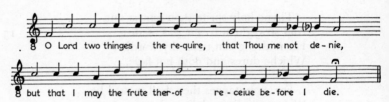

O Lord two thinges I the re-quire, that Thou me not de-nie,
but that I may the frute ther-of re-ceiue be-fore I die.

The first shall be that vanitie   15
Thou wilt from me restrayne,
And eke the lips that luste to lye,
To flatter glose and fayne.

K2   The

136

The seconde that thou make me not
To poore in any wyse,
Ne yet to riche: but meane lyuyng,
Of necessary cyse.　　　　　　　　　5

Least when I am to full of welth
I thee forget and saye:
What felowe is the lorde? when I
Forgotten haue thy waye.

And lyke wyse least that pouertie　　10
Constrayne me out of frame,
And me prouoke to steale O God
And to forsweare thy name.

Ecclesiasticus. xxiii.

⟦ *Syng this as, I am the man whome*　15
　　God. &c.

OH lorde I the desyre
Of thyne abundant grace,
That pryde & scornefull counte-
Appeare not in my face.　(nance　20

Thy goodnes nowe extend,
Oh for thy mercies sake,
Disdeyne and all voluptuousnes
Witsafe from me to take.

The fylthy fleshly lustes　　　　　25
That to our bodies leane,

　　　　　　　Destroye

Destroye therof the fyery rage,
And make me chaste and cleane.

Of pitie oh good Lorde
Extincte in me this fyre: 5
And let my mynde be mundifyd
Of eche vncleane desyre.

Oh leaue me not I saye
To myne owne lust and wyll:
Thyne ayde doe not from me withdrawe, 10
But be my succour styll:

Least wanting of thy helpe,
I runne in error blynde:
And fall into vnshamfastnes,
And obstinate of mynde. 15

Oh be thou my fortres,
That I may prayse thy name:
So shall I other men exhort
Also to doe the same.

⟦ The songe of *Esechia,* 20
Ego dixi in dimidio. &c.
Esaie. xxxviii.

⟦ *Syng this as, I am the man whome*
God. &c.

VNTO the gates of hell 25
I wente I should haue wende,
Amid my days whē as I thought
My yeres were at an ende.

K3   With

138

With in my selfe I sayde,
I neuer shall agayne
Visite the Lorde (the lorde I saye)
In this lyfe whyle I reigne.   5

I neuer loke agayne
Before men to appeare,
Nor to beholde no worldly wyghtes
That haue their dwellyng heare.

Myne age is folded vp   10
Together at this daye :
As one should from the shepeherd poore
His cottage take away.

And through my synnes my lyfe
Is cut of and vndo,   15
As when the weuers worke is done
His webbe he cuttes ato.

This pynyng sycknes wyll
My lyfe in sunder rende,
For in one daye I well perceyue   20
My lyfe shall haue an ende.

Vntyll to morowe yet
I thought to lyue so long :
But he my bones hath brused sore
Moste lyke a gyant strong.   25

For in one daye thou wylt
Myne ende brynge on me lo :
As swalowes chatter in their laye,
Then gan I to doe so.

                              I cryed   30

I cryed lyke the crane,
And morned as the doue:
Directyng euer more myne eyes
On hyghe to hym aboue.   5

O lord then sayde I tho
This sycknes doth me presse:
O ease thou me for in thy powre
It is, the same to ceasse.

What shall I saye, the lorde   10
His promis made to me,
And he hym selfe performed hath
The same as we may see.

All whyle I lyue therfore,
It shall not from my mynde,   15
My bytter life, and howe therin
I founde hym good and kynde.

Beyonde their yeres I see
O lorde that men may lyue,
Whiche I to all men wyll declare,   20
And knowledge wyll them gyue.

In those prolonged yeres
Howe I in ioye doe reigne:
And that thou causedst me to slepe
And gaue me lyfe agayne.   25

My pensifnes beholde,
As bytter was as gall:
And for my health I longed sore
Out of that wofull thrall.

K4   Thy   30

Thy pleasure was to saue
Me from the filthy lake:
For thou O lorde hast all my sinnes
Out trowne behinde thy backe.   5

For hell geues thee no prayse,
Nor death magnificence:
And in their graue none praise thy truth,
That parted be from hence.

The lorde hath wrought my health,   10
Our songes we therfore sure
Wyll always synge within thy house,
Whyle our lyfe dayes indure.

Ieremie .ix.

⟦ *Syng this as, I am the man whome*   15
  God. &c.

O WHO wyll geue my head,
Of water perfecte store:
And to mine eyes a wel of teares
To flow for euer more?   20

So should myne outward acte
Expresse myne inwarde payne,
To wepe and wayle both nyght and day,
My people that are slayne.

Would God I had elswhere   25
A cottage in some place,

                                     That

That from the people I myght be
A farre distance and space.

That I myght leaue my folke
And be from their resorte,   5
Adulterers because they be
And eke a shrynkyng sorte.

Lyke bowes they bende their tongues,
Wherwith they shoote out lyes:
And grow on earth, for why the worlde   10
Doth alwayes truthe despyse.

From wickednes they goe
To wickednes agayne,
And wyll not knowe me sayth the lorde,
Nor in my lawes remayne: 15

One from an other nowe
Abstayn and shurnish muste:
For no man in his brother may
With saftie put his truste.

Men doe their brethern seke,   20
To wrong and vnder mynde:
Disemblyng styll they practise guyle,
No truthe in them I fynde.

Their tongues they exercyse,
To lye and eke to fayne: 25
And mischiefe so they may commyt,
They force not for great payne.

K5   Why

Why doe I then remayne,
In this despitfull throng?
Whiche doe dissemble, and nought els
But falshod them among.   5

They wyll not knowe the lorde,
But wander styll awry:
Therfore thus sayth the lorde of hostes,
I wyll them melte and try.

For what should els be done   10
To suche a people vyle:
Whose tongues are like to arowes sharpe,
To vtter fraude and guyle.

For with their mouthes they speake,
As though they ment but peace: 15
To hurte their neyghbour priuily
Yet wyll they neuer cease.

Should I not punysh them
For this thyng (sayeth the lorde)
Or should not I aduenged be   20
Of people so abhorde?

I shall them cause therfore
On mountaynes to lament:
The desertes and the plesant playnes
To mourning shall be bent.   25

For burned shall they be,
Their cattell and their store:
Of byrde or beaste there shall no voyce
Be heard there any more.
                                  Iere-   30

Ieremie .17.

[[*Syng this as, The sixt of Mathewe*
if ye reade. &c.

O LORDE I shall be whole in dede,　　　　5
If I be healed of the:
If thou witsafe nowe me to saue,
Then shall I saued be.

　Thou arte my prayer and my prayse,
I haue none other forte:　　　　10
To geue thee thankes for all my helpe,
To the I must resorte.

　Beholde those men that say to me
In mockage and in scorne,
Where is the worde of God say they?　　　　15
Let it come vs beforne.

　Though not withstanding when I led,
Thy flocke in godly trayne,
Into thy wayes by violence
I did them not constrayne.　　　　20

　Ne yet the death of any man,
I neuer dyd desier,
Thou knowste right wel that before thee
My tongue was not a lyer.

　Be not to me to terrible　　　　25
O lorde, but me refrayne:
For thou arte he in whom I hope
In perill and in payne.

Con-

Confound me not, but confound thē
That doe my lyfe pursue:
Nor feare me not, but make thou them
To feare and eke to rue.   5

And powre on thē their painful plague
When thou shalt see the tyme,
And them destroye that haue thee done
So detestable cryme.

Ieremie .xxxi.   10

[*Syng this as,* On tabrets to the
Lorde. &c.

O LORDE thou hast corrected me
For my sinfull lyuyng,
Though I did as a calf vntame   15
Receyue thy chastening.

Conuert me from my sinne, and so
Shall I conuerted be:
Thou art my God and only Lorde,
And others none but thee.   20

So sone as thou hast turned me
From sinne, I shall returne:
Before whiche tyme I haue no powre
My selfe for to reforme.

Which when thou madest me perceiue   25
And vnderstande the same:
I smote my selfe vpon my thyghe
In my great zeale and shame.

For

For shamful thinges sure haue I done
Oh let my youth therfore
Confounded be, with his reproofe:
For nowe I them abhorre.   5

⟦ *Out of the thirde chapiter of*
Ieremies lamentations.

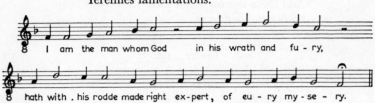

I am the man whom God   in his wrath and   fu - ry,

hath with . his rodde made right ex-pert, of eu - ry my-se - ry.

He droue and led me forth,   10
In darknes to endure:
But as for lyght I myght none see,
So weare my wayes obscure.

He only agaynst me
Doth turne his hande and powre,   15
And laith the same vpon me styll
At eury tyme and howre.

                                                        My

My flesh and skyn waxe olde,
My bones are brused all:
He buylded round, and closde me in,
With trauell and with galle.   5

In darknes he me sette
As dead for euer more,
He hedgd me in and fettered me
With heauy linkes and sore.

With clamors pitiously   10
Though I to hym did call,
My prayer and my painfull playnt
He heareth not at all.

My wayes he stopped vp
With stones of cubike forme: 15
My pathes are made so crokedly,
I not where me to torne.

As doth the cruell beare,
Lye wayting for his praye,
And as the lyon in his hole   20
To take me in my waye.

He marred hath my wayes,
In peces he me brake:
He altogether layde me waste,
And brought me all to wrake.   25

And when he bente his bowe,
He made his marke of me:
The arrowes of his quiuer lo
Into my raynes shot he.

                        I lau-   30

I laughed am to scorne,
Of people in the throng:
They make deridyng songes of me,
And mocke me all day long.　　　　　5

He fylde my hungry soule,
With bale and bitternes:
And wormwod was my drynke also
In my great thyrstynes.

In peces weare my tethe,　　　　　10
In dust he did me roule,
All good thynges then I cleane forgot,
No reste had my poore soule.

Then in mynde I thought
My selfe vndone to be:　　　　　15
For in the lorde I see quod I
There is no helpe for me.

O yet remember then
My misery and wo,
The wormwod and the bitter gall　　　　　20
And my troubles also.

Yea some rememberaunce
I truste and hope thou hast:
For why my soule within me lorde
Doth melte away and waste.　　　　　25

Whyle I dyd these thynges thus
Consyder in my harte,
I gat some houlde of hope agayne
That was so long aparte:

　　　　　How　　　　　30

148

How thy mercies oh lorde
Are not gone clene awaye
And howe thy louyng kyndnes doth
Not cease from vs for aye.   5

Thy faythfulnes is great,
And euer doth renewe:
As after the most darkest nyght,
The mornyng doth ensue.

The lorde quod my soule tho,   10
He is my porcion:
Therfore my faythe and perfect hope
Is fixte on hym alone.

O howe good is the lorde
To them that in hym truste?   15
And to the soule that seketh hym
With feruent mynde and luste?

Lo then howe good it is
Vpon the Lorde to staye,
And tary for his sauyng health,   20
With stilnes daye by daye.

Howe good is it for man,
His yoke on hym to take:
And from his youth vp weare the same,
Whiche wyll hym perfect make?   25

Suche one alone wyll syt
And holde hym selfe ryght styll:
Who by hym selfe wyll euer dwell,
And quiet be from ill.

                              Hym   30

Hym selfe he doth prostrate,
To harke for hope with loue,
And offreth styll his cheke, to them
That smyte or wyll reproue.   5

In hope thus wyll he reste,
And purely styll perseuer:
For god the lorde wyll not forsake
His chosen flock for euer.

But though he seme somtyme   10
To cease of for a space:
By multitude of mercies he
Receaues agayne to grace.

He suffreth sonnes of men
Not from his harte to fleete,   15
Nor all the prisners on the earth
He treades not vnder feete.

He doth not iudgment geue
By mans desertes in syght:
And to condemne man in his cause,   20
The lorde hath no delyght.

What kynde of man is he,
How mad is suche a one,
Without the lordes commaundment
That sayth ought may be done?   25

Out of the holy mouth
Of God the lorde moste hye,
Both ill and good doth not procede.
What man can this denye?

L   Why   30

Why doth the lyuyng man
Then grudge and murmur so?
At his owne sinne let him repyne
And so commit no mo.   5

Behold we our owne wayes,
And eke bethynke vs well,
And turne agayne vnto the lorde,
From whom we did rebell.

To heauen let vs lyfte   10
Our heartes and handes on hye:
And to the Lorde that there in is,
On this wyse let vs crye.

Dissemblers haue we bene
And did thee sore offende: 15
O lorde let vs intreat thee yet,
That thy wrath nowe may ende.

We hid are in thy wrath
And persecutyng payne,
Without all fauor and regard,   20
O lorde thou hast vs slayne.

For in a cloude from vs
Thy selfe thou hydest so,
That through the thicknes of the same
Our prayers can not go.   25

For outcastes are we nowe,
The Heathen vs despyse:
Our enmies all on vs they gape,
And mocke in sondry wyse.

                              And   30

And subiectes are we made,
To feare and to the snare:
Destruction on vs is come,
And we despysed are.   5

Whole ryuers from myne eyes
Of teares doe styll increase,
My peoples hurte doth cause myne eyes
From wepyng not to cease.

For why there is no reste,   10
O lorde consider this:
O when wylt thou from heauen loke,
And mende that is amys?

Myne eyes haue causde my hearte
In sonder for to ryue: 15
The daughters of my citie made,
My wo so to reuyue.

As foulers seke to haue
The byrdes within their pawes
Myne enmies sharply hunted me   20
And that without a cause.

Into a pit moste depe
My lyfe put downe they haue,
Because I should not ryse they layde
A stone vpon my graue.   25

They powred water then
Vpon my head also:
Nowe am I quyte and clene vndone
To my selfe thoughte I tho.

                    L2   Yet   30

Yet from this pit profounde
I called to the lorde,
Whiche heard my playnt & piteous crie,
And hath my lyfe restorde.   5

When I did syghe and crie,
And for redemption praye,
Thou heardst my voyce, and turnedst not
Thyne eares from me away.

Thy selfe thou didst inclyne,   10
Thy name when I dyd call:
And vnto me thus hast thou sayde,
Haue thou no feare at all.

For thou O lorde arte he
That dyd my soule mayntayne,   15
And hast from death redemed me
And gaust me lyfe agayne.

O lorde auenge my cause
On them that me blaspheme:
Thou knowst how thei would worke me   20
Against me what they meane.   (wo

Thou knowest lorde their spyghte,
And all that they inuent
Against me what their lyps deuyse,
And their moste vyle intent.   25

Howe they syt downe and ryse
O lorde thou doest beholde
And how all day in songes on me,
They nothyng els but scoulde.

     Accor-   30

According to their workes,
Their rewarde them disburse:
And geue them that their hartes doe feare
That is to saye thy curse.   5

O lorde persecute them
With indignation,
From vnder heauen roote them out,
And leaue of them not one.

Oseas .xiiii.   10

O Lord our God we turne to the, thy word we doe em-brace:
For-geue vs our in - i - qui - tie re - ceyue vs vn - to grace.

To offer then in Godly wyse
Shall be our whole intent:

L3   Our   15

154

Our lyps the lyuly sacrifice
Of prayse shall the present.

    To man for helpe and fortitude
We wyll not seke therfore,   5
And strength of horse we wyll conclude
To trust in them no more.

    The workes eke that our handes dyd
That vayn are & must fall,   (make
We doe determine to forsake   10
No more on them to call.

    For it is thou that art our God
And euer shalt remayne:
For mercy at thy fatherhod
The fatherles attayne.   15

    O that they would haue this remorse
(Sayth God) and them conuert:
I would them heale of all their sores,
And loue them with mine hearte.

    My wrath I would from thē decline,   20
To them that I may be
As dew doth make the lylye shyne,
So beutifull to se.

    Their roote lyke vnto *Libanus*
Shall breake out of the ground,   25
And as the olyfe bewtious
Their branches shall abound.

                      As

As *Libanus* so excellent
Theyr swetnes shall excell:
Wherof (as all men doe assent)
Ryght plesant is the smell.   5

For as the corne vnder that tree
Doth floryshe well and growe:
So are they shadowed by me
From hurte and ouerthrowe.

And as the growyng of the vyne,   10
So shall they spryng in dede:
Of *Libanus* as doth the wyne,
So shall their name excede.

Propose I wyll this thee vnto
O Ephraim therfore: 15
From henceforth what haue I to doe
With Idols any more?

I wyll thee heare and geue thee grace
And leade thee forth aryght:
And I wyll be to thee lyke as   20
The grene fyrre tree in syghte.

On me set thy foundation,
Whiche am to the so kynde:
Thy lyuly frutes then eury one
Vpon me shalt thou fynde.   25

This vnderstand the godly wyse
That repe for this rewarde:
The ryght instruct wyll exercyse
The same with good regarde.

L4   The   30

The lorde his wayes be iust and ryght
The godly walke the same:
The wycked folke doe stumble quyte,
And fall out of the frame.   5

Ionas. Cap. ii.

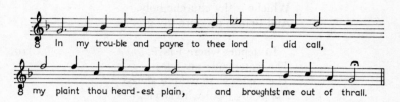

In my trou-ble and payne to thee lord   I did call,
my plaint thou heard-est plain,   and broughtst me out of thrall.

Out of the womb of hell
To the when I did crye,   10
My voyce thou heardest well,
And holpe me louyngly.

Thou threwst me downe as dead
Full depe into the sea,
And made about my head   15
The floudes to compas me.

The

The water waues in haste
Went ouer me with myght:
I thought I had ben cast
Away out of thy syght.   5

But yet agayne shall I
Go to thy holy place:
Whiche is thy churche holy,
And thanke therfore thy grace.

In depnes where I laye,   10
The water sude my lyfe:
The wedes were wrapte alwaye
About my head with stryfe.

Into the helles depnes,
Descendyng I did perseuer,   15
In wo and great distresse
Barde in with earth for euer.

But thou oh God my lorde,
Hast brought my lyfe agayne,
And hast my soule restorde,   20
From corruptible payne.

When that my soule did faint
Vpon the lorde I thought,
My prayer and my playnt,
Was to thy temple brought.   25

Therfore they that delyght
In vanitie so vayne,
Forsake his helpe and myght
That mercy doth retayne.

                    L5   But   30

But I wyll prayse and paye
That I hym vowed haue :
And thanke the lorde alwaye,
That did me helpe and saue.   5

⟦ *A consideration of the vnryghte-*
  ousnes of the vayne & miserable world.

⟦ *Syng this as, Of Ielousy who so*
  wyll heare.

DIRECTLY who so nowe wyl walke   10
In pathes of plain & perfect way :
Whose hartes & mouthes together
Not glosing by deceit astray.   (talke

That flatter none for mede nor loue,
Nor ruled by affection,   15
Nor wyll for worldly glory moue,
Nor yet for brybes infection.

Such mē had nede their countes to cast
In what maner to thriue and gayne :
For here let them be sure and fast,   20
No frendshyp doth for suche remayne.

Requisitly they doe regarde
The ioyes layde vp in lyfe to come :
And that is only the rewarde,
Wheron their mynde is all and summe.   25

Wherfore we may with truthe cōclude,
That suche as loue this worldly pelfe,

From

From heauen doe them selues seclude:
As doth that wretch who kylles him self.

And those agayne that doe despyse
These mundane gaudes, as vyle & vayne: 5
May well be called godly wyse,
For heauens blysse they shall obtayne.

⟦ *A ditie of lamentation against*
the dissemblyng and hipocriticall false
dealynge, vsed of moste folke in these   10
dayes: that is to saye, holy and honest
talke, myxed with wicked and vicious
dedes.

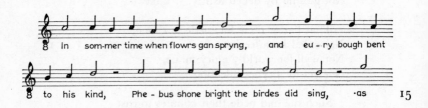

In som-mer time when flowrs gan spryng, and eu-ry bough bent

to his kind, Phe-bus shone bright the birdes did sing, ·as   15

natures

na-tures or-der hath as-signd: I walked to re-cre-at my mynde, which out of so-rowe might not starte: but saide as du-ty did me bind, lord Christ help eu-ry wo-full hart.

My wittes were tossed to and fro,   5
That truthe is preached sincerly,
Yet wycked lyuers neuer mo
Were in this worlde ryght sikarly:
Wherfore I wepte full bitterly,
None but God only knew my smarte: 10
Whiche me constrayned lowd to cry,
Lorde Christ helpe eury wofull harte.

None doth in his vocation walke,
But eche estate wandreth awry:
Yet haue the moste part godly talke,   15
And commit deedes cleane contrary.
Thus walke they in hypocrisie,
In well doyng none doth his part:
Wherfore I cryde ryght hartily
Lorde Christ helpe eury wofull hart.   20

The

The man that is most couetyse
Wyll talke most against wrongful gayne,
Thinkyng by speakyng in suche wyse
His subtill purpose to obtayne: 5
As though perfection did remayne
In flattring tongues & myndes peruert.
This caused me to crye agayne,
Lorde Christe helpe eury wofull heart.

How doth the ryche oppresse the poore?   10
Punyshing them that therof tell?
Howe doth the wolfe the lambe deuoure?
And enuy in his venym swell?
Howe falsly doe men buye and sell?
To speake of this it is my part: 15
For sure these frutes came out of hell,
Lord Christ helpe eury wofull heart.

In dronkenes they haue no pere
That conterfet moste sobernes,
Their talke is often chaste and clere   20
That moste frequent lasciuiousnes,
Whordom, adultrye, and excesse:
And none can cause them to conuert,
Wherfore I crye in heauines,
Lord Christ helpe eury wofull heart.   25

Who reigneth nowe but pryde alone?
Eche man in his owne sight is wyse,
And graue councell regardeth none:
But rather doth doctrine despyse.
Dissimulation and lewde lyes   30
Is nowe excepted as an arte:
Whiche made me crye out in this wyse,
Lord Christ helpe eury wofull hart.

                                        Suche

Suche are most wyse and honest now,
As sonest can their friendes beguyle :
Suche doth the most sorte best allowe,
Whose talke is fayre & dedes most vyle, 5
Simplicitie is in exyle,
And as for truthe can make no marte :
Which made me morne & crie this whyle,
Lorde Christ helpe eury wofull harte.

Gods worde both to and fro is toste, 10
As men doe with a tenis ball,
And wrested from pyller to poste,
To serue mens tourne for sinne and all :
But fewe from wickednes doe fall,
In godlynes to doe their parte : 15
Wherfore thus crie I euer shall,
Lorde Christe helpe eury wofull hearte.

Of wexe they make scripture a nose,
To turne and wryng it eury waye,
With many a false and filthy glose : 20
Suche as by errors walke astraye
The same doe wrythe soules to betraye,
And from the truthe doe them peruerte :
Wherfore I shall crye day by daye
Lord Christ helpe eury wofull hearte. 25

No error synce Christe did ascend,
But nowe it starteth stoutly forth :
The seamles coate of Christe is rend,
And vnitie is nothing worth :
Wherfore plentie is tournd to dearth, 30
And many plagues shall make vs smart :
Wherfore my crie styll forward goeth,
Lorde Christe helpe eury wofull heart.

But

But sure such hartes as here haue wo,
And in this worlde doe mone and morne,
The lorde Christe hath promysed so,
That they shall ioye his face beforne: 5
When suche as here deryde and scorne
Shall suffer sorowe for their parte:
Which lewdly haue them selues forlorne,
Lorde Christe helpe eury wofull hearte.

Wo be to you that here reioyce,   10
Ye shall hereafter wepe and wayle:
For that ye would not heare the voyce
Of Gods worde for your owne auayle.
Which (although heauē & earth doe faile)
Shall styll remayne and byde in quarte: 15
Wherfore my voyce shall neuer fayle,
Lord Christ helpe eury wofull harte.

For all the byrdes with mery songe,
And the bryght shyning of the sonne
And plesant floures I went among,   20
Frō wo my hearte myght not be wonne:
To see what worldly men had done:
For all doe ryde in sinne his carte.
Wherfore I ende as I begonne
Lorde Christe helpe eury wofull hearte.   25
                              Amen.

⟦ *A ditie named blame not my lute*
   whiche vnder that title toucheth, re-
   plieth, and rebuketh, the wycked state
   and enormities of most people, in these   30
   present miserable dayes.
                              Blame

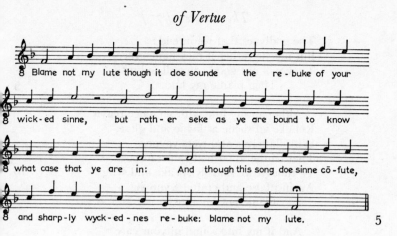

Blame not my lute though it doe sounde the re-buke of your wick-ed sinne, but rath-er seke as ye are bound to know what case that ye are in: And though this song doe sinne cō-fute, and sharp-ly wyck-ed-nes re-buke: blame not my lute.

5

My lute and I sythe truth we tell,
(Meanyng no good man to offende)
Me thynke of ryght none should refell

The

The godlynes that we intend :
But muche rather if they haue grace,
They will our good counsell imbrace,
    Then blame my lute.   5

   Although my lute with sentence playn
Rebuke all suche as fayne and glose,
With flatterers and lyers vayne,
That truthe to falshod can transpose :
Ye though we sharply speake and syng   10
Against false and craftie wynnyng,
    Blame not my lute.

   And if my lute sound in your eare
The priuy hate and lacke of loue,
And howe ye should sclander forbeare,   15
Syth gods word doth ill tõgues reproue :
Though as saint Iames we doe expresse
The same, a worlde of wickednes :
    Blame not my lute.

   Though my lute doe expres and show   20
That prayer and holy fasting,
Is tourned nowe with hyghe and lowe
To vncleane talke and banqueting :
Although we saye that chastitie
Be gone, and in place lecherie,   25
    Blame not my lute.

   Though with their own fewe be cõtent,
Chastly to lyue with one good make :
But rather the moste part be bent
Their constant vowe for to forsake :   30
Though some in Sodom rather byde,

        M   Then

Then honest mariage to prouide,
> Blame not my lute.

If my lute blame the couetyse,
The glottons, and the drunkards vyle,   5
The proud dysdayne of worldly wyse,
And howe falshod doth truth exyle:
Though vyce and sinne be nowe in place,
In sted of vertue and of grace,
> Blame not my lute.   10

Though wrong in iustice place be set,
Committing great iniquitie:
Though hipocrites be counted great,
That mainteine styll idolatrie:
Though some set more by thynges of nought,   15
Then by the lorde that all hath wrought,
> Blame not my lute.

Although eche man finde faulte with other,
And no man will him selfe acuse,
But eche man blameth his brother: 20
Though he him selfe as great faulte vse,
Though we see none their owne fault fynde,
Nor call repentance vnto mynde,
> Blame not my lute.

Though my lute say that suche as preache   25
And should men leade in wayes directe
Doe lyue amys, though truth they teache,
Whiche causeth truth to be suspect,
Though my lute say suche cause offence
Through their great slouth and negligence,   30
> Blame not my lute.

> Though

Though some gods worde doe still despyse,
For beggerly traditions:
Aduancing highly fayned lyes
Of mens imaginations. 5
Although my lute doe suche accuse,
As by errors gods worde abuse,
  Blame not my lute.

Although we see the clergie slack,
Wrong wayes by ryght for to redres: 10
Though some also goe rather back,
Then procede forth in righteousnes:
Although we saye that auarice
Doth stop the mouthe, and choke the wyse,
  Blame not my lute. 15

Though offendors be borne withall,
Although the wolues in corners lurke
That haue and will the lambes make thrall,
And daily doe their false feates worke.
Though whispryng treason in the eare 20
Burst out somtyme without all feare,
  Blame not my lute.

Though some also abuse the lute
With sinfull songes of lechery:
Though some goe forth as beastes brute, 25
In false treason and trechery:
Though at eche sermon we may see
Gods holy worde scorned to be,
  Blame not my lute.

Blame not my lute I you desyre, 30
But blame the cause that we thus playe:

   M2 For

168

For burnyng heate blame not the fyre,
But hym that blowth the cole alway.
Blame ye the cause blame ye not vs,
That we mēs faultes haue touched thus   5
  Blame not my lute.

 Blame not my lute, nor blame not me,
Although it sound against your sinne:
But rather seeke for to be free,
From suche abuse as ye are in.   10
Although we warne you to repent:
Whiche grant you God omnipotent.
  Blame not my lute.

⟦ *A song of the lute in the prayse of*
 God, *and disprayse of Idolatrie.*   15

⟦ *Syng this as,* My pen obey. *&C.*

MY lute awake and prayse the lord,
My heart and hādes therto accord:
Agreing as we haue begon,
To syng out of gods holy worde.   20
And so procede tyll we haue done.

 Prayse we the lord in this our song,
And syng it Christen men among,
That in a godly race doe ronne:
The whiche although it be not long,   25
Shall be right good or it be donne.

 This plesant song shall not song be,
To the goddesse of lechery:

      Nor

Nor to nothyng vnder the Sunne,
But praysing of the almyghty,
My lute and I tyll we haue done.

This teacheth vs Dauid the kyng,   5
With harpe and lute geue God praysyng,
All men that in this worlde doe wonne
To God therfore geue prayse and synge,
As my lute and I haue begonne.

This lord first made al things of nought,   10
And when against his lawe we wrought
From heauen he sent downe his sonne:
Whiche with his gospell vs all taught,
After the whiche we haue not donne.

Although in man weare nothyng good   15
Hym to redeme Christ shed his blood,
With thornes ỹ Iues our lord did crown,
He suffred death vpon the roode:
Lo thus our sauyng health was donne.

On this therfore we fix our fayth,   20
That Iesus Christ (as scriptur sayth)
Is only our saluation.
Vpon this rocke who so him stayth,
Thus sayth the lord it is well don.

But one thing sore my harte doth greue   25
That hipocrites made vs beleue
In Idols both of wodde and stone:
From Christ our rock they did vs dryue,
Wo be to them what haue they done.

M3   Whiche   30

Whiche canker still within their heartes,
Doth yet remayne and fewe conuertes:
For at gods worde they frete and frown,
Therfore my lute it is our partes   5
Them to rebuke as we haue done.

God sent his worde vnto this ende,
That we our synfull lyues should mende:
And yet repenteth fewe or none:
My lute therfore let vs intende   10
To say the truthe tyll we haue done.

If in our songe we should recyte,
Howe eche estate doth not vpright:
(Whiche will be their confusion,)
Whiche knowe the truthe and do not ryght,   15
My lute when should our song be done.

But to be short my hartes intent,
Is to prayse God omnipotent,
Whoe of our helth the thred hath spunne,
And hath his worde to vs nowe sent,   20
To mende our lyues tyll we haue done.

Mans soule to saue Christ died therfore,
Who of vs men doth aske no more:
But this lesson to lerne and conne,
With loue to kepe his holy lore: 25
In whiche all perfect workes are donne.

Lorde graunt vs to thy worde to cleaue,
That no man other doe deceaue:
And in that zeale that I begunne,

                                  Lauding   30

Lauding our lorde God here I leaue,
Be styll my lute my song is done.

⟦ *A ditie shewyng the office of all e-*
states : warnyng them to repent, & walke   5
euery estate accordyng to their callyng.

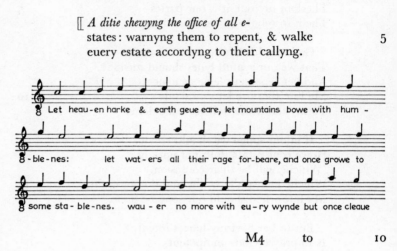

Let heau-en harke & earth geue eare, let mountains bowe with hum-
-ble-nes: let wat-ers all their rage for-beare, and once growe to
some sta-ble-nes. wau-er no more with eu-ry wynde but once cleaue

M4   to   10

to a con-stant mynde. In fayth and loue, for why the lord him
self doth speake, and will you els in son-der breake, euen from a-boue.

Let not god speake now to deafe eares,
Nor vnto hartes made of flynt stone :   5
But rather with repentant teares
Bewayle your synnes now eury one.
And let a godly lyfe all newe
Shew forth frutes of repentance true,
And them expresse.   10
That from henceforth in such new lyfe,
We may remayn without all stryfe,
In righteousnes.

Let suche as shewe the heauenly muse
Haue godly conuersation,   15
Least through their vyle and great abuse
They worke abhomination :
When as in synfull wayes they walke,
Contrary to their outwarde talke,
And gods true worde.   20

For

For who that sclandreth so the truthe,
Their myrth shall turne to wo and ruthe
Before the lorde.

Let kynges that mountains sygnifie,   5
In iustice doe styll their due part:
Supporte no more iniquitie,
Nor mainteyne suche as are peruart.
Se that henceforth with all your myght
Ye put downe wrong & mainteine right.   10
Or els surely
The lord God whiche is kyng of all,
Your glory turne to shame he shall
Moste ryghteously.

Let nowe the waueryng multitude,   15
That signifyd is by the sea,
Oh let I saye this rable rude
Still henceforth cleaue to constancie.
And not them selues as waters showe,
Vnstable for to ebbe and flowe: 20
But styll depende,
Vpon the churche to lerne their due,
And serue their kyng w^{t} hartes most true,
Euen styll an ende.

Let not the churche be temporall,   25
Let not rulers be rude and vayne:
Let no man from his calling fall,
But eche man in his state remayne:
Let not the common people deale
With matters highe of common weale.   30
For why I saye,
If one anothers callyng vse,

M5   All

All equitie they doo refuse
From day to daye.

Let all men nowe repent therfore,
And leaue theyr synne without delay,   5
And henceforth vse the same no more:
Least by theyr goyng thus astray,
Gods wrathe in hast they doo procure:
For this theyr doyngs so vnpure
In synfull trade.   10
Knowe that the Lorde his mercy styll,
Dothe offer all with ryght good wyll,
That he hath made.

Let men whyle mercy then doothe last,
Haue mynde of this theyr onely meane,   15
Abhorre theyr yll lyfe that is past:
Lyftyng their eyes vp into heauen.
Lokyng from thence for theyr reliefe:
Whiche is a salue for all our griefe,
Swete Christe Iesu.   20
Your hartes and eares I say attend,
That you to blysse without all end,
May hence insue.

⟦ *A Ditie declaringe the daungerous*
abuse of all degrees, whyche go astraye   25
from theyr vocation.

PERFORME O penne I thee desyre,
The thyng that we dyd late deuyse:
Blowe to this cole, kyndle thys fyre:
That suche may know as truth despise   30

That

That darknes shall no more them hyde:
No secrete place shall they prouyde
To couer guyle:
For now the lyght shall them bewray,   5
That secretly haue gone astray,
A ryght long whyle.

Suche Princes as the poore oppresse,
Vnder title of gouernance,
And wyll no poore mans cause redresse,   10
But all theyr ioye and fyne pastance,
Is nowe with craft in couerture,
They may in theyr yll wayes indure,
And styll remayne.
It shall appeare at the laste day,   15
That they haue wrongly gone astray,
Vnto theyr payne.

Suche prelates as for fylthy gayne,
With errors doo mens soules destroy,
And on theyr flock lyke lordes wyll raigne,   20
Wherin Gods woorde they doo anoy:
The fleece to take is all theyr care,
And for the soule no foode prepare,
But venym vyle.
Suche prelates shall once know, I say,   25
That they haue falsly gone astray
With fraude and guyle.

Suche men of lawe as wyll for golde
Make thyngs seme right the which ar wrong
And wyll for gayne with falshode hold,   30
And eke delaye the tyme to long:
Suche as in Iudgement wrest the lawe,

                                        And

And wrongly doe the sentence drawe:
Wrong to supporte.
Poore innocentes for to betraye,
For brybes they goe from ryght astraye,   5
In wicked sorte.

 Suche marchantes as are not content,
With right and reason for to wynne,
But daily doe false fraude inuent,
To gayne by wickednes and synne,   10
Vnlawfull gayne and vsury,
And counterfetyng wyckedly
Muche marchandyse,
In hell they shall once fele I saye,
Howe they by fraude haue gone astraye,   15
In vniust wyse.

 Suche leches as wyckedly vse
Medicines arte, but not aryght,
But falsly doe the same abuse,
And to that arte doth wrong and spyght: 20
They rob and murder where they go,
From place to place, workyng muche wo
Without cunnyng,
The Diuell shall them fetche away,
By suche deceyte that goe astraye,   25
With false wynnyng.

 Suche as in any kynde of arte
Doe worke both slyghtly and vnsure,
For to deceyue with a false harte
His neighbour, by his worke vnpure: 30
Slightly they worke and all for haste,
Wherin this day is wrong and waste:
Yea hatefull wrong.

     Syth

Syth now ther is no faith nor fay
But all from truth are gone astray,
Wo be our songe.

Suche as breake vnitie and loue,   5
Suche as by couetyse contende,
Such as wyll sweare & great othes moue
Suche as on whordom doe depende,
Suche as in pryde doe leade their lyfe,
Suche as by wrath doe lyue in stryfe,   10
And great debate:
Satan with suche must make afraye,
For their walkyng so farre astraye,
Whiche god doth hate.

God for his mercie graunt therfore,   15
That men may nowe repent their ill,
And that they may their synnes abhorre,
Wherin they walked with their wyll:
It is hyghe tyme for to redres,
And to absteyne from wyckednes,   20
For feare of payne.
And for Gods mercy call and praye,
That we through grace frō this our stray
Come home agayne.

⟦ *A voyce from heauen to you shall*   25
    come, Venite adiudicium.

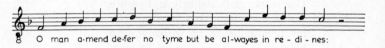

O man a-mend de-fer no tyme but be al-wayes in re - di - nes:

For

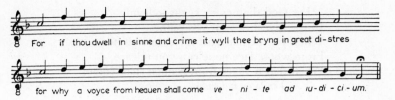

For if thou dwell in sinne and crime it wyll thee bryng in great di-stres

for why a voyce from heauen shall come ve - ni - te ad iu-di - ci - um.

Then blessed shall that seruant be
Whom God shall fynde in perfect mynde,   5
To doe his due in eche degree:
For great reward then shall he fynde.
When that a voyce from heauen shall come,
 Venite ad iudicium.

Contrary wyse the seruant yll,   10
That walked in offences great,
Contrary to his maisters wyll,
With many strypes he shalbe beate:
When that a voyce from heauen shall come,
 Venite ad iudicium.   15

        For

For God shall come ryght sodeynly
In the mydst of your wyckednes,
When you thynke least appeare wyll he:
From whose face none can you releace.   5
When that a voyce from heauen shall come,
    Venite ad iudicium.

Eche lorde and lady, kyng and quene,
Before that lorde muste bowe theyr knee:
And then shall theyr rewarde be sene,   10
Lyke as their dedes and lyfe hath bee.
When that a voyce from heauen shall come,
    Venite ad iudicium.

What shall auayle you then your pryde,
Your welthy pompe and dignitie: 15
Your ryches then must stande asyde,
And not helpe your necessitie.
When that a voyce from heauen shall come,
    Venite ad iudicium.

The shynyng face of God the Lorde,   20
Your stony hearts shall then appall:
Because that ye so muche abhorde,
His preceptes euangelicall.
When that a voyce from heauen shall come,
    Venite ad iudicium.   25

Then shall ye say, Wo worthe the tyme,
Your lawes agaynst the Lorde of blis,
That you made in despyte of hym,
And all that hys true members is:
When that a voyce from heauen shall come,   30
    Venite ad iudicium.

              And

And you shall gnashe your tethe and saye,
Lo those whom we did hate and mocke:
We see them sytte in quiet staye,
Beyng the lordes elected flocke.   5
For nowe a voyce from heauen is come,
  Venite ad iudicium.

And we lyke fooles haue erred styll,
Our worldly wyt is nowe all spent:
To plead our cause we haue no skyll,   10
Before the lorde omnipotent:
For nowe a voyce from heauen is come,
  Venite ad iudicium.

The sonne of wisdom and of lyght,
Of vnderstanding, and of grace,   15
Did geue to vs no kynde of lyght:
We are vndone alas alas.
For nowe a voyce from heauen is come,
  Venite ad iudicium.

In payns of hell thus shall they crye   20
That nowe doe Christ his flocke oppresse,
Tormented styll eternally
With diuels for their wyckednes:
When that a voyce from heauē shal come,
  Venite ad iudicium.   25

Therfore let vs defer no tyme,
But be alwayes in readynes:
That we may all to heauen clyme,
With Christ the kyng of ryghteousnes:
When that a voyce frō heauen shal come,   30
  Venite ad iudicium.

     Against

⟦ *Against pryde.*

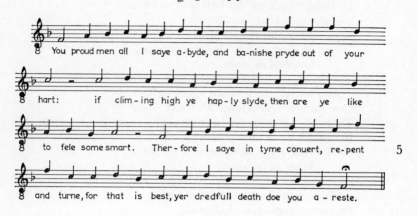

You proud men all I saye a-byde, and ba-nishe pryde out of your hart: if clim-ing high ye hap-ly slyde, then are ye like to fele some smart. Ther-fore I saye in tyme conuert, re-pent and turne, for that is best, yer dredfull death doe you a-reste.

5

N   Study

Study therfore in holy wryte
And knowe howe that lucifer fell,
Whiche beyng once an angell bryght
God for his pryde dyd hym expell   5
Out of all lyght, downe into hell.
Lo here you see the frute of pryde,
I say therfore laye it asyde.

Before your eyes fixe also this,
Howe Nebucadnezar the kyng,   10
(Whose dedes in Daniell wrytten is)
Who praisde him selfe aboue all thyng,
And gaue not God his due praysing
Was made an oxe and did eate haye
Seuen yeres, his great pryde to alaye.   15

And kyng Herod (as sayth scripture)
As he was clad in proude araye,
His owne honor for to procure,
To his own praise great wordes did say:
Therfore Gods angell that same day   20
Dyd stryke him for his harte vnwyse,
Who vnto death was eate with lyce.

Lo if God would such kings not spare
To punysh, for ambition,
What shall we thinke he wyll prepare   25
To plague our sinfull nacion:
Whiche forsake their vocation,
And will in no wyse pryde eschue,
Nor seke to serue swete dame vertue.

For Salomon in sentence playne   30
Calles fauor a deceyuyng thyng:

Yea

Yea beautie is a thing moste vayne,
Wherin some haue suche delyghtyng:
Which in ill case once wyll them bryng,
Gods heauy wrath they so procure: 5
Through their proude hartes vayn & vn-
                                        pure.
  For from the course of reason true
They seme to be vnknowne and strange,
That doe delyght in the vayne hewe,   10
Of beautie, that so sone wyll change:
For that wherin their rude wittes range,
Is muche more britle then is glasse,
And fades as doth in fieldes the grasse.

  More inconstant it is also,   15
That vnto pryde doth you prouoke,
Then wynde that wandreth to and fro:
Yea much more vain thē smothring smoke
Lo thus of vyce you beare the yoke,
Of beautie proude more vyle then slyme,   20
And fleteth faster then tyme.

  A thousand thynges may beauty fade,
As wyse men dayly see and saye:
For if a feuer you inuade,
And shake you but one simple daye: 25
Is not your beauty gone strayghtwaye?
Your colour shewes your substance iust,
Euen earth and ashes doung and dust.

  If men were bent the truth to tell,
Is beauty any other thyng,   30
Then color in the skyn or fell?
Wherin some haue suche reioysing?

       N2   But

But if as well were appearing
Their inwarde partes, then myght we see
A sacke, stufte full of doung fylthy.

What syght more strange may there apeare,   5
Vnto our eyes so fantsy full,
Then see one bewtifull and clere,
Declare it selfe so vnfruitfull?
And cause hym whose wites be not dull
Hym self to knowe, a dounghill dyght   10
As with a cloth purple and whyght.

What impudence, yea what madnes
Is it in beutie to glorie?
Forsakyng all sober sadnes,
For thynges that bene transitorie?   15
Sythe more delectabilitie,
It is to some that see the same,
Then those that therof beare the name!

I leue of here, for to recite
What other hurtes your bewtie doth,   20
With your apparell proude and lyght,
Tempting the frailtie of weake youth:
Therefore vse nowe meknes and truth.
This olde sayde sawe may warne you all,
That pryde wyll surely haue a fall.   25

⟦ *An inuectiue against the most hate-*
   full vyce enuy.   ⟦ Syng this as Let
nowe thy power be great O Lorde. &c.

                                        All

ALL they that will of enuy here,
Vnto my song let them attend:
If you will lerne, then draw you nere,
Let enuious mē their mysse amēd. (nere,   5

   Vnto my lippes haue good respect,
And marke what shall from them insue:
Enuy with blyndnes dothe infect,
And styll disprayseth dame vertue.

   Within this worlde so full of sinne,   10
It is a scabbe sayth *Tullius*,
If that suche men as be therin
To vertue shall be enuious.

   Oh wicked worlde, full of enuy,
Polluted with despight and hate: 15
Receiue agayne simplicitie,
Take loue, and banysh all debate.

   Salomon sayth in sapience,
I wyll none enuy nor disdeyne:
Banysh them cleane from my presence,   20
Wisdom wyll none suche enterteyne.

   For hatefull enuie is mother
Of wycked wordes, fond, ferce, and fell:
Contrary wyse loue doth couer
The wordes whiche are not spoken well.   25

   Sythe loue then is the remedy
Against enuy that wycked vyce:
Take loue to you continually,
It is a treasure of great pryce.

        N3   *Against*   30

⟦ *Against slouthe.*
  Syng this as, Of Ielousye who so
  wyll heare.

MARKE and geue eare ye slouthful mē,   5
And to my song geue good respect:
Aryse out of your drousy den,
To Idlenes that are subiect.

  Ryght truly sayde kyng Salomon,
As smoke the tender eyes offende: 10
So slouthfull men are wrathe anon,
Wyth suche as moue them to amend.

  Go to (sayth he) thou slouthfull beast,
Go to and slumber out thy fyll,
Wyth folded armes lye downe to rest,   15
Accordyng to thyne idle wyll.

  As one that iourneyth all day long,
So pouertie shall on thee lyght:
And as a souldier fierce and strong:
Necessitie shall shew her myght.   20

  But who so is industrious,
And wyll his labour well apply:
His increace shall be plentious,
And he shall haue abundantly.

  In slouthfull soules, thus saith the Lord,   25
My wysedome it can take no place:
Oh be conuerted by Gods word,
Ye slouthfull men, and calle for grace.

                  Who

Who so to worke no payne wyll take,
But liues in slouth (thus saith S. Paul)
His company we must forsake,
And geue to hym no meate at all.   5

Thus sayth the lord, therfore awake
Thou that dost slepe, and stande vpright:
Stande vp from death, for Christes sake:
And Christ the lord shall geue thee lyght.

[*A description of auarice*   10

Saint Ber-nard saith the cha-ri-ot of a-ua-rice is borne, on

fow-er wheles of vic-es ill: through which the poore are torne.

The first is courage faynt and fonde,
The next vngentylnes,
The thirde contempt of God, the fourth   15
Of death forgetfulnes.

N4   And

And horses two this chariot drawes,
That is as muche to saye,
As Raueny and Nygardshyp:
Whiche are in it alwaye.   5

The Carter whiche dooth dryue them bothe,
He is a greedye knaue:
And who so would hys name were knowen,
It is Desyre to haue.

That Carter dryueth with a whyp,   10
Whych whyp of cordes hath twayne:
That is, Great appetite to get,
And Lothe to yeld agayne.

Ryght many of the cart haue scorne,
And them that cartes doo dryue: 15
Yet moste men for to dryue thys cart,
Thys daye contende and stryue.

And they that take in most yll part,
Of carters to heare name:
Doo dryue thys carte of couetyse,   20
And muche delyght the same.

And suche as weare bothe sylke and golde,
(That strange is for to see)
Doo sue to master Auarice,
His carters for to bee.   25

Where some were wont with speare & shield,
Theyr countrey to defend:
Haue layde asyde theyr armour quight,
And to this carte attend.

                                    The   30

The Clergy whych should preache and teache
If they dyd playe theyr parte,
Doo laye asyde the worde of God,
And dayly dryue thys carte.   5

The Merchant and the learned leche,
And eke the man of lawe,
Forsake theyr artes, and dayly doo
This carte bothe dryue and drawe.

And they that common carters be,   10
(Of moste men called so)
Doo knowe least how to dryue this cart
And farthest are therfro.

Our money (as sayth Seneca)
Ought ay to be our drudge,   15
To serue for our necessitie,
And at our wyll to trudge.

But yf we (as a lady dere)
Make her our souerayne:
She wyll not mysse to bryng our soules   20
Into eternall payne.

God of hys mercy therfore graunt,
This cartynge we may leaue,
To loue and lyberalytie,
That we may alway cleaue.   25

Free from the thefe and from the mothe
That we may horde our store:
Forsakyng gredy auarice,
And dryue hys carte no more.

A   30

⟦ *A dittie of the pen inueiyng against*
vsury and false dealyng.

My pen o-bey my wyll a whyle till I see good to ende this
stile: for if all men would sinne ab - horre such songs 5
we nede not to com-pile, nor my pen should write so no more.

If all men of their worde were true,
Promis to kepe and paye their due:
What nede had pennes to worke therfore?

But 10

But sythe no whyght wyll truthe ensue :
Pennes were as good to wryte no more.

Pennes are abusde, and that dayly,
About all craft and vsury :   5
We may well say alas therfore.
And yet least we make them angry
It semes as good to wryte no more.

Yet let vs shewe the lordes intent,
Howe that for gaynes nought should be lent,   10
All falshod God wyll plage ryght sore.
And yet my penne least we be shent,
It semes as good to wryte no more.

For all in vayne we speake scripture,
To suche as wyll in synne endure :   15
For they amende neuer the more,
But hate all godly counsayle pure,
That warneth them to synne no more.

Yet if all men with suche pretence,
Should cease to shewe their conscience,   20
They should transgresse gods holy lore.
Yet sythe none wyll it reuerence,
It semes as good to wryte no more.

The scripture thus doth specifie
In Dauids psalmes, blessed is he,   25
That lendeth freely ryche and poore.
Without all gayne of vsury :
Yet doe they vse it styll the more.

Though scme for writing wyl vs blame,

These   30

These crafty men, whome we not name,
These false gotte goodes they must restore,
To those of whom they got the same,
Or els be damnde for euermore.   5

   For though some men haue bene er thys,
In vsury that dyd amys,
And haue bene warnde of it before :
That doo repent yet fewe there ys,
But rather vse it more and more.   10

   But sure in hell theyr bed is made,
And all that vse of crafte the trade
Are lyke the same to rue ryght sore :
In crafte and guyle yet syth they wade,
It were as good to wryte no more.   15

   God graunt as in this song is ment,
We may amende all and repent :
Rootyng out vyce to the harde core,
To serue the lorde omnipotent,
In loue and truthe for euermore.   20

⟦ *An exhortation to wrathfull men.*
  Syng this as, I am the man
  whom God. &c.

IF wrathe were paynted out
In perfect lyuely hue,   25
As coulde Apelles in hys lyfe,
Wyth colours fyne and true.

   Or as Demosthenes,
Descrybe it coulde with pen :

                    As   30

As it is yll it would appere,
Vnto these wrathfull men.

Or he that cunnyng had
In metre to recite,   5
Both soule and body how it noyes,
As sheweth holy write.

Then should these wrathfull men,
That anger wyll sustayne,
Perceaue the incommodities   10
That therwith doo remayne.

Concernyng body fyrste,
Diseases it doth bryng,
As feuers vyle of euery kynd,
Whiche mortally doo styng.   15

It causeth phrenesie,
And madnes of the brayne:
Of visage great deformytie,
And palseys this is playne.

Concernyng soule also,   20
(The whiche is worste of all)
It maketh men blaspheme their frendes,
And euell them to call.

Outrage and wycked othes,
And loue put out of place: 25
Reuengement is theyr whole desyre
That banysht be from grace.

All benefytes forgot,

                              That

That to thee dyd thy frende:
Obedience true and reuerence,
Wrathe putteth out of mynde.

Wherof succedeth oft,   5
Contention full of cost:
By trouble and vnquiet mynde,
Thyne appetite is lost.

To scorne dysdeyne and hate,
Ye thynke it is no shame: 10
All though nothyng can hynder more,
A good report or name.

These wycked fruites of wrathe,
Remember he that can:
Full lytle haste (as I suppose)   15
To wrathe they would haue than.

Harke and geue eare ye men
That thus to wrath are bent,
Attend a whyle vnto my tune,
And holde your selfe content.   20

For as thou art a man,
Thynke also so ys he:
With whō thou doest cōceiue such cause,
So wrathfull for to be.

Is it not laufull then,   25
And as conuenyent,
That he with thee should be as wrathe,
And as muche discontent?

                                        Leaue

Leaue of your wrath therfore,
I saye to you agayne:
Assure your selues that angry men,
Doo alway lyue in payne.   5

And calle to mynde howe Christ
The sonne of God moste hye:
Whyche in a moment by hys power
Hys enmies myght destroye,

How dyd the Iewes hym greue!   10
Hauyng no cause wherfore:
Hys most swete face they strake in spight
And buffeted hym sore.

It nothyng irked them,
At hym to spyt in scorne,   15
Wyth wytnesse wrong accusyng hym,
And crowned hym with thorne.

Hys vertous body lo,
They haled to and fro:
An heauy Crosse on hym they layde,   20
The more to doo hym wo.

All faultlesse as a lambe,
To suffer deathe he went:
They dyd hys body all to beate,
And yet was he content.   25

They naylde hym on the crosse,
Thys shoulde we beare in mynde:
Thys suffred he of his good wyll,

For

For sauyng of mankynde.

And they that dyd all thes,
As scripture telleth playne,
Were his owne kynne and countreymen,   5
That put hym to thys payne.

For all whiche hatefull dede,
(As worse there coulde none bee)
Yet to be wrath at any tyme,
No creature coulde hym see.   10

Thus Christ went vs before
Example vs to geue,
Of mekenes and of pacience,
And godly for to lyue.

Some make excuse and say,   15
That wrathe is naturall:
To whom I saye of natures power,
Christ lacked none at all.

For Nature neuer was,
The cause of suche abuse,   20
Nor neuer taught her perfect workes,
Them selues so to mysuse.

For wrathes moste wycked rage,
Is contrary to kynde:
Whiche dothe by accidentall power,   25
Possesse the wycked mynde.

Yet some wyll say agayne,
(My purpose to asswage)

That

That wrathe is vertue in a man,
And token of courage.

    I answere that in Christ
Was courage thorow out: 5
For angels trembled in hys syght,
And dyuels dyd hym dout.

    Eche man I truste therfore,
Of ire wyll take good hede:
And folowe Christ wyth pacience,   10
In worde and eke in dede.

    I would not yet ye thought,
My meanyng to be here,
Of zeale, the whych in godly men
Ryght often dothe appere: 15

    As when a wyse man doth
His seruantes fault rebuke,
Or moderatly punyshe hym,
His euell to confute.

    Displeasure proprely   20
This passyon we may call:
Whych yf we vse in discrete wyse,
We doo not synne at all.

    As holy wryt recordes,
This hath full oft bene sene,   25
In Prophets and in holy men,
That God dyd well esteme.

       O   For

For Moses in this zeale,
The Tables brake of stone:
In whych God with hys fynger wrote,
His ten precepts eche one.   5

As Dauid ment when he,
Ryght holyly dyd saye:
Be angery, but doo not synne,
By no maner of way.

It was in Christe also,   10
(As holy wryt dothe tell:)
When he out of the temple whypt
Those that dyd buye and sell,

Within his holy place,
Where nothyng els should be,   15
But prayer to the lyuyng God,
In secrete that doeth see.

And at an other tyme,
It shewde in hym agayne,
The hypocrites when he rebukt,   20
As Mathew telleth playne.

This symple song all ye,
That heare or doo it reade:
It is enough to cause you all,
Of wrathe to take good hede.   25

Of synfull wycked wrathe,
Beware in any wyse:
To all men that haue wyt in store,
Let this as nowe suffyse.

                                    In   30

In hearyng of theyr faultes,
That they may mend them soone,
And after stand at Gods ryght hand,
When they receyue theyr doome.   5

[*An Inuectiue agaynst wrathe.*
  Syng thys as, The lyuyng God
  our only Lorde, that. &c.

SALOMON sayth, A foole his guyse,
Is to be wrath immediatly: 10
But he is to be counted wyse,
That well can hyde hys iniury,
Therfore saynt Paule doth say of trauth,
Let not the sunne rest on your wrath.

And Plato beyng demaunded,   15
Wherby a wise man knowne should be:
Sayd, yf wyse men be rebuked,
Therwith they wyll not be angry.
Therfore saint Paule doth say of trauth,
Let not the sonne rest on your wrath.   20

Byas also dothe ryght well shewe,
Of wrath the discommoditie:
Saying that it in hygh and lowe,
To counsayle is chiefe enemye:
Therfore saint Paule doth say of trauth,   25
Let not the sonne rest on your wrathe.

The chiefest helpe agaynst the same,
Seneca dothe describe ryght playne:
Take Pacience that godly dame:
In her syght wrath can not remayne.   30

              O.ii.   Ther-

200

Therfore saint Paule doth saye of trauth,
Let not the sonne reste on your wrath.

Of wrathfull men it is the wunt
To sowe discorde with eche estate: 5
But pacience doth alwayes hunte
For to appease strife and debate.
Therfore saint Paule doth say of trauth,
Let not the sonne reste on your wrath.

Therfore with men replete with ire   10
Vse no familiaritie,
And those whom wrath sone settes on fyre,
Byde thou not in their company:
But as sainte Paule doth saye of trauth,
Let not the sonne reste on thy wrath.   15

As sayth saint Iames be swyft to heare
The thyng that may thee edifie,
Be slowe in speache in lyke maner,
But slowe to wrath especially:
For why saint Paule doth say of trauth,   20
Let not the sonne reste on your wrath.

By wrath as sayth saint Gregory,
Wysdome is hid and out of syght,
And puts all out of memory
That should be done by wisdomes myght.   25
Therfore saynt Paule doth saye of trauth,
Let not the sonne reste on your wrath.

My brethern here to make an ende,
I you commit to pacience,
As seruantes true doe you intende   30

                                        To

To serue hyr grace with diligence,
Because saynt Paule doth say of trauth,
Let not the sonne reste on your wrath.

⟦ *Against drunkennes and gluttony.*   5

⟦ Syng this as, Of Ielousy who so wyll
  heare. &c.

A DRUNKEN workeman certeynly
By labour neuer getteth ought:
A lyttle he settes nothyng by,   10
But from a litle commes to nought.

For learned men howe may suffice,
Their wyne in litle quantitie:
So in their reste and exercise,
It doth none incommoditie.   15

Wo be to those that early ryse
(The prophet sayth) to make great haste,
And drynke tyll nyght (as is their guyse)
Tyll reason banysht be at laste.

A drunkard (as saint Austen sayth)   20
Offendeth nature very sore,
Castyng asyde both grace and fayth,
He hedlong runnes to hell therfore,

The moderate vse of drynke and meate,
No wyse man hateth, this is true: 25
But luste inordinate and great,
Ought euery good man to eschue.

                    O3   Saint

Saint Ierome sayth, Cursed be they,
That in theyr meate haue suche delyte,
That reason can not cease nor stay
Theyr vyle and gredy appetite.　　　　　5

Saynt Ambrose playnly doth expresse,
A worse to serue can none inuent
Then gluttony, that yll maystresse:
Desyryng styll, and nere content.

Nor nothyng more insaciate　　　　　10
Then glottons bellyes most lyke hell,
For that whych they receyued late,
Ryght early they agayne expell.

These farsted panches aye abhorre,
Good continence and chastitie:　　　　　15
Before digestion they craue more,
Forsakyng vertue fylthyly.

All Christians therfore I exhort,
Voluptuous excesse to forbeare:
To moderation now resorte,　　　　　20
And frugally lyue in gods feare.

⟦ *Lecherie rebuked.*
　Syng this as, On tabrets to the
　Lorde. &c.

LIKE as the fowler wyth hys bayte,　　　　　25
Soone brynges the byrd in snare,

So

So are mens soules through lechery,
Destroyde yer they be ware.

   For lechery (Gods ennemy)
With vertue is not plaste: 5
Of present lust a fowle delyght,
And of substance a waste.

   It blyndeth men, that they thynke not
On dreadfull pouertie:
Whych from great vse of lechery,   10
Long absent can not be.

   To bryng a man to beggers state,
Of harlots is the trade:
Therfore absteyne from lechery,
Let it not thee inuade.   15

   For yf we shall consyder well,
Mans nature excellent:
The hyghnes and the dygnitie,
That God therto hath lente,

   It is a fowle and wycked synne,   20
To vse it wantonly:
Resoluyng it vnhonestly,
In fylthy lechery.

   How honest and howe beautyfull
To lyue contrary wyse,   25
In continence and temperance,
Sobernes to deuyse.

                 O.iiii.   For

For lechery and synfull lust
In youth who so doth vse:
Shall wythred be with feblenes,
In age for thys abuse.   5

    Take hede therfore, let not your hartes
In harlots snares be caught:
Absteyne from them, frequent them not,
Theyr pathes be very naught.

    The houses of suche harlots are,   10
Of helle the very snare:
Theyr chambers vnto dredfull death,
Full well we may compare.

    For grace therfore pray we to God,
And vnto wedlocke cleaue: 15
Of lechery and synfull lust
That we may take our leaue.

[*An earnest complaint agaynste*
  Idolatry. Syng this as, In my
  trouble and payne.   20

SOMETYME that I haue sene,
To see agayne were strange,
In place where I haue bene,
In hope no more to range.

    In wyckednes and synne,   25
And in Idolatrye:
Whyche who so vse, shall wynne
Helle euerlastyngly.

                       For

For from the face of GOD
There can be nothyng hyd:
Who hath full oft forbod,
That we agaynst hym dyd.　　　　　5

To worshyp an Image,
The Lord dothe most abhorre:
But in our pylgremage,
We honoured great store.

That tyme I trust be past,　　　　　10
For custome made vs blynde:
And I am sore agast,
Lest worse be lefte behynde.

Beware whyle you haue space,
That Idoll of the harte:　　　　　15
Leste at the laste it chace,
Your soules in hell to smart.

Beware and take good hede:
Leste that er ye be ware,
Ye doo so farre procede,　　　　　20
That ye no more repayre.

Example ye may see:
As Salomon doth saye,
Take tyme whyle tyme may bee,
For tyme wyll soone away.　　　　　25

Repent therfore in space,
Whyle tyme to you is lent,
And call to God for grace,
With true heart and intent.

　　　　　　O.v.　　　Lest　　　30

Lest when ye would ryght fayne
There shall no grace be sent,
As subiect to hell payne
In sorowe to be shent.   5

⟦ *An inuectiue against sclanderous*
  tongues.
⟦ Syng this as, If truthe may take no
  trusty hold. &c.

IN sadnes set with wo opprest,   10
Oft did I sighe by my constraynt:
From depnes of a pensiue brest,
Thus carefully came forth my playnt.

O sclander vyle and tongues vntrue,
Unbridled lo thus ye procede,   15
And cause the carefull harte to rue,
That did no faulte by worde or dede.

Not all for nought (I well perceyue,)
Kyng Dauid did on you complayne:
Sythe nought may let you to deceyue,   20
And vtter frutes of your disdayne.

Delyuer lorde my soule sayeth he,
From lyps that lye for me in weyght:
And from suche tongues as euer be,
In vse with falshod and deceyt.   25

What rewarde then may we deuyse,
For tongues quod he that speake vnright,
The whottest coles in burnyng wyse,
With arrowes sharpe and full of myght.

                                    Among   30

Among men mortall on this mould,
I thynke there is no vyce nor cryme,
So wycked by a thousand fould:
As ill tongues are this present tyme.　　　　5

Whiche ernestly hath geuen me cause,
If Dauid ment not fyre of hell,
That I may ad therto this clause,
With Lucifer that they may dwell.

For nothyng in this lyfe certayne,　　　　10
We may so well to hell compare,
As enuious tongues that not refrayne,
To gender styll both stryfe and care.

For as they are a punyshment,
A hell to good men and a stryfe:　　　　15
So may in hell be their torment,
When they departe out of this lyfe.

And as they burne till they burst out
In wicked wordes and sclander vyle:
In hell so may they beare a route,　　　　20
From heauen hauing their exile.

⟦ *A complaint against euel tunges*

⟦ Syng this as, I am the man whom
　　God. &c.

WELL may the wyse deteste　　　　25
The frutes of tongues vntrue:
Whiche neuer cease but styll prouyde
Their malyce to renewe.

　　　　　　　　　There

There is no tyme nor place,
That may them ones refrayne,
No vertuous mynde nor exercise,
That may their vice restrayne. 5

To sclaunder and detract
And blab the same about:
A wycked thyng when they conceyue,
They streyght waye put it out.

As Socrates hath sayd, 10
No worse thyng can be found,
Then wycked tongues, from whō deceyt
And falshode doth redound.

What wyckednes is there,
That maye compared bee: 15
Vnto the false and fylthy tongue,
In any one degree?

For where all other hurtes
By death are vanquisht quite:
Euen after death the wycked tongues 20
Doo vtter theyr despite.

Whych causeth me to thynke
As Chilon dyd yer whyle:
No sworde that cutteth halfe so kene,
As wycked tongues and vyle. 25

Of which most wycked vyce,
I neuer yet could fynd:
Not halfe so muche in any wyght,
As in the female kynde.

In 30

In whom it doth abounde,
With detestable rage:
That no deuice nor yet constraynte
May cause it to aswage.   5

O detestable tongues,
O fylthy sinkes of hell,
O wycked vyce whose hatefulnes
All other doth excell.

Ryght aptly was it calde,   10
A world of wickednes:
Syth nothyng in this lyfe so muche
Doth innocentes oppres.

By paynfull profe I founde
Such frute, that wrought me wo: 15
For wycked tongues haue caused me
My playnt to vtter so.

Do me not blame therefore,
That I on them complayne:
The simple worme when ye him treade,   20
Wyll turne his tayle agayne.

[[*A ditie made in the tyme of the*
  sweatyng plague. Anno. *1552.*

O PLAGUE possest with mortall myght,
(So farre as god doth geue precinct)   25
Well mayst thou moue the christian right
Vpon his lorde and God to thinke:
And shew him well by tokens playne,
How that he shall from sinne refrayne.

My   30

210

My flesh is frayle and shakes for feare,
My soule is strange and hath no doubt,
And hopes for health, and seketh where
It may be had, to fynde it out. 5
The scripture saith be strong in fayth:
And then be not afrayd of death.

In this my nede thy helpe to haue
To thee O god I crye and call,
I thee beseche my soule to saue, 10
From Satan synne and hell and all,
Though I O god haue done amysse:
Thy death shall me directe to blysse.

Then welcom plague the guide to helth
And death also the porte of lyfe. 15
Sythe that this change is perfect welth,
Out of this vale of moste vyle stryfe:
Why should we then thus feare to dye,
And end our fatall destenie.

O folysh flesh so fonde and frayle 20
To rage against all ryghteousnes,
I wyll that thou shalt not preuayle,
To folow thyne own filthynes:
For I wyll set my whole delyght,
To fight against thee with my sprite. 25

[*That vertue excelleth both ryches*
and beautie.

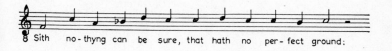
Sith no-thyng can be sure, that hath no per-fect ground:

how

how can the thyng en-dure, vn-cer-teyne that is founde.

What so begynning had
Must haue his fatall ende:
And nothyng good or bad   5
Hath other waye to bende.

All those that buylders be
Vpon vncerteyne staye:
Their workes as we may se,
Doe vanysh sone awaye.   10

And those contrary wyse
That grounde their matter well:
Their worke shall well aryse,
And perfectly excell.

When mariage then is made   15
For ryches or for goulde:
If goodes and ryches fade,
The loue doth lose his houlde.

If beautie eke so gaye
The cause be of thy loue: 20
When beautie fades away,
Thy fantsye wyll remoue.

For

For if the cause doe quayle
Whereone the mynde is bent:
The effect then must fayle,
What so therin is ment.   5

Then vertue shall be best,
Who so wyll it retayne:
All other beyng cest,
She euer doth remayne.

For beauty beyng gone,   10
Whose dwellyng is not sure:
Dame vertue styll alone
For euer wyll endure.

And when gould hath his ende
The causer of muche strife: 15
Yet vertue shall extende,
And garnysh well the lyfe.

A good rewarde also
To louers doth she gyue:
In kepyng them from wo,   20
A quiet lyfe to lyue.

If mariage then be wrought,
On vertue buylding loue:
No suche thing can be sought
To stande without remoue.   25

Ye that wyll wed therfore,
On vertue set your cure:
All contraries abhorre,
So shall your loue be pure.

For   30

For better were the tyme
Of death, and of the graue:
Then otherwyse to clyme,
A wedded loue to haue. 5

For goulde doth cause and gayne
Contention and vnreste:
He that hath moste, wyll fayne
Hym selfe to be the beste.

And beautie ofte doth brede 10
Mistruste and ielousy:
But vertue hath no sede
Of suche iniquitie.

Then happy is the loue
On vertue whiche is knytte, 15
That styll without remoue
Continue wyll and sytte.

Whiche in this lyfe cause is
Of prayse and godly fame,
And also after this 20
Of heauen for the same.

✿ *Nomen Authoris.*

In hope I doe endure
Of that whiche I intende,
Hauing my fantsy sure 25
No false thyng to pretende.

P   Hope

214

Hope styll dothe me allure,
At theyr handes whom I serue,
Lyke goodnes to procure,
Lo as I doo deserue.　　　　　　　　　　5

〖 *A godly warnynge to put all men*
　in remembrance of theyr myserable
　estate, and that they are subiecte to
　death and corruption. Syng this
　as, If truthe maye take no trustye　　10
　holde. &c.

REMEMBER well ye men mortall,
From whence ye came, & go ye shall,
Of earth god made thy shape & forme
And vnto earth thou shalt returne.　　15

　Remember well, O man I say,
Thou art wormes meate, and very clay:
Thou art none other, thys is iust,
But earth and ashes dung and dust.

　Remember well though thou be young,　　20
Thou art nought but a sacke of doung:
Deferre no tyme tyll thou be old,
For of long lyfe thou hast no hold.

　Remember well though now thou seme
As beautyfull as kyng or quene,　　25
That when thou shalt departe and dye,
Thou shalt rot, stynke, and putrefye.

　Remember well thou dounghyll, dyght
With garments gay to please mens syght,

　　　　　　　Remem-　　30

Remember earth thy first estate,
Thy lyons harte it wyll abate.

Remember well that thou shalt come
At the last day vnto thy dome: 5
Wher if thou doe thy selfe exalt,
In extreme payne remayne thou shalt.

Remember well I saye aloude,
Thou earth and ashes be not proude,
Suche coste on earth why doste bestowe? 10
Leue of thy pryde be meke and lowe.

Remember and in fyne marke this,
Who so of hym selfe humble is,
The lorde wyll hym exalte on hye,
In heauen aboue the sterry skye. 15

[[*The faithfull souldiour of Christe,*
desireth assistance of God against his
ghostly enemies.

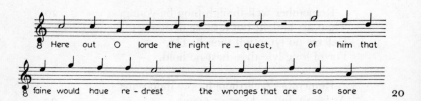

Here out O lorde the right re - quest, of him that

faine would haue re - drest the wronges that are so sore 20

P2   increst

in - crest, with in my soule so sore op - prest.

O lord to thee with wofull crye
I call for grace and for mercy:
And if thou helpe not, then truly 5
In deadly wo remayn must I.

The world, the diuell death and hell,
With great assaultes against me swell:
Lorde let thy grace in me excell,
Against their fury fierce and fell. 10

O lorde my God to the I praye
Suffer me not to goe astraye:
And haue in mynde the pryce and day,
Wherwith thou didste my ransome pay.

Oh haue in mynde thine own great cost 15
And let not this thy payne be lost.
In the O lorde my trust is most,
To dwell among thy holy host.

Thou knowst wherin my help doth stād,
Whereuer I be on sea or lande: 20
Good lorde put to thy helping hand,
Saue me from hell that fierce fyre brand.

⟦ *An exhortacion to brotherly loue*
and vnitie.

Beholde 25

Be-holde it is a ioy-full thyng, that breth-ern should con-tin-u-al-ly to-geth-er haue their good dwel--ling, in con-cord and in vn-i-tie.

This godly loue Dauid lykned   5
Vnto that precious vnction,
Which descended vpon the head,
And into the beard of Aron:

Whiche being powred on his crowne,
Was euer more styll descendyng: 10
And from his beard it dropped downe,
Into the skirtes of his clothing.

And as this precious oyntment swete,
Did smell all of one swete sauour:
For Christen brethern it is mete,   15
To be all of one behauour.

He that loues God aboue all thyng,
His neighbour as him selfe lyke wyse,

P3   Ful-

Fulfyls the lawe in so doyng:
Whiche Christe would haue vs exercyse.

For where this godly loue doth byde,
There present is the lorde Iesus: 5
Whiche neuer from his flock wyll slyde,
If they in loue continue thus.

Loue not ẙ world (thus saith S. Iohn)
Ne any thing conteynde therin:
For who so settes his loue theron,   10
The loue of God is not in hym.

And none can loue the lorde aboue,
Whom with our eyes we neuer see:
If we our brethern doe not loue,
That alway present with vs be.   15

Let loue therfore be among vs,
And from it let vs neuer swarue:
As we are loude of Christ Iesus,
Muche more then euer we deserue.

The dewe that fell on Syon hyll,   20
The whiche descended plesantly,
Is nothyng lyke this loue vntill,
Beloude of god eternally.

For god from tyme to tyme doth geue
To this loue his holy blessyng: 25
For all that doe with loue beleue,
Shall reigne in ioye without ending.

He

He (sayth the lorde) that loueth me,
Doth kepe my lawe and holy lore,
And vnto him geuen shall be,
A crowne to reigne for euer more.   5

Lorde in this loue we thee beseke,
To set vs in a quiet staye:
That we beyng louyng and meke,
May reigne with thee in blys for aye.

⟦ *The iust and true mā complaineth,*   10
that flattery and falshod is more regarded then truthe, and reioyseth that he is
hated for the truthe.

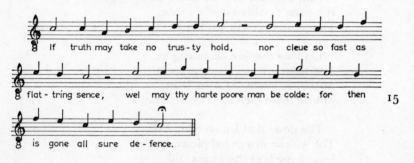

If   truth may   take   no   trus-ty   hold,   nor   cleue   so   fast   as

flat-tring sence,   wel   may thy   harte poore man   be colde: for   then   15

is   gone   all   sure   de-fence.

The Nyghtyngale must change her note,
And of the Cucow learne to syng:
The modest mynde must learne to dote,
Or conne some other fayned thyng.   20

P4   If

If meanyng well may take no place,
Nor dealyng iust haue no regarde:
Thou must deuyse an other space,
To fayne suche thyngs as may be heard.   5

Shall vertue dwell in such disdayne,
And honestie be had in hate?
Then must we learne to glose and fayne,
Or els remayne in vyle estate.

But yf there be none other way,   10
To purchase fauor and good wyll:
Better it were I dare well saye,
In vyle estate to tary styll.

What call ye then the vyle estate?
As some doo iudge this is the thyng: 15
If my superior doo me hate,
And would me to displeasure bryng,

And that also without desert:
(If reason may the cause decerne)
And haue disdeyn for my true heart.   20
Wherfore to please I am to lerne.

Yet is myn heart determind sure,
If truth and reason take no place:
Of suche disdeyne to take no cure,
But wyse men rather wyll imbrace.   25

For yf wysedome were noblenes,
As noble byrthe and ryches is:
Then should not truth be in dystres,
And flattrye should of fauor mis.

                                    So   30

So flattrye and bland eloquence,
Should (as they are) be compted vyle,
And truth should then make none offence
Nor vertue reigne in suche exyle. 5

Blamd, but not shamd, the prouerbe is
And truth can haue none other wrong:
So may they hap theyr marke to mys:
That thinke them selues in falshod strōg.

Then hated lo I must reioyce, 10
And fonde regarde despyse as vayne:
Closing my mouth stoppyng my voyce,
From speache in presence of disdayne.

⟦ *An holsome warning for all men*
that beare the name of Christians, to 15
lyue Christianly.

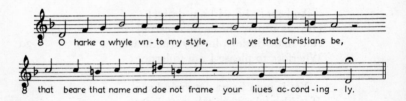

O harke a whyle vn-to my style, all ye that Christians be,

that beare that name and doe not frame your liues ac-cord-ing - ly.

P5   Is

Is fayth in syche,
As beyng ryche,
(Though they doo Christ professe)
That euery houre   5
Do Christe deuoure,
And his poore flocke oppresse?

For we are all,
As sayth saynt Paule,
Membres of one body: 10
Of Christe Iesu,
Ground of vertue,
And of all veritie.

Then the poore man,
(As proue I can)   15
Is Christ his member true,
As well as he,
What so he be,
That ryches doth endue.

Why should ye then,   20
To symple men,
Beare suche despight and hate?
Syth they be all,
In Christ equall,
With you in all estate.   25

Christ his kyngdome,
Was neuer wonne,
By wealth or hygh degree:
All though that here,
Some doo appere,   30
To reygne in dignitie.

Then

Then let none thynke,
That Christ wyll shrynke,
When he shall iudge vs all:
Of all your wealth   5
So got by stelthe,
You to accompt to call.

When yf he fynde,
Ye were vnkynde,
To your poore brethern dere: 10
Then wyll he say,
Go from me aye
Into eternall fyre.

When I lackt meate,
And fayne would eate,   15
In sycknes thyrst and colde:
In all my nede,
Not one good dede
That you to me doo wold.

Then wyll ye say,   20
Wythout delay:
Lord when dyd we see thee
Lacke any foode,
To doo thee good,
And dyd it not to thee?   25

And he agayne,
Shall answer playne,
I truely say to you:
Ye styll oppreste,
And muche detest   30
The poore my members true.

When

When ye therfore
Did them abhorre
That are of lowe degree:
To me alone   5
And other none
Ye did that iniury.

Saint Iohn doth proue,
We can not loue
God whom we doe not see   10
If we doe hate
Our brethern, that
Are present to our eye.

Nowe call for grace,
Whyle ye haue space,   15
Your wycked lyues amende:
And so procede
In worde and dede,
True Christians to the ende.

⟦ *A short song exhorting all men to*   20
abstayne from the vse of false weyghtes and measures.

My harte constraines my mouth to tell,   the du-tie of eche worldly wight,

howe

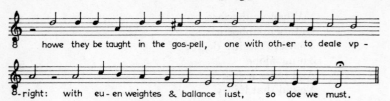

howe they be taught in the gos-pell, one with oth-er to deale vp -

-right: with eu - en weightes & ballance iust, so doe we must.

> So doe we must, this is no naye,
> Also with measure iust and true: 5
> Who so doth not at the last day,
> Ryght sore are lyke for it to rue:
> When he shall goe for wante of breath
> Vnto his death.

> Vnto his death when he must goe   10
> With painful panges and torment strong:
> Then is he lyke to suffer wo,
> For that his dealyng false and wrong.
> Suche one is lyke, in extreme payne
> For to remayne.   15

> For to remayne, wo worth the whyle
> That any man so fond should fare,
> With othes his neighbour to beguyle,
> When he should truly sell his ware.
>
> Oh   20

Oh wherfore then doo ye vnwyse,
Prudence despyse?

   Prudence despyse? that should so well
Leade you in Godly wayes and ryght: 5
And teache you also how to deale:
With your neyghbours iustly vpryght.
For he that to amend denayes,
Thus the Lorde sayes:

   Thus the Lord sayes very certayn,   10
Such measure as ye mete to other,
Suche measure shall ye haue agayn:
How then yf you deceyue your brother?
Thynk you that God wyll forget thys?
No no Iwys.   15

   No no Iwys ye may be sure,
For heauen and earth shall ioyntly fayle:
But Gods word shall for euer dure,
In force and strength styll to preuayle,
All false dealers for to expell   20
Downe in to hell.

   Down in to hell, therfore take hede,
And call for gods grace and mercy:
Amend your wycked lyues with spede,
Lamentyng them repentantly,   25
God geue vs grace so to intende,
And there an ende.

⟦ *A Ditie declarynge the stedfast*
  hope and trust that the faythfull afflicted soule hath in Christ Iesu.   30

                                 Lyke

Lyke as cer-tain, the hart wold faine of the foun-tain ob-tain
the spring: so hath my sprite his whole de-light, in God al-
-might a-boue all thing.

Myne enmies strong,　　　　　　5
All the daye long,
To doe me wrong
Is their intent:
Euery howre
On me they loure,　　　　　　10
Me to deuoure
They doe inuent.

This doe I see,
For to myne eye
It is truly　　　　　　15
Alwayes obiect.
With might and mayne,
Them selues they strayne,
My soule to gayne
And to infect.　　　　　　20

My

My soule therfore,
Doth tremble sore,
And euermore,
Doth stande in feare: 5
And all the whyle,
Myne enmies smyle.
Me to beguyle
They not forbeare.

Therfore I say,   10
My soule alway,
Reioyce and stay,
Thy selfe in Christ.
Though men extold,
Agaynst thee hold,   15
In Christ be bold,
Them to resyst.

Who is alyue,
That dareth stryue,
(Strong dyuels fyue)   20
Although they were:
Thys can I proue
O Lorde aboue,
If thou me loue,
I nede not feare.   25

O God of myght,
Strengthen my spryte,
That doth delyght
Only in thee.
O holy Lord,   30
Let thy swete word,
Wyth one accord,
Styll be wyth me.

O Christ

O Christ Iesu,
Ground of vertue,
Messias true,
As sayth Scripture:
To thee I pray, 5
Graunt that I may,
In heauen aye,
With thee indure.

⟦ *A song shewing that no commo-* 10
ditie is without a discommoditie.

⟦ Syng this as, I am the man whome
God. &c.

AS I dyd sytte and muse
Once by my selfe alone, 15
The wretched state of worldly
The mind was fixed on: (wights

Howe no commoditie
May here with man indure,
Without some discommoditie, 20
To shewe it selfe vnpure.

By fyre we haue great ayde
In colde vs for to warme:
Whiche in an houre somtime doth burne,
Rewarding vs with harme. 25

We may lyue certayne dayes,
Without both drinke and meate:
But without ayre not one moment,
The lack would be so great.

Q   Yet   30

Yet somtyme by his rage
We mortall men doe fynde,
That trees houses and cattell eke
Are ouerthrowne with wynde. 5

The water who can lack,
That in this worlde doth byde?
Yet many one therin is drownde,
By great aboundyng tyde.

The earth wheron we dwell, 10
And seke great welth to fynde,
In sekyng to possesse the same,
With iudgement vayne and blynde:

When we thynke to possesse
This earth that we attende, 15
Behold the same possesseth vs,
In it we take our ende.

The Sommer whiche doth repe
Our sede, both corne and frute,
Alas to hot, this heate to hot, 20
With men thus goeth the brute.

And as with sommers heate
We doe complayne and scoulde:
So do we wayle on wynters chere,
And blame hym for his coulde. 25

No welth without some wo,
No Ioy without some care,
No blysse without his dolefull bale:
Thus wretched men doe fare.

We 30

We seke for sugred welth,
As we should aye dwell here,
The bytter galle of mysery,
Therfore doth strayte appere. 5

The wyne that cheres the hearte,
Doth ofte tymes vexe the brayne:
And woman made was for mans helpe,
Who doth hym ofte great payne.

Sometyme we call for dryth, 10
Some tyme we aske for rayne:
Some tyme we saye we haue to much,
Of eche thus we complayne.

In musyke we delyght,
And calle for it some tyme: 15
Wherof we sone be wery lo,
And blame our selues of cryme.

And iudge our selues to be
Both vayne, fonde, and vnpure:
Because our myrth without sorowe, 20
No long tyme doth indure.

And whyle this dredfull care
Had fraughted thus my breste,
I me bethought what myght be founde,
To purchase here moste rest. 25

And that we myght let passe,
With lesse disease of mynde:
These contraries that vs assaulte,
Of so repugnant kynde.

Q2 And 30

And temperance was the thyng,
That then came to my thought:
A better ayde in suche a case,
Is no where to be sought.   5

And therin seke to fynde
The wyll of God aboue:
And doe the dedes prescribed vs,
Within the lawe of loue.

⟦ *The iust innocent complayneth*   10
on sclanderous tongues.

Like as the larke with-in the mar-lions foote from so-lace sup-plan-ted it were with me, if thou lord wert not my buck-ler and boote: at whose hand I hope sal-ua-cion to see.

My   15

My hope and helth lord is only in thee,
My castell of comfort my shylde and defence:
From sclanderous tongues Lorde delyuer me,
That thei no iust cause haue through myne offence.   5

So shall their deceites turne to their own shame
Although for a tyme they chance to preuayle:
When truthe shall be tryde, and vtred by fame,
Their falshod may faynte and vtterly quayle.

For they doe reporte that I neuer did,   10
My iudgement and cause I yelde vnto thee,
That out of this wo ryght fayne would be ryd,
And neuer did why so sclandred to be.

Oh mercifull lord creator of all,
I doe remember men sclandered thee: 15
Great diuell and Belzebub they did the call,
Thy myracles daily though they did see.

If thou se it good thy seruant to trie
By sclander of tongues and vntrue reporte:
For pacience thy gifte, to suffer I crye,   20
Rememberyng thee, my selfe to comforte.

For helpe at thy hande I only resorte,
Resolue their harde hartes and cause them relent:
For they that loue euell doe alwayes suporte
All suche as to lyes and sclaunder are bent.   25

Yet if thy wyll weare that they myght repent
Confessing their fault, their falshod and guyle:
To comfort somwhat the poore innocent,
That falshod and lyes hath put in exyle.

Q3   Thy   30

Thy glory so should we largely expresse
And teache it to men, and cause them to feare,
Whiche were for this crime a perfect redresse :
For nothyng so much could make thē forbeare.   5

Thus all my whole cause to thee I commit,
My matters with thee I alway decyse :
Iustly in iudgement because thou doest syt,
And ryghteousnes is thy whole exercyse.

O lord geue thē grace, to leaue ther great crime,   10
And me for to suffer, & walke without blame :
So wyll I endeuor from tyme to tyme,
To blesse and to prayse thy most holy name.

⟦ *The innocent sclaundered complaineth*
   praying for the conuertion of his enemies.   15

Al cō-fort-les lo with-out an-y ayd, now shuld I
re-mayn if God wer not he, which in y̔ de-fēce of
good mē hath sayd, in all their dis-tresse their hel-per to be.

My

My hope is therfore sure fixed O lorde,
That thou dost abhorre all vntrue reporte:
And as thou dost byd in thy holy worde,
All only for helpe to thee I resorte.   5

From thee O good lord ther is nothyng hyd,
Prouoke them by force their lyfe to refrayne:
For they doe reporte that I neuer dyd,
Accepted of suche as lyes doe maynteyne.

Good lord let not them their purpose obetyn,   10
Which in these my days wold turn me to shame:
Not that I refuse to suffer the peyne,
But only that it turne not to their blame.

My harmes be heinous whē they me defame,
But yet the moste harme to them doth returne,   15
When they vpon me doe reporte the same,
That they can not proue, it maketh me morne.

Lo thus am I bent in good part to take,
The sclander of tongues, rememberyng thee,
Contented to suffer all thynges for thy sake,   20
For vengeance only belongeth to thee.

Oh mercifull Lord I render therfore
To thee condygne thāks, which art my defence:
O strengthen me then good lorde euer more,
That I may styll suffer with pure pacience: 25

And finally graunt oh mercifull lorde,
That these false lyers may turne and conuert:
And being instructed by thy swete worde,
They may be ryght sad and sory in heart.

Q4   To   30

To God our Creator and lord omnipotent,
The Father, the Sonne, and the holy ghost,
Thre persons and one God most excellent,
Be all prayse and honour as worthy most.   5

⟦ *The complaint of Christ our sauiour*
  agaynst the Ingratitude of mankynde.

THYS of the Lord is the complaynt,
Of man, how he was sold and bought:
And thus he sayd hym to attaynt,   10
Myne own people what haue I wroght?
For towards me thou art so faynt,
And I thy loue so dere haue bought.
Thy answer loke thou nothyng paynt
To me, for why I knowe thy thought: 15
Haue not I done all that I ought?
Or els what haue I left behynd?
Thou sterst my wrathe, I hurt thee nought,
Why art thou to thy frend vnkynd?

  I sought thy loue it was well sene,   20
When I thee made so lyke to me,
Myne earthly workes both quicke and grene,
To thee I gaue bothe frutte and tree:
From Pharao that was fierce and kene,
Out of Egypt delyueryng thee,   25
I kylled hym and all hys men,
And the redde sea in twayne dyd flee:
Which I commaunded drye to bee.
The water serude thee and the wynde,
From bondage so I made thee free.   30
Why art thou to thy frend vnkynd?

                                              Full

Full forty yeares in wyldernes,
To wyn thy loue I dyd the lead,
Toward a land of great ryches,
With Manna also I thee fed: 5
To thee to shewe my great kyndnes,
Thy kynde to take I had no drede.
I left my myght, and toke mekenes,
Myne owne heart bloud for thee I bled:
To buy thy soule my selfe I led,   10
And bound my selfe thee to vnbynde.
Thus with great peyne thy turne I sped.
Why art thou then to me vnkynde?

For thee I ordeynd Paradyse,
And shewde to thee my Testament,   15
And thou agayne dydst me despyse,
In breakyng my commaundement.
Thy synnes were great in dyuers wyse,
For to my foes thou dydst consent:
Downe I thee thrust, thou couldst not ryse,   20
Thy wyts from thee away they went,
A naked wretche poore, shamd, and shent:
And as for frendes thou couldest none fynd,
But I whych on a crosse was rent,
Why art thou to thy frend vnkynd?   25

Thus I loude thee, but whom loust thou?
I am thy frend, why wylt thou fayn?
I gaue thee lyfe, and thou me slew.
Who parted thus our loue in twayn?
Turne thee to me, bethynke thee how   30
Thou hast done yll, come home agayne,
And thou shalt be as welcome now,
As he that free from synne dyd raigne,
Thynke howe dyd Mary Magdaleyn.

What   35

What sayd I to Thomas of Inde?
I grant the blysse, why wylt thou payne?
And art thus to thy frend vnkynde?

Of frends I am the beste and chiefe,   5
Thou wylt me neyther dreade nor please,
Of thy true loue to se a prefe,
My loue to thee would much increase,
For thy mysdedes I suffred grefe,
And thou dydst me that same disease,   10
Hanged I was most lyke a thefe.
I suffred death thy payne to cease:
Yet to loue me thou dost not prease,
Nor bearest not my payn in mynde:
But seekst Idols in thy dysease.   15
To me why art thou so vnkynde?

Vnkynd, for thou hast slayn thy Lord,
And euery day dost wound hym newe:
If thou be brought vnto accord,
Of couenant made, thou art vntrue: 20
To thy old synne thou dost resorte,
Thou louest vyce hatyng vertue.
All false Idols that I abhorde
To honour thou wylt not eschue:
But to my lyuely Image true,   25
The poore, the halt, the lame and blynd,
To offer thou wylt not insue,
Bur rather art to them vnkynd.

Thryse dyd the fiend tempt me truly,
And thou doste tempt me day by day,   30
Wyth synne and vyce most wyckedly,

To

To stirre my wrath thou wylt assay.
Thou dost as who so would me buye,
As false Iudas dyd me betraye:
For at my workes thou hast enuye.   5
There is nothyng that would thee stay,
If thou on me myghtst as I may.
Full cruelly thou wouldest me bynd:
If I forgyue thee thou sayste nay,
Why art thou to thy frend vnkynd?   10

⟦ *A Ditie warnyng all townes and li-*
berties to chose theyr gouernours for ver-
tue wysedom and lernyng: and by all mea-
nes laudable, to kepe from rule the proude
enuious and wylfull wycked men: lest the   15
prince be dishonored, and they them selues
abused and oppressed.

⟦ Syng this as, If truth may take no
trusty hold. &c.

VVHER pride doth hold the helme in hand   20
The shyp to rule by wylfull wyll,
Oft tymes we see on rocke or sand,
Both shyp and goods do ioyntly spyll.

  As Phaeton prowde, most wylfully,
Hys father Phebus charyot,   25
Would prease to rule, tyll foolyshly
He nygh spylde all, suche was hys lot.

                              Wherby

Wherby as Ouide playne doth tell,
The wrathe of Ioue he did prouoke,
In floud of Po hym downe to fell,
Wyth dreadfull dynt of thunder stroke. 5

    The lyke thyng may be sene eche day,
In shyp of publike gouernance,
Where onely pryde and wyll beare sway,
Sekyng all discorde to aduance.

    For reason there is captiuate, 10
Reiect and cast out as a slaue,
Tyll theyr owne swynge doth bring the quade
Whose end doth shew how much they raue.

    Wherfore yf I myght counsell geue,
When as the matter lyes in choyce, 15
Blynde ignorance should not acheue,
To wyn to rule by common voyce.

    For by theyr rude and fonde abuse,
The prince they doo dishonor muche,
And subiectes poore they muche mysuse, 20
Of pryde and wyll the fruites are suche.

    Then best it is for to reiect,
The blynde the ignorant and rude,
And vertues chiefly to respect,
And wysely so your choyce conclude. 25

    If that ye knewe the difference,
Betwene the wyse and learned men,
And rude vnlearned negligence,
Muche more respect ye would haue then.

For 30

For loke howe farre a lusty wyght,
That can doo all actiuitie,
As go, runne, wrestle, playe and fyght,
Dothe styll surmount in eche degree   5

The infant yong that can not go,
But muste of force be led or borne,
So farre extendeth learnyng lo,
The rude and ignorant forlorne.

He that in all his lyfe and dayes,   10
His owne affections can not rule,
But beastly is in all his wayes,
As any saluage horse or mule,

Or he that hys house howe to guyde
Or household yet coulde neuer tell,   15
Can such be mete at any tyde,
A towne of folke to gouerne well?

Haue this therfore before your eyes,
Whom hencefoorth ye doo chose or take,
Vertue imbrace, and vyce despyse,   20
A ryght good choyce so shall ye make.

Esteme hym euer as moste yll,
Whiche by his froward mynde vniust,
Despysyng lawe wyll maynteyne wyll,
To lay good order in the dust.   25

If any man perceaue this case,
Or haue experience of this cryme,
Vertue hencefoorth let hym imbrace,
And take more hede an other tyme.

A   30

242

⟦ *A briefe description of wysedom and*
  folly in gouernance.

VVHERE wysedome beareth sayle,
In shyp of common wealth,   5
Lyke are they not to fayle,
Lawe, loue, good hope and health.
Iustyce shall there auayle,
All wrong to ouerthrowe,
Mendyng both hygh and lowe.   10

    In lyke wyse and maner,
Of folly to defyne,
Ryght may no rule beare there,
Debate so doth enclyne:
And peace can there be none,   15
Ye may therof be sure:
Nothyng but payne and mone,
Euer doo fooles procure.

⟦ *A briefe Description of truthe*
  and falsehode.   20

TRUTHE shall triumph and falshode fayle,
Hope in the Lord so hath vs taught:
Of falshode shall the cunnyng quayle,
Most, when she hath her malice wrought:
As of the truth it is the guyse,   25
Suppressyng wrong, and then to ryse.

    Why then doth falshode make her bost,
Of her dedes as they should endure?
Only a whyle they rule the rost,
Doubtles theyr buyldynges are not sure.   30
Myschief to doo they men allure:

                                        And

And yet is all that they inuent,
Nothyng stable ne permanent.

[[*An exhortation to truthe,*
   fayth and vertue.   5

EXAMYN well thyne inward spryte,
Directe thy wayes with perfectnes:
Make streyght the thynges that are not right,
Vexe not thy frend with vnkyndnes.
No lye for gayne see that thou make,   10
Do nothyng yll for frendshyp sake.

   Haue styll in mynde the truth, which sayth,
All thynges are vayne that haue an ende.
Let all thy workes be done in fayth,
Lyke that whych Christ doth most commend.   15

[[*A description of mans lyfe both in*
   his owne affections and vertues.

WE may by profe behold and see,
In thys world what is mans delyghte,
Lewde is our lyfe naturally,   20
Lacke yf we doo gods holy sprite,
Iniurie, hate, wrath, and despyghte.
All that to payne shall vs procure,
Most we frequent and put in vre.

   In vertue yet those that doo dwell,   25
Occasyons yll they wyll eschue,
Remembryng that suche as doo well,
Doubtles the Lorde wyll them endue,
All goodnes that they may ensue.

                              Yea   30

244

Yea and them kepe so safe and sound,
None ill shall them hurte or embrace,
Endeuoryng styll iust to be found.

A frendly aduertisement.　　　　　　　5

REIOYCE in him that did thee make,
In welth and wo haue him in mynde,
Conceaue none ill, all vyce forsake:
Helth in thy soule so shalt thou fynde.
And where thou art a louyng frynde,　　　10
Reuoke it not, but stay thee there,
Decaye no loue but hate forbere.

To proued frendes commit thy trust,
And flee from suche as fayne and glose,
Note one thing well, and kepe it iuste,　　15
No secret of thy frende disclose,
Except counsell, disdaine it not,
Repent thou mayst els, well I wot.

That selfe loue and auarice, weare
　　　neuer true friendes.　　　　　　20

MARUELL not, though the faunyng tongue
All other doth excede in guile,
Rather thinke howe the foulers song
Into the net doth byrdes bewyle.

In couetise or in self loue,　　　　　25
Se that ye put no stedfast trust:
Leste confused your fansie moue,
Euer complainyng of thuniust.

A

A description of frendship.

IN frendship true there surely is
Of nothyng lacke, or scarcetie,
He whiche is frendly doth not mys,   5
No tyme his frende to gratefye.

Neuer therfore was frendshyp found,
In selfe loue, or in auarice:
Contrarily it doth abound,
Occasion shewde in exercise,   10
Loue neuer doth his frende despyse,
Sure frendshyp knoweth not hir owne.
Of this description to the wyse,
Now hēceforth may frēdship be knowne.

An opening of the rude peoples   15
inconstancie.

READE who so wyll in wyse wryting,
It shall be easy to conclude,
Commonly how the rashe doynges,
Haue of the moste fonde multitude   20
Always bene vayne and very rude.
Rauyng they doe reuers certayne,
Deuise of wyse men to disdayne.

Haue in their mynd therfore this feare,
Of their dedes be suspicious: 25
Out of all doubt theyr fond maner
Can not be but pernicious.
At all tymes therfore let the wyse
Reuoke their wayes and enterpryse.

      R   *That*   30

That flattery and sclaunder
are of all wyse men to be
taken hede of.

RIFE in this life is rude reporte,   5
Of suche as order doe disdaine:
But who so wyll to blysse resort,
Auoyde must all their scouldinges vayne:
Regardyng in his mynde all whole,
To runne a pace and wynne the gole.   10

   Trust not to much the faynt frendshyp
In suche as flatter for a gayn,
Ne yet the leude and lying lyp,
Lyke one lyke other is certayn.
Ye therfore ought him well to proue,   15
Endeuor that ye doe to loue.

    That a cõstant mynde is a great
pyller of bodily health.

HEALTH of body for to procure
Expediente is a constant mynde: 20
Nothyng doth better be you sure,
Direct you helth and welth to fynde:
Remember that the lyfe vnstable,
Is founde in no man commendable.

   For custome (Aristotle sayth)   25
Is lyke to an other nature,
So that he whiche him therin staith,
Hath good assurance long to dure,
And who the same to rente is ryfe,
Regardeth neither helth nor lyfe.   30

Respect

RESPECT euer and haue regarde,
Ill men from good for to deuide,
Constantly kepe both watche and warde,
Hate ill mens dedes on euery syde.   5
Agayne with iust men at eche tyde,
Regarde to dwell, and them frequent,
Decyse with them your whole intent.

  Beneuolence se you bestowe
Alwayes on suche as loue vertue,   10
Regarde also to ouerthrowe
Hatefull synners, who vice ensue,
And alwayes company the wyse:
Make spede from vyce and fooles despise.

A commendacion of vertuous   15
exercise.

INUENTION of the mynd ingenious
Of godly thyngs and of humane science,
Hath & shall be ẘ men good & righteous,
Noted styll as a poynt of excellence.   20

  Continue styll then in thy diligence.
Let not the world pluck back thy good intent,
And sure god wyll alwayes be thy defence,
Regardyng thee and thy doynges decente.
Know that the lord is styl the good mās guide,   25
Enuyronyng his ways on euery syde.

Against vndecēt busy medlers in other
mens vocation neglecting their owne.

REASON would that in the publique estate,
Of eury realme, where order would be had,   30

        R2   Because

248

Because therby the better to voyde hate,
All suche should be estemed to be mad,
Rudly that wyll his own calling forsake,
To vse others, hym self a foole to make.   5

Better it were that eche in their degree,
Endeuour would to folow their own art,
Then fondly as experience we may se,
In breaking order cause thē selues to smarte.
Nothing on earth, the which hath vndone mo,   10
God for their plage hath wylde it to be so.

For certeynly the vncontented mynde,
Extreamly doth hym selfe therby torment,
Lyuing to get they do many fetes fynde,
Dotyng in all that euer they inuent,   15
Euer therfore to constancie be bent.

Of fortune.

VVHO so would know what fortune is
To *Chilons* answer take god hede.
When lyke demande as nowe is this   20
To hym was put, he sayde in dede :
A leche right leude, they did hir fynde
That trusted hyr : she made them blynde.

Or thus out of Iustinus.

EXAMPLES great were without ende,   25
Vneth possible to be toulde,
I myght vnto the mynde commend,
Therein to stay if now I should :
Howe changeable howe frayle and fond
Is fortune for to vnderstonde.   30

Whiche

Whiche neuer yet made any ioye
But sorowe strayght ensude the same,
And doth hir selfe prepare to noye
Moste when she semes to noryshe fame: 5
Nor neuer strake the sorow stroke,
But where she first with ioye did mocke.

Of honor out of Tully.

HONOR as Tully doth wysly repete
In wyse men doth norysh both wisdom & skill,   10
And prayse in the wyttes doth kyndle a heate,
And also to study doth sturre vp the wyll.

Of glory.

IN thre thinges it doth well appeare
Where perfect glory doth remayne.
The first is where as far and nere   15
The multitude in loue doth reygne,
The second is as I perceaue,
Where they to good opinion cleaue.

The thyrd is where they maruel much   20
At vs, and doe vs well esteme,
And thynke vs able to be suche
As they of worshyp worthy deme:
And so with loue and good pretence
Doe gladly geue vs reuerence.   25

Of vain glory.

OF this vyle worlde the vayn glory
Is a swetnes full of deceit,

R3   A feare

A feare fyxed continually,
Aduancement bydyng dangers bayte:
A thyng begon without foresyght,
And endes without repentance quight.   5

⟦ *Or thus.*

By clymyng hyghe did neuer ioye
So swyftly yet ensue,
As (in the fallyng downe to wo)
Our sorowes doe vs rue.   10
Nor yet renoume by victory,
Doth not so muche inflame:
As doth in ruyne vyle reproche
Of follye, vs to shame.

Of grace out of S. Bernarde.   15

In three thinges lo consisteth grace:
Ryght well to knowe as I doe thynke,
Of faultes nowe paste abhor the trace,
And present ioyes despyse and shrynke:
Desyryng only thynges to come,   20
Prepared for vs all and some.

Of temperance out of Plutarche.

WHAT may we thynke that mā to lack
In any one degree,   25
To lyue in ioye and perfect welth,
And pure felicitie.
Whose vertue lo doth hym discharge
From sorowe and from feare,
His temperance constreigneth hym   30

All

All extremes to forbeare :
And calleth hym from carnall luste,
In thoughte, in worde and dede,
That in reioycing folyshly   5
He neuer doth excede.

Of talebearers out of saynt
Hierome.

The tale bearer that wicked man
Whiche by his synfull sleyght,   10
Doth mynysh loue betwene true frendes,
Through his most vyle deceyte,
Offendeth in muche worse degree,
Then he that would constrayne
The meate out of the beggers mouth,   15
Whom hunger sore doth payne,
For loke howe muche the soule excedes
This mortall body here :
So is the foode that fedes the soule
More precious and more dere,   20
And much more ought estemde to be,
Then that whiche here doth fede
Oure carein vyle, that dayly doth
Offende in worde and dede.

Of virginitie.   25

THE holy man saynt Ciprian
In praysing of virginitie,
Syster of angels cald it than,
To vanquysh lustes valiently :
Of vertues lo she is prynces   30
All good thinges eke she doth possesse.

R4   A

A maydens speache should be therfore,
In sobernes ryght circumspect.
Let bashfulnes also be more
Then eloquence in all respect, 5
Apperyng seld, few tymes and rare,
Vse well the eares, the tongue to spare.

When that ye speake, speake so that men,
May wonder at your shamfastnesse,
When ye speake not prouyd that then, 10
They may lykewyse your sobernesse.
Lo these fewe thyngs that I haue sayd,
Should be the garments of a mayd.

⟦ *Of Arrogancie in studentes.*

ALL arrogancie from study seclude, 15
Lest thou remayn styll vnlerned and rude.
For all that the best learned man doth know,
Would make a baren and very bare showe,
His knowyng w^t vnknowing, if wer in sight,
For why hys ignorance is infinit, 20
Wherfore the cumbrance of arrogancy,
The greatest hyndrance is vnto study.
For many myght haue come to wysdoms lore,
If they had not thought thēselues there before.

⟦ *Of reuerence to age.* 25

AGE and discretion in any wyse,
Loke that thou reuerence, and therto arise:
Geue place and hede therto with diligence.
For therein consysteth great experience.

For 30

For if thou wilt here an vpryght lyfe lyue,
At theyr handes thou shalt that knowlege atchiue:
Wyth godly lyfe, and true felicitie,
In graue iudgement and worldly policy.   5

⟦ *Of truth and falshode.*

Truthe doth wyth truth foreuer consent,
But falshode with falshode nor truth nor content.

⟦ *Of Inhumanitie.*

OF great rudenes it is an argument,   10
And that he is both proude and insolent,
In stout disdeyn that wyll styll remayn mute,
To those that gently hym greete and salute.

Or yf that we should not agayne for our part,
Shew the ryght fruite of a gentyll heart,   15
To wyshe well to them that wyshe well to vs:
We might wel be thought beastly and barbarous.

⟦ *Of constant temperance.*

Though fortune her face turne from the & fayle,
Be of good chere, let not thy hearte quayle,   20
For oft after mornyngs carefull and sad,
Succedeth euenyngs both mery and glad.

Of truth and lying.

As profyt by lying is vncertayne gayne,
Which can not long dure, nor stedfast remayn: 25
So damage that men by truth get among:
Such trouble I say can not hynder long.

Of the errors of the common
rude multitude.

Lodo-   30

254

LODOUICUS Viues in sentence playn,
With words that be wyse affirmeth certayn,
That thopinions of people tumultous,
Is commonly hurtfull and pernicious.   5
Theyr braines and heads so grossly vnderstond,
That all theyr iudgements are foolysh and fond.
For truly the vulgar people ay is,
Scholemaister of errores, and thynges amys.
There is nothyng vpon this earth therfore,   10
That in our study we should seke for more,
Then hym to bryng that knowlege would obteyn,
By wysedomes rule, in which he taketh peyn,
That he eschewe the iudgement vayn and rude
Of the most waywarde wauryng multitude.   15
   Fyrst therfore that he then be not infect,
It doth behoue hym styll for to suspect,
What so the multitude with great assent,
Seme to allow with theyr common consent:
By suche wyse mens rules tyll he them well try   20
Whose measure is vertue, to proue matters by.

⟦ Agaynst vayne apparell, out of
Lodouicus Viues.

GARMENTES of profyt to couer the body,
Were fyrst inuented by necessitie,   25
Ryches and ryot found garments precious,
Which vanitie formde with trycks superfluous.
Thus in vestures the dyuers inuention,
Hath drawne folke to prowd and folish contention,
And brought them to toyes hurtfull and vayne: 30
For eche one would now great honor attayne,
By that whych sheweth most our infirmitie,
Our folly weakenes and great miserie.

Agaynst

THE angry man for his countenance fell,
His sharpe words and his dedes fierce & cruell,   5
Doth oft lose much of his authoritie,
Men from hym withdraw beneuolencie,
His frends him forsake, and no man therfore
Will gladly him mete, but all hym abhorre:
Wherfore all wyse men of graue experience,   10
Eschue nothyng more, nor more diligence
Do vse in ought, then theyr anger to cloke,
And all workes of yre to shunne and reuoke,
In so much that they wrastle not only,
Agaynst theyr nature and infirmitie,   15
But spyght of her beard they put her to flyght.
Ye gyue her the fall, and banyshe her quyght.

⟦ *Of frendes, out of the same*
Author.

CHOSE them for no frendes in dede nor in woord,   20
That wyll at thy lyfe styll gest mocke or boord,
And suche as passe lyttle to scoffe at eche tyde,
At that which most secrete thou woldest hyde:
But yet most of all auoyde shun and flee
The frendshyp of suche as quyckly wyll bee,   25
For thynges of naught streyght at defyance,
With theyr best frendes, kyndred and alyance,
Reuengyng also themselues muche more
Vpon suche as they haue loued before,
Then on those foes whych they always dyd hate,   30
And with whome they styll haue ben at debate,
Persuadyng them selues most barbarously,
That of theyr most frend the small iniury,

It is

It is to be forborne or suffred lesse,
Then of theyr chief foe the most wickednes,
Which vayne & vile wordes do shew forth & moue
Declaryng most playn they neuer dyd loue,   5
Sure yf they had, loue would haue extended,
That they could not so much haue ben offended.
Make neuer no frendes of suche as be those,
For better it were to haue them for foes.

Dulce bellum inexpertis.   10

As flyes oft tymes in candle flame,
Doo play tyll they be burnt and dye:
So many thynke the warres but game,
Wyth danger tyll the truth they trye.

Or thus.   15

As Flyes delyght is oft to play,
In candell flame tyll death they tast,
So many wyll the warres assay,
That after soone repent theyr hast.

That the riche and myghtie should   20
not hate the poore and lowly.

AS the grape bearyng vyne lyuely,
The lyttle tree doth not despyse
That doth hym beare, so should perdye,
No great estate yf they be wyse,   25
Dysdeyn the subiect or seruant,
Whose ayde of force they may not want.

Or thus.

Lyke as the vyne that flourysheth,
With lyuely grapes and leaues moste green   30
The small tree neuer despyseth:
That beares hym vp as it is seene,

So

So ought no ryche nor hygh estate,
The poore or symple wyght to hate.

⟦ *Of formed fyllets and de-*
formed forheddes.   5

A LADY had a forhed fayre,
Formed very feateously.
For in the mydst a typ of heare
Came downe before ryght proprely.

Bothe sydes were bare and cowlyckt hye,   10
Wherfore she dyd in hast deuyse,
As in her glasse she late dyd prye,
To forme her geare after that guyse.

Her forhead clothes and other tyre,
Were altred streyght vnto that lyke,   15
On both sydes crokyng lyke a wyre,
And downe before a pretty pyke.

All other women great and small,
That dyd this trym newe trycke behold,
Olde, yong, yea ryche and poore and all,   20
Theyr forhed clothes so cut and fold.

But some that fayne would so be drest,
Dame Nature streyght denyd them that,
They could not be trym lyke the rest,
Theyr forheds lowe weare lyke a cat.   25

To that whiche was to some decent,
To others dyd as muche disgrace :
Whiche caused them streyght to inuent,
To plucke the heare of from theyr face.

Wher-   30

Wherfore fyrst as the fayre lady,
Her fyllet lyke her forhed formde,
Some worked the cleane contrary,
Theyr forheds lyke fyllets deformde.   5

⟦ *Sentences of the wyse.*

Plato.

OF all thynges the newest is best for behoue,
Saue only of frendshyp and of frendly loue,
Whych euer the elder and longer it dure,   10
Is so muche the better more perfect and sure.

Seneca.

Wel may he be counted right valient in dede
In ioye nor in sorow that doth not excede:
The temperate man possesseth this treasure,   15
Whose modesty moues hym styl to mynd measure.

Socrates.

Socrates calles it a great poynt of madnes,
To be without measure in ioy or in sadnes.

Plato.   20

Idlenes doth ignorance as her fruite render,
And ignorance euer doth error ingender.

Aristoteles.

Auarice doth gentlenesse styll away chase,
Whiche good liberalitie ay doth purchase.   25

Bias.

Of Flatterers Byas dothe byd vs beware,
And sayth that theyr speach is a hony swete snare.
        Salo-

Salomon.

As vnmete is honor fooles to assayle,
As snowe in the sommer, or in haruest hayle.

Plato. 5

Small errors not stayd at the fyrst but procede,
Wyl grow to great and huge mischefes in ded.

Plutarchus.

The wyts which in age wyll excellent byde,
By honest delyghtes in youth wyll be spyde. 10

Chilon.

Who can deny that man enuious to be,
That sory is at good mens prosperitie.

Socrates.

An ignorant foole he is without mys, 15
By counsell of women that gouerned is.

Aristippus.

He is without doubt a ryche man in dede,
To borow or flatter that neuer had nede.

Cicero. 20

Wysdome as Tully doth wysely defyne,
Is knowlege in thynges humane and deuine.

Xenophon.

For worldly ryches be not to studient,
Syth God hath prouided for eche man sufficient. 25

Plu-

Plutarche.

For sufficient thynges ought no man to pray,
For that doth God geue vnasked alway:
But praye that thy selfe mayst alwayes be bent,   5
With that whiche God geueth to be styll content.

Pithagoras.

Do ryght in your dedes to serue God if you lyst,
In workes not in words doth Gods worship cōsist.

Socrates.   10

Speake euer of God whyle talke doth endure,
And God in thy mouth wyll good words procure.

Solon.

The soule that is iust, and purely doth meane,
Doth neuer delyght in matters vncleane.   15

Seneca.

The good soules plant goodnes whose frute is saluatiō,
The wicked plante vices, their fruite is damnation.

Truste not this world I saye in no wyse,
Whiche neuer doth paye that it doth promyse.   20

Pithagoras.

True frendship and frendes, ye surely shal finde:
Where many pure hartes are made in one mynde.

Xenophon.

There neuer was frendshyp nor iustice certayne,   25
Where nothyng among them in cōmon doth rayne.

To lyue

To lyue without frendes would no man be glad,
Of all kynd of welthe though plenty he had.
Theyr frendshyp was neuer yet perfect and sure,
That did become frendes for profite or pleasure.   5

Socrates.

Let wyse men aske counsell for that is good skyll,
Lest somtyme theyr wits be myxed with wyll.
To the wrathfull man or dronkard infect,
Or he that is to a woman subiect,   10
Commyt no secretes to any of those,
For surely they can no counsell kepe close.

Isocrates.

He which to others good councell doth geue,
Hym self to profyt begyns to atchieue.   15

Seneca.

He (sayth Seneca) is ryche and welthy,
Which is contented with his pouertie.
None in this lyfe lyue more certayn and sure,
Then those that doo lacke ryches and treasure.   20

Hermes.

Receyue with patience the wordes of correction,
Though they seme greuous in thyne intellection.
Discipline my sonne see thou apprehend,
To grace and vertue so shalt thou extend.   25

Plutarchus.

Forget sone thy wrath, quench quickly that fyre,
And to be reuenged haue no desyre.

Socrates.

A man well brought vp that doth so procede,   30

S   Incre-

Increasyng mo vertues, is perfect in dede.

Shame and dyshonour, yll end, and damnation
Doth lyght vpon lecherous abhomination.

Socrates. 5

A ryght good gyft is eloquence,
Whyche doth in truthe shyne bryghtly styll:
But vsed in falshodes defence:
It doth corrupt and worke muche yll.

Pythagoras. 10

They which to sclander or to rob
The dead haue theyr delyghte:
Are lyke such dogges in fury that
At stones do barke and byte.

Plutarchus. 15

Nothyng so muche dysprayseth one
As dothe a mans owne prayse,
And chiefly when he bosteth of
His owne good dedes and wayes.

Hermes. 20

He that dothe good vnto hys frendes,
Is counted wyse therfore:
But who so dothe his enmy good,
He is a man and more.

As well men ought that benefytes 25
In mynde shoulde euer cleaue,

As

As they are glad in tyme of nede,
Wyth handes them to receaue.

The gyftes of a frynde,
Whose loue is not colde,   5
Ought neuer in mynde
To weare or waxe olde.

The good wyll of the geuer ought
To be regarded more,
Then ys the value of the gyft   10
Though it be great and store.

Seneca.

Of welth he shall haue no,
That can not suffer wo.

Smalle knowledge is in suche   15
As vse to babble muche.

Seneca.

The wyse in deede,
Dothe nothyng neede.

Hermes.   20

Beware well of spyes,
And tellers of lyes.

Aristoteles.

To delyght in treasure,
Is a dangerous pleasure.   25

S.2.   *Seneca.*

Seneca.

In a lyer doubtlesse,
There neuer was goodnesse.

⟦ *A description of dignitie or true*   5
      Noblenesse.

IF thou a noble man wylt knowe,
A great estate and honorable,
He is (as Chrysostome doth showe)
To vices nothyng seruisable :   10
But dothe detest and muche disdayne,
Subiect to be, to vyces vayne.

      If thou (as Seneca doth tell)
A man wylt in sure wyse esteme,
Or knowe hym perfectly and well,   15
What he is, and so truely deme :
Thou must hym see in fashion rare,
That is to say naked and bare.

      Possessions let hym laye asyde,
And put from hym authoritie :   20
And let nothyng wyth hym abyde,
But natures gyft and propretie :
All fortunes fables in lykewyse
Thou must in this thy serche despyse.

      In fyne and last of all the rest,   25
Let hym put of hys owne body :
And then behold wythin his brest
His soule, and vewe it certaynly :
For so shall it be truely knowne,
What he hath of his very owne.   30

                    For

For it in me deserues no prayse,
That I of others do receiue,
For looke what nature me denayes,
I can not haue, but doo deceiue, 5
As wyth a false and fayned synne,
Bragging with that which is not mine.

He that can vices ouercome,
Is then the chiefest conquerour.
He that wyth vertue beareth roome, 10
He is a man of great honour.
He is noble and of great myght,
That shunnyng wrong imbraceth ryght.

[*The anotomy or particular description*
of a byrchē broome or besome: In the compo- 15
sition or makyng wherof, are conteyned, iii.
notable Iustices or purgers of vices.

A BYRCHEN besome that ye a broome calle,
Is made of a wyth, a staffe, and twygs smalle:
By whych all folke of eche age and estate, 20
May gouerned be, yf nourture they hate,
As fyrst the smalle twygges do serue a good shyft,
The buttockes of boyes to hoyse vp or lyft.
From which it is sometymes nedefull to draw,
Abundance of bloud to kepe them in awe. 25
The haft of the broome lyke purpose shall serue,
To shrub well theyr backs that strypes do deserue,
And namely such knaues that are growne so bygge
That they nothyng set by any small twygge.
Therfore is the staffe a toole for the nones, 30
To canuys theyr backes, or kydgell theyr bones.

S.3.   Then

266

Then thyrdly the wyth wyll hang by the necke
Such theues as feare not the strype nor the checke.
Thus in euery house .iii. Iustices reigne,
Whyche the byrchen besom well doth conteyne :　5

The hygh and the meane, and also the lowe,
Theyr offices all, ought eche man to know :
By whom al such men must nedes passe theyr way
The rules of reason that wyll dysobaye.

The highest Iustice the necke wyll out stretche,　10
The low from buttockes wyl skyn & bloud fetche,
The meane must nedes shrobin the shoulders stout
Of eche stubbern varlet lubber or loute.

The lowe Iustyce nowe he that wyll reiect,
Nor his lyfe by rule and compas direct,　15
Neglectyng the small, he stireth the great,
The hafte of the broome the shoulders must beat.

By which back beatyng yf he wyll not mend
The with must hym hang, and so hys lyfe end.
Lo thus may they see that wisely behold,　20
The besome hath vses many a folde,

Besides that for which most men do them kepe,
Namely theyr kitchens or houses to swepe :
For he hath office mens vices to purge,
By thre Iustice rules, that sharply wyll scurge.　25

For who so euer they doo in hand take,
Either good or dead they wyll hym sure make :
Good, if by vertue from vyce they wyll vary,
Dead, yf by vyces they doo the contrary.

The　30

⟦ *The description & declaration of a mon-*
strous chyld, borne in the towne of Maydston
in the Countie of Kent, in the yeare of oure
Saluation .1561. the .xxix. daye of Sep-   5
tember, beynge Sayncte Mychaell the Ar-
changels day, betwene two & thre of the clock
in the mornyng.

SITH monsters as some lerned men declare,
Doo demonstrate to vs oure monstrous lyfe,   10
Repentantly let vs our hartes prepare,
Synne to aduoyde, wherin our fete be ryfe:
For why we walke deuoyde of loue in stryfe,
And for the most part councell men doo scorne,
Which mōstrous ways cause monsters to be borne.   15

Behold those eyes which monstrously strout out
Which typeth foorth our boldnes to doo yll,
And where it hath no forhead without doubt,
The lacke of shame ryght playnly shew it wyll:
Suche shameles grace we se frequented styll,   20
Whyles we stoutly our naughty ways defend,
And seme gods word to mocke and reprehend.

It hath no necke, whych may also expresse,
That lacke of loue doth reigne in euery wyght.
No paps nor teats whiche signifieth no lesse,   25
But that we doo regard no truth nor ryght:
To nouryshe vertue few haue nowe delyght,
But pryde, and foolyshe fonde and vayn attyre,
Of women chiefely nowe is the desyre.

S.4.   Such   30

Such ruffes, such rolles, such folysh tricks beside,
More heathenlyke then any Turke doth vse:
In wycked waies thus boldly do we glyde,
And holsom counsell most folke do refuse,   5
Thus monstrously we walke in great abuse,
As God by tokens dothe to vs declare,
That paynfull plagues he doth for vs prepare.

A hole it hath depe in the head behynd,
Couered ouer with a fleshy flappe,   10
Thus were these partes contrary vnto kynde:
Which may declare and signify perhap,
With feigned maners how we do vs wrap,
Apperyng outwarde honest fayre and gay,
Corrupted inward with most wycked way.   15

The buttockes also ioyned are in one,
Without a twyst the same for to deuyde,
Yet some there were that looked it vpon,
That toke great payne the matter for to hyde,
Ascribyng it to chaunce that myght betyde   20
Vnto the woman, whyle she therwith went,
As hurt or bruse, so vayn heads dyd inuent.

But who that wyll discretely the same vewe,
Shal fynd that God therin hath wrought his will
And their surmyse to be false and vntrue,   25
With lies that would our eares and wyt so fyll,
That we shoulde not repent vs of the yll,
That caused God therby vs to amend,
Thys token great before our eyes to sende.

Presumpteous boldnes in vnshamfast wayes,   30
Is termed courage or audacitie,

But

But shame to sinne is counted now a dayes
Great folyshnes, and doltysh dastardy.
So ryfe so rype is nowe iniquitie,
That fearful signes must faine be vs to teache,   5
That no man els can doe although he preache.

Let vs therfore haue sufficient regarde
To these great workes of God shewed to vs:
Least death and hell doe shortly vs rewarde,
For these our sinnes that we committed thus,   10
Let learned wits now more at large discusse,
By these great mōstrous tokens what is ment
But in the meane space let vs all repent.

⟦ *An exhortation to al preachers of the*
   Gospell, that they ought to preache as well   15
   in workes as with wordes: if they wyll
   preache profitably, namely to the conuertiō
   of soules to the truthe.

THE first mouer from easte to weste,
That turnes the starry sphere,   20
Vnder the whiche the seuerall orbes
The wandryng lyghts doe beare,

  By endles turnyng in that course
That all men doe perceyue,
Contrary to their stryuing waye,   25
Whiche few folke can conceaue,

  Twelue thousand tymes hath borne the
This endles balle about,   (sonne

            S5   Be-

Beshyning all our hemisphere
With beames, most clere and stoute,

   (Which cutting crosse our horizon
The night away did dryue,   5
And frō this arke by glistryng light,
Dyd darkenes styll depryue,)

   Synce parentes procreation
My lyfe did fyrst beginne,
And nutriment performyng it,   10
Tyll that I breth did wynne.

   And yet in this number of dayes
I neuer could espie,
Or on that wyght once fyx my looke,
Or see hym with myne eye,   15

   That cary could a good report
Vnto his finall graue,
Whiche in this lyfe dyd not subdue
The fleshe when it dyd raue:

   Or could not with a moste sharp byt   20
The heady synnes refrayne,
Subduyng frayle affections,
As with a brydle rayne.

   No though he could well prophesie
And profitably preache: 25
And as a heauenly messenger,
The gospell purely teache,

                  If

If lyfe and conuersation
Doth not therto accorde,
His labours are abandoned,
His preaching is abhorde.   5

For in bare wordes doth not cōsist
The pure sinceritie:
But perfect works doth chiefly shew
The Christian veritie.

And only wyt in speakyng well,   10
Doth shewe his force and myght:
But wysdome euer is exprest,
In dealyng iust and ryght.

Thus wyt can say, but wisdō doth
All thynges godly and iust.   15
Wit in good words, wisdom in dedes
Is knowne and well discust.

As workes then doe all wordes excede,
And doyng speache excell:
Though wit may make a glorious shew,   20
Yet wysdom beares the bell.

How many preachers haue ben staynde
That spake eloquently,
Which wanting wisdom, could not work
Therwith accordingly.   25

Wherfore the wyse philosopher
Vnhappy dyd them call,
Whiche had a wyt, and neuer could
Attayne wisdom withall.

                                        For   30

272

For wytte doth serue wisdom to learne,
In eche reasnable wyght:
Wherfore they are but beastes, who not
In wisdoms schole delyght.   5

If wysdoms worke then folowe not
Of wyt what is theffecte?
To what ende are these goodly wordes,
If good workes be reiect?

What are the frutes of lyuly fayth?   10
Whiche are the tokens true,
Of those whom God in Christ our helth
With grace doth styll renewe?

Is it not lyfe agreable
To that ye teache and saye?   15
Howe can ye otherwyse with glose
These verities denaye?

To what end speake ye all these wordes
Wherin ye so glory?
Ist not as good of godly dedes   20
To tell an history?

Who best think you should mē perswade
Their churche and fayth to loue?
Or who to folow or beleue
Should the moste mens hartes moue?   25

Of him that sayde, and no good dyd,
Or he that helde his peace,
Walkyng a good and Christian lyfe
Among the peoples prease?

Though   30

Though faith by hearing come in dede,
Whiche I will not denye:
Wordes voyde of workes did neuer yet
Worke halfe effectually.   5

It is but lyke the flowers gaye
That floryshe fayre and grene,
And wyther streyght as sone as sonne
Doth whot vpon them shyne.

Lyke wytherd haye vpon house tops,   10
That many tymes doth growe:
Whiche sodeynly doth spring and spreade,
Makyng a braggyng showe:

But streyght for lack of perfect roote:
Or grounde wheron to staye,   15
It wytherd is, that no man can
His handfull beare away.

Wherfore vnles ye preach with works
The frutes of wysdom pure,
Your wytty wordes are vanitie,   20
Your ground is nothyng sure.

Howe some haue geuen vyle offence
I nede not here to name,
For wyse men wyll my meanyng see
And doe but reade this same.   25

And who so by an others fall
Can staye and take good hede,
That man to be wytty and wyse
We shall beleue in dede.

A buyl-   30

274

Nor scripture studie
In suche a long space,
Made at hande redy
Assistance of grace?   5

How canst thou thy selfe
Gods messenger name?
Syth in this vyle pelfe,
Thou semest past shame?

But what man hath sene   10
As yet other frute,
In suche as haue bene
So beastly and brute?

With God and man to
Dissemblyng to lye: 15
Where all that they doe
Is Hipocrisye.

For he that wyll cloke
The enmies of God,
And saye they reuoke,   20
(That God hath forbod)

To shelde them from lawe,
And danger of cryme,
By crafte for to drawe
And detract the tyme: 25

How shall we hym thinke
The brydgroms true frende,
That falsly doth shrynke
From hym to the fende?

                    And   30

And that to make truse
Betwene wolues & shepe,
Good men to misuse
That dyd the flock kepe?   5

Betwene saynctes & dogs
What feloshyp is?
Betwene fylthy hogges
And chyldren of blis?

Betwene the elect,   10
And vyle reprobate?
Betwene the reiect,
And blessed estate?

Betwene good and bad,
Betwene heauen and hell?   15
Betwene subiect sad
And traytrous rebell?

Then those that proteste,
Suche vyce to forsake,
Howe can they requeste,   20
A peace for to make?

Making but one churche
Of vertue and vyce?
How falsly suche lurche,
Is knowne to the wyse: 25

If riotously
To lashe out and waste,
Moste prodigally
Of deynties to taste,

       T   The   30

The redyest waye be,
To please God aryght,
And Gods face to se
And serue hym in spryght,   5

If to be careles,
To burden ones frende,
And to make redres
Haue neuer in mynde,

Borowyng frankly,   10
No caryng to pay :
And somtyme falsly
To shyft so away :

If to be wandryng
So fugitiuly,   15
Leauyng the lyuyng
Sure and constantly,

Intendyng therby
With sleyghtes to deceaue,
With subtiltie slye,   20
Both to take and leaue,

If bybbyng of wyne
Tyll belkyng boyle out,
Be the true ryght lyne,
To fynde heauen out,   25

If lasciuious talke,
Prouokyng to synne,
Be the way to walke
Heuen blysse for to wynne,

                         Then   30

279

Then fare well saye I
All workes and vertue,
We may well defie
All good dealyng true.   5

But wo worth that suche
Had euer the place,
That so and so muche
The truthe doe disgrace.

Why takste in thy mouthe   10
My worde sayth the lord?
That hast from thy youth
All vertue abhord.

Thy lyfe to accord,
Doste also despyse: 15
Myxyng with my word,
Papystry and lyes.

If these causes nowe,
Be full sufficient,
Suche to dysallowe,   20
And from hym discent,

Also to abstayne
Hym to hyde or cloke,
Hys doynges refrayne,
And also reuoke: 25

My frendes I desyre,
That they beare wyth me,
Though I doo retyre,
And from suche one flee.

                    T.2.   For   30

For I thynke the pot
Scant whole wyll appere,
Nor from fylthy spots
The water be clere.   5

And rather I sure
Had lyfe to forgo,
Then with mynde vnpure,
Affectionat so,

With suche one to beare,   10
In suche confusion,
That can not forbeare
His frayle affection.

⟦ *A song against the sinful time*
    wherin all thynges are out of or-   15
    der, and synne groweth nere vnto
    rypnes.

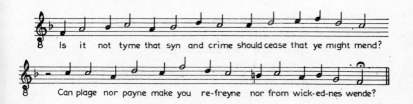

Is it not tyme that syn and crime should cease that ye might mend?

Can plage nor payne make you re-freyne nor from wick-ed-nes wende?

Shall eche brother   20
Malyce other?
Can nothyng you perswade,
Once to tender
Eche good member
Whom Christ hath bought & made?   25

                            Syth

Syth ye professe
Of faythe no lesse
Then the Apostles all:
Should you despyse 5
Thus eche good guyse,
With lyues most sensuall?

Can one vessell
At once expell
From hym both swete and sowre? 10
Or can a man
Any tyme whan
At once both laughe and loure?

As wolues wroth
Your selues ye cloth 15
In lambe skinnes to seme good,
Hipocrites subtill
Haue hartes styll britle,
Two faces in one whoode.

Commend they wyll 20
Gods swete worde styll,
As though they loud it well:
Yet they vary
Most contrary
Vnto that pure gospell. 25

In psalmes saying
And in praying
They seme to haue perfection:
Yet their delyght,
Is all in spyght, 30
Whiche is a great infection.

T3 In

In wrathe and pryde,
From grace they slyde,
Wyth fylthy fornication:
Enuy and hate,   5
Excesse, debate,
And all abhomination.

In auarice,
Beyond all cyse,
And arrogant ambition,   10
Although they feyne,
An other veyne,
They maynteyne superstition.

And he is well,
That can excell,   15
In vice and fylthynes:
Suche stryfe to wynne
The price of synne,
Was neuer sene I gesse.

Fylthy lucur,   20
Dothe them procure,
To parcialytie:
For worldly gayne,
They all are fayne,
To worke iniquitie.   25

They prate and pray,
And well can say,
To purchas them promotion,
The worlde to wynne,
They susteyne synne,   30
So vayne is theyr deuotion.

                    Flat-

Flattryng they fleare,
Eche other in theare,
To worke theyr wycked mynd.
They sclandryng slay,   5
Good men eche day,
As beastes that passe theyr kynd.

They feyne a face,
To runne the race,
As men of Christ elect: 10
And yet in dede,
They doo procede
Wyth lyues synfull infect.

They flatter can,
With euery man,   15
Where gayne may so be wonne:
Longer then gayne,
They not remayne,
Their frēdshyp streight is done.

They wyll be meke,   20
And humbly crepe,
Where they no frendshyp beare:
Tyll theyr purpose,
They may vp close,
And thēstreight ways they leare.   25

On promyse they,
No farther stay,
Then lucre doth extende:
No fayth nor truthe,
In age nor youth,   30
But falshode all attende.

T.4   Muche

Muche they pretende,
Fautes to amende,
And doe for common welth:
Wher in the end   5
They nought intend,
But priuate gayne and stelth.

Ca me ca thee,
This styll we see,
They wynke at wyckednes: 10
None but the poore
Doth wrynge therfore,
And suffer the distres.

With hartes moste stout,
They snuffe the snout,   15
Lyke swyne ỹ smell their swyll,
With haulty harte,
And mynde peruarte,
To worke their wicked wyll.

Suche they oppresse   20
As in distresse,
Do wante both helpe and ayde:
Their cruell myndes,
As fierce as fyndes,
By no meanes can be stayde.   25

No fayth we see,
On earth to bee,
Nor yet iustice or ryght:
But bearyng out
Of falshod stout   30
By office poure and myght.

Wher-

Wherfore the day,
At hande I say,
Of force muste nedes appere,
This worlde to burne,   5
That thus dothe turne,
To worse from yere to yere.

[*A meruaylous dreame of the*
   Author: Anno .1561.

WHEN in the lyon Phebus had,   10
Obteynde the seuententh grade,
And on the bulles necke, Ioue ridyng
The twyns for to inuade.

    And Saturne slow had in the Crab
Then entred one degree,   15
Mars from the waterman regrest,
The goate agayn to see.

    And Venus by coniunction,
Wyth Phebus late had lyne,
By backward course as she returnde   20
In *Leone* the sygne.

    And Mercury the messenger,
In May last past, was sent,
By myghty Ioue, from out the bull,
And nowe in vyrgyn went.   25

    Dyrectly walkyng through that sygne,
The balance to peruse,
And in September turne and shew
To Phebus all the newes.

                    T.5.   Diana   30

Diana, rydyng on the ramme,
Dyd on her brother looke:
Wyth tryne aspect, as wyth the lyke
Dame Venus late she tooke.   5

Intollerable was the heate,
That Titans burnyng beames
Gaue on the earth when he put foorth
His bryght and shynyng leames.

Which parching heat, had made ẙ corne   10
Eche where to change hys hewe,
Whych warning gaue, that husbandmen
Wyth sythes and sycles newe,

Should nowe prepare to cut and bynd,
And in theyr barnes preserue,   15
Suche necessary foode as myght,
For wynters nede well serue.

What was the cause I leaue to say
But sodeynly that nyght,
Suche tempest rose of wynd and rayne,   20
And lyghtenyng in syght,

With thunder strokes most terrible,
And hasty stormes of hayle,
As though God wyth destruction,
Would then the world assayle.   25

When .iii. long howres this sturdy storme
Had hys continuance,
It dyd asswage, and gan to go,
In farre other dystance.

                              And   30

And the deepe nyght approchyng fast,
From prayre to slepe I fell,
And suche a dreame to me apperde
As strange is for to tell.   5

Me thought I stoode vpon a hyll
Where I hard by myght see,
In a lowe playne of all estates,
A multitude to bee.

Where euery sort and eche estate,   10
Dyd stryue and muche contend,
The gredy gayn of gold to wyn,
Theyr hunger had none end.

So muche to gold theyr loue aperde,
That nought els myght be founde,   15
To wyn or please, or to haue fame,
Or in wealth to abounde.

There saw I kyngs and rulers great
By tyranny to reigne:
Wheras the great consumde the small,   20
And wysedom dyd disdeyne.

Theyr subiects when they had opprest
By heapyng of muche golde:
They straight became ambicious,
Yea arrogant and bolde.   25

Theyr own realms could not thē cōtēt,
Theyr spendynges to discharge:
But they must conquere others ryght,
Dominions to enlarge.

                                            And   30

And so wyth bloudy victory,
Great terrour and dystresse,
Of many poore, at last by force
They others lande posseste.   5

Which notwythstandyng of .iii. heyres
Was not inherited:
But was agayne wyth losse and shame
Forgone and home rendred.

And others as ready agayne,   10
Wyth lyke them to acquite,
As they before weare for to wynne,
And conquere others ryght.

There sawe I iudges in lyke case,
Whose mynde dyd whole depende,   15
For hym to doo that most wold geue,
And plentyfully spende.

For brybes & giftes bare all the sway,
In matters of the lawe,
For gayne of golde, and for no ryght,   20
All matters dyd they drawe.

All officers I dyd beholde
From moste vnto the least:
Whych without brybes had no regard,
To any mans request.   25

Yea offices were solde and bought
And not for vertue gaynde:
But all for gould, thus went the world,
For gould were all retaynde.

A foole   30

A foole as sone should haue to doo,
To rule a common weale:
As should the wyse: vnles by mede
He dyd his offyce steale.   5

Yet some desyre (I not denye)
Of gold was to this ende:
The glutton gutte of Epicure,
To fyll full and extende.

For in some place no dronkard can   10
So ofte yll rule repayre,
Nor yet frequent the tauerne more,
Then shryfe Iustyce or Mayre.

The spectacle of all excesse,
And mysrule to infect,   15
Was sene of them that ought of due,
Suche vyces to correct.

The ryche dyd poore men vndermynd,
To make them trauell sore:
And yet drue backe beneuolence,   20
And wages not the more.

But rather dyd wythdrawe the due,
They ought to haue of ryght:
For pryuate gayne thus waded they,
Wyth all theyr powre and myght.   25

To promyse or to counant made,
There no man had regarde:
For gayne of golde all thynges vndyd,
Theyr doynges well declarde.

No   30

No lease so good had any man,
Nor bonde so surely made:
But golde was able to vndoo,
And vtterly to quade.   5

Who had no gold, vnable was,
Hys owne ryght to retayne:
Ne without gayne no kynde of force
Myght permanent remayne.

Ryght many that good science had   10
Vpryghtly wyth to lyue:
To tauerne and to typple fell,
Therto them selues to gyue.

Estemyng gayne therby to ryse,
Muche more abundantly,   15
Then by the former trade they vsde,
With lyuyng decently.

And dyuers artes theyr trade did leaue,
Wyth hurt of common weale:
Forstallyng corne and victuals all,   20
Vyle gayne therby to steale.

The cobler, tynker, and the smyth,
Theyr labour gan to leaue:
More gold to gayne by phisykes art,
And therwyth dyd deceaue.   25

So leapt foorth Loy the loyterer,
That no man myght hym let,
To be a priest or mynister,
An ydle gayne to get.

                                            Wyth   30

Wyth gold some bought theyr benefice
In hope more gold to reache:
Whych to attayne is all theyr cure,
For nothyng els they preache.   5

   Vnlearned though they latine lappe
Before the symple folcke,
As yf a sowe should spyn and twyst
Of from a lynnen rocke.

   The byshops once confirmde in see,   10
Regarded idell thryft:
To preache or teache they toke no care,
For golde was all theyr dryft.

   The superstitious hipocrite,
Styll helde antiquitie,   15
In hope to gayne if change may hap
To buylde iniquitie.

   Eche varlet in hys brauery,
Affyrme may what he lyste:
Yea openly agaynst the lawes,   20
They dayly doo resyst.

   Thus gayn of gold hath made the lawes
Voyde, and of none effect,
The godly preachers rayled on,
And theyr doctrine reiect.   25

   Thus is theyr golde or Mammon vile
Theyr onely lorde and God:
For it they onely seke and serue,
Though Christ haue it forbod.

                The   30

The laboryng man would for his payn,
Be wagde with double hyre,
Or els would loyter, and not worke
At any mans desyre.   5

For whiche at last some did pretend
To make a quick redres:
But all their dedes did rather turne
Vnto double distres.

For as the common saying went,   10
Who so a tree would fell,
Hard to the roote must put his axe,
If he wyll doe it well:

And not begyn small toppes to shred,
And let the stock alone: 15
For so mo twygs wyll growe agayne,
Lo thus dyd poore men grone.

The pryce of fermes must fyrst fal down
Vnto their ancient rate,
Or els ye shall reforme to ryght   20
No degree or estate.

If ye meane right, first bate the pryce
Of that whiche is your owne:
So howe to mende after that rate
Shall easyly be knowne.   25

But whylst your selues wil not debate
Your rentes and gredy gayne,
Your study of amendement
In others is but vayne.

                                    Of   30

Of takers and commyssioners,
There myght one see a sort,
For gayne of gold begyle theyr prince
And his subiectes extort.   5

Of all thyngs would they double take,
And sell the resydue:
Thus bothe to prince and people to,
These wretches were vntrue.

In lyke sort bayliffes playd theyr part   10
In gettyng gold with wrong:
And somners whyche causde many one
To syng a sory song.

These could make one wryte double serue
As many mo as nede: 15
And for a brybe the same discharge:
Thus falshode hath decrede.

All marchants ther me thought I saw
Wyth many a subtyll shyfte,
The gredy gayne of gold to wyn,   20
By false and theuysh dryfte.

So saw I crafts men leaue theyr art,
And fall to husbandry:
Leases ouer theyr neyghbors head,
To that intent they buye.   25

Whiche made the rent of lands to ryse,
From fyue vnto a score:
Suche great enormitie as thys,
Euen Nature doth abhore.

                   V   Vn-   30

Vnlawfull gayne and vsury
That execrable vse
I sawe frequented commonly:
Whyche was a great abuse.   5

Ryght many heyres full rychely left
Were therby cleane vndone,
By craft and guyle therin conteynd,
Wyth crafte thus haue they done.

Some gasyng vp vpon the sterres,   10
Wyth vayne deludyng Iapes,
Deceaued many symple folkes,
And mocked them lyke apes.

Theyr learnyng in Astronomye,
Was scarsely worth a myte: 15
Although of it was all theyr boste
To blynde the peoples syght.

The dyuels arte they do frequent,
And therwith tell muche newes:
The christen flocke thus they peruert,   20
Wyth moste hatefull abuse.

For chyldren now are scarsly borne
But streyght they wyll apply,
Theyr goodes to spend on such as bost
They can well domifye.   25

And calculate what shall become
Hereafter of that chylde:
Wyth vanitie for gayne of gould
Thus was that place defylde.

                              When   30

295

When things were lost or stolne by theues
These hypocrites dyd gase,
Vpon the sterres, and sometymes told
That dyd the people mase.   5

For easy sure by suche deceyght,
Among the people rude
It is, with counterfeatyng face,
Them to mocke and delude.

And hatefull wytches euery where,   10
With hurtfull wordes and charme,
Both men and cattell dyd destroy,
Committyng endlesse harme.

And thys they dyd, that dayly men
Myght seke that trade vnto: 15
The grysly grefes by wytches done,
By wytche crafte to vndoo.

And in thys wyse some gayned so,
That nought were worthe of late,
That they could buy and trymly buylde,   20
At thys present estate.

And some for gayn wyth the lyke arts,
Diuyne and prophecie,
And promyse many thyngs to come
By suche fals trechery.   25

From crowned kyng to pesant poore,
No degree or estate,
Escape could, that they would not be,
With them bold to checke mate.

                    V.2.   Noble   30

Noble princes that diademe
And scepters iustly beare,
To Iudge theyr endes most hatefully,
These dyuels doo not feare.   5

Suche trayterous kynd of prophesies,
Wherin they closely mell,
And dayly doo the same frequent,
A strange thyng were to tell.

For which cause some by coniuryng,   10
The wycked spirites rayse,
And trouble all the elementes
In these moste hatefull dayes.

Howe they doo offer sacrifice
Vnto the fende of hell: 15
Sometyme of theyr owne flesh & bloud
Whyche therfore they doo quell,

And how they cast theyr soules away,
In most damnable wyse,
By felowshyp with damned sprites,   20
Is knowne vnto the wyse.

I sawe also lyke fugitiues,
Ryght many foorth dyd straye,
With beastly gaudes & makyng shiftes,
With fonde and theuyshe playe.   25

Of these many were Iuglers lewde,
And some had apes and beares,
And some had foolyshe puppet playes,
And therby great gayne reares.

                               Some   30

   Some throw a houpe would trimly daunce,
And some with hoby nagge
For gayne of gold wold play trim tricks,
With turne round kycke and wag.   5

   And many mynstrels there I sawe,
Whych money to attayne,
For eche mans fansy had a song,
Though they were naught and vayne.

   Yea popysh songes for popyshe folke,   10
And eke for men demure,
They wold haue songs that framed were
Out of the gospell pure.

   And fylthy songes for fylthy folke,
That therin had delyght,   15
And gold to wyn they would not shunne
To doo all thynges vnryght.

   And some agayn by palmestry,
Mens fortunes would disclose:
As beggers throng vnto a dole,   20
So many went to those.

   And gaue them money liberally,
To tell them lying tales:
Of which these wreches haue great store
When they vndoo theyr males.   25

   To these vayne women much resort,
The chiefe cause is to heare,
Howe many husbandes they shall haue
As it dothe oft appeare,

              V.3.   And   30

And robbe theyr husbands on this sort
Suche lewde men to reward:
So muche to change and gayn therby,
It semeth they regard.   5

These knaues would whyster in theyr eares
And would dysclose eche marke,
That on theyr bodyes these folkes had
In secrete place or darke.

O mystresse ye haue suche a mole   10
Or marke in suche a place:
And suche a wart I know it well
By lookyng on your face.

Vpon your belly is a marke,
A wart vpon your brest,   15
And on your foote a lyttle mole,
(I know them most and lest.)

And more than thys iwys I know,
If all I should you tell:
Then would ye blushe and be abasht,   20
Therfore I wyll not mell.

But wyll be sylent in all thynges,
Saue that you do require,
In whych I shall my mystresse fayre,
Accomplyshe your desyre.   25

Lo streyght these folks are mad in lust
And most beastly affection,
To heare these lyes of crafty theues,
O most hatefull infection.

How   30

How long shall suche consumyng mothes,
And hatefull caterpyllers,
Be suffred thus to hurt and spyll,
The fruits of honest lyuers?   5

How longe shall they be maynteyned,
And scape all punyshment?
Suche theues I mean as gather gold,
By craftes that they inuent.

From shyre to shyre, from towne to towne   10
And styll from place to place,
These theues dyd fleete vnpunyshed,
And none dyd them deface.

The rable rude of ruffyen roges,
Dyd furnyshe vp the trayne   15
Of such as lyude by robbery,
Gold to gette or obtayne.

Of these some cut the poore mans purse,
An other dothe conuaye:
And worse then this they cut mens throtes   20
To gette that wycked pray.

Some in a bushe would closely lurke
For thys most fylthy gaynes,
And wyth a club most murderously,
Knocke out the true mans braynes.   25

But others in more stoute order
In companyes would wayght,
Of suche as trauayle by the way,
To make theyr golden bayght.

                    V.4.   Stand   30

300

Stand sayth the thefe, and streyght his mate
Sayth, Delyuer thy purse:
Lo thus they snatche that others get,
Among them to disburs.   5

There sawe I also rat catchers,
And suche as teethe dyd drawe,
Lyke fugitiues and vagabundes,
Contrary vnto lawe,

Cloke ouer many shyftyng mates,   10
That lyue by rape and spoyle.
Among that flocke I you assure,
They kept a shamefull coyle:

And many wyth a pedlers packe,
To sell bothe pynnes and lace,   15
Resorted to eche cockbeld fayre:
Onely but for a face,

To make folk thinke they come to sell,
Where they come but to steale:
What nede I say, how hurtfull these   20
Be to a common weale?

When some of these were spyde & take
And before Iustyce brought:
Then theyr moste wonder was of all,
What wyckednes gold wrought.   25

For golden brybes there myght a man
See false theues lette slyp go:
And where no gold was, pickery
Enough was them to slo.

Where   30

Where golde dare rule wylful murder
Was made but chaunce medlye,
And chaunce medlye was murder made:
Where golde was but skantye.   5

Thus lyfe & death, yea payne and ease,
Hong all on wycked mede:
For the attaynyng of the same,
All mens maners agrede.

For gredyly they gryped it,   10
By hooke or crooke eche where:
And to be briefe none other thyng
Authoritie could beare.

For God nor kyng none dyd regarde
In respect of the same: 15
And other ende saue onely it,
Had neyther worke nor game.

For some there were with testyng tricks
That laughter coulde prouoke:
And golde to gayne wyth thys theyr art,   20
They had a ready stroke.

Some were so vayne to laugh at suche
That measure cleane they mys,
As though they had wyth myre & wyne
Dronke Gelothophilis.   25

Yea wyse men wold them surely deme
Cleane gone besyde theyr wyttes,
If they should see them gape and laugh,
And gygle so by fyttes.

V.5.   Corne,   30

Corne, lether, leade, wood, and salte hydes
By stealthe some dyd conuaye,
For priuate gayne they brake the lawes,
To common wealthes decay.   5

Suche wayes to wyn, and goulde to gayn,
No othes but they were sworne:
Thus as they myght the lorde hym selfe,
Wyth othes was all to torne.

Some by the foote, some by the handes,   10
Some by the head, and harte:
Some by hys guts, some by hys eyes,
Some by his deathe and smarte.

Some by the fayth they owe to God,
Would sweare and falsly lye: 15
And some as God should be theyr iudge,
Dyd vse theyr falshode slye.

Eche science eke in theyr degree,
I sawe tosse and turmoyle,
Falsly to wyn they counterfete,   20
In theyr trauayle and toyle.

True workmanshyp was turnde to slyght,
Wyth falshode to beguyle:
The trusty trade eche man refusde
For gayne of gold so vyle.   25

No man myght at hys worde be trust,
For vnder sugred talke,
Deceyt was ment and subtiltie,
In falshode thus they walke.

                          Eche   30

Eche man to hys inferiour
A cruell Cyclops semde:
The great the small dyd quite consume,
Wherfore hell I it demde.   5

With balance false, and weyghtes vntrue
And measure of lyke cyse,
Eche one an other dyd deceaue,
And truthe all dyd despyse.

The husbandman and other lyke,   10
Dyd benefyces buye:
Wherby the man should lyue that taught
The people faythfully.

So were the people all vntaught,
And blyndly were they led,   15
Whyche made them irreligious,
For fayth was from them fled.

Thus simony and sacrilege,
And all extortion,
Was laufull gayn, naught came amys,   20
That profyte hanged on.

Wyth colour of symplicitie,
And fayned holynesse,
Me thought I sawe muche gold was got,
Oh wofull wyckednes.   25

False wytnes, whordome and excesse
Were vsde for gayn of golde:
And fynally all wyckednesse,
For lucre was extolde.

                                              Great   30

Great murder, theft, and robbery,
Thys gredy hunger bred :
Rauyn, dysdeyne, and periurye,
For golde was commytted.   5

I well perceaue no kynd of folke
There were, but all were bent
To brybes and to vnlaufull gayne,
Wyth moste wycked intent.

What shall I say, yf I should here   10
Theyr whole deceytes reherse?
An huge long boke I myght well fyll,
Wyth thys my ragged verse.

If some of them in theyr desyre,
Theyr gredy wyshe myght haue,   15
All that they touche shold turne to gould,
As Midas once dyd craue.

Who sterued had because his meate,
Dyd all to golde conuert,
If Bacchus had not then wytsaft   20
That sentence to reuert.

Who taught hym then for remedy,
Pactolus to washe in,
Whyche is a streame in Lydia,
Wyth golden grauell fyne.   25

I musyng muche at theyr vsance,
It caused me to feare,
(Theyr mynds so beastly semde to be)
That Circe had ben there.

                            Who   30

Who feygned was, that she by craft
Of sorcerye coulde change,
Bothe formes & myndes of mē to beastes
Whyche was a matter strange.   5

For neuer tygre was more fierce,
Then some dyd there appere,
No swyne so fylthy nor so drunke,
Nor glutton nothyng nere.

In lechery they passe the Goate,   10
And in theyr pompous pryde:
The Lyon stoute they muche excede
And that on euery syde.

The subtyll foxe, the rauenyng wolfe,
The enuyous serpent,   15
The gredy Gryppe, the hasty Hounde,
His game that fayne would hent,

The cruell beare, the foolyshe asse,
The harmefull mockyng ape,
The gryffon, or the Antilope,   20
Or Bygorne that dothe gape,

The goryng Bull, the buttyng ramme
The scratchyng cat wyth clawe,
In beastly actes may not compare,
Wyth those that there I sawe.   25

O God (quod I) what place is thys?
Is hell more odious?
My heart in great perplexitie,
My clamor made I thus.

     Ye   30

Ye Muses nyne my comfort swete,
Take pitie and drawe nere,
Coequally by one consent,
Lette come Arete dere.   5

That she thys doubt may me dissolue,
And that she may me learne,
Howe I may knowe what place is this,
And all this folke decerne.

Of mercy oh my dere delyght,   10
Arete I thee calle:
Approche vnto thy seruant poore,
Or peryshe els I shall.

O dulcet dere Arete fayre,
Thy promys nowe fulfyll,   15
With me made when that I me bound
To serue thee at thy wyll.

Wyth thys me thought a thunder clap
Made all the earth to shake:
That I abasht and muche afrayde   20
Dyd tremble sore and quake.

Wherwith me thought Arete bryght,
From heuen dyd descende:
As swyft as is the arrow flyght,
The ayre can she rende.   25

My seuant dere quod she to me,
What happe is thee befall,
That thou in suche lamentyng wyse
To me dydst crye and call?

                                    Was   30

Was Satan lyke to vanquyshe thee,
Or dryue thee to dispayre?
Or what myght cause thy voyce so shrill
Thus to deuyde the ayre?   5

My dyamonde moste dere, quod I,
Myne onely luste and wyll,
Is that thou lose me from thys doubt,
Through openyng of my skyll.

What name myght haue thys present hyll   10
Where desolate I stande?
What kynde of folke are they alow,
And of what vncouth lande?

That valey lowe should seme to be,
Some vyle vnhappy soyle: 15
What hyll is thys, where thought so strang
My mynde doth thus turmoyle?

The hyll (quod she) that thou art on,
Is an hygh diuine mynde,
From whyche all worldly wyckednes,   20
Is separate by kynde.

And as eche thynge by contraryes,
Is best knowne and decernde:
So on thys hylle the vyle estate
Of worldlynges lowe are lernde.   25

The chyldren of thys wretched world,
Be those in yonder vale,
Whyche gredyly doo payne them selues,
In sekyng paynfull bale.

                                        Know   30

Know they not God (quod I,) nor doo
They nothyng feare hys force?
No not all (quod she) no more
Then dothe the mule or horse.   5

They feare God as the dyuels feare,
But fayth or loue is none:
Philargery they onely serue,
And set theyr myndes vpon.

Who as the poets haue feynd doth liue   10
By fedyng styll of golde:
And therwith neuer satisfied
He wasteth manyfolde.

Although he dayly doo consume,
And euer styll deuoure: 15
Yet craueth on hys clyents styll
To fede hym euery houre.

Whose labour eke is infinite,
Theyr hunger hath no ho
Abundance can not slake theyr thyrst,   20
So wycked is theyr wo.

Wyth hauyng is not satisfied,
The heart of auaryce:
For as the ryches doth increase,
So dothe the couetyse.   25

A hell wythout all order is,
That realme where suche do wonne,
A flocke of folke vngodly bent,
In synfull pathes to ronne.

                          A packe   30

A packe of people sekyng gayne,
And priuate welthe prefer:
And common wealth doth none seke for,
But eche dothe it hynder.   5

Eche man is there all for hym selfe,
The dyuell is for all:
Hys kyngdome onely doo they seke,
And thyther shall they fall.

Saynt Paule hath called couetyse   10
The only roote of synne:
How then can those men be but yll,
That walke so farre therin?

So vnrepentant is theyr hartes,
As hard as any flynt: 15
Nought can resolue or mollifye,
Or make them once to stynt.

Great tokens from the Lord aboue,
Ryght many hath ben sent,
At London, and at Hungerforde,   20
And in some place of Kent.

The elementes to repentance,
Wyth dyuers tokens calles,
As hath ben sene, when fyre consumde
The piramid of Paules.   25

And other places haue well felt
Theyr rage, whome I not name:
Yet se we few whose hartes relent,
Or repent by the same.

                    X   Whych   30

Whych manyfestly dothe declare,
That greater plagues then those,
God hath preparde and redy bent,
For to consume his foes.   5

So lytle fayth is found on earth,
Whyche sheweth certaynly,
That the last day is not farre hence,
But wyll come sodeynly.

Whych reprobates most damnable,   10
Haue cause to doubt and feare:
But Gods elect doo dayly wyshe
To see the same appeare.

Farewell (quod she) I must departe,
I haue done thy request: 15
As swyft as thought she perst the clouds
To wynne eternall rest.

And I wyth care for her absence,
And sodeyne presence change,
Awoke from sleape, much meruaylyng   20
At thys my sweuen strange.

[[*A Poesis in forme of a Visyon,*
   briefly inueying against the most hatefull and prodigious Artes of Necro-
   mancie, Wytchcraft, sorcery, Incan-   25
   tations, and diuers other detestable &
   dyuelyshe practises, dayly vsed vnder
   colour of Iudiciall Astrologie.

                                            From

311

FROM out the Ramme into the Bull
As Titan last gan crall:
By order in hys endles pathe
Ecliptike that men call.   5

    Whyche pathe dothe so the zodiak,
Iust in the myddest deuyde:
That syxe degrees thereof are founde,
From it on euery syde.

    When day was fled, and night in place,   10
As was natures request:
I went to bed full hopyng there,
To take some quiet rest.

    Whyche long before I lacked so
Through trouble of myne hart,   15
That thus I made my playnt to God
Who only knewe my smart.

    Almyghty Ioue, graunt now that I,
Wyth sleape thys nyght begyle:
As dyd Vlysses, when from care,   20
He eased was a whyle.

    When most frendly *Alcinous*,
Good kyng of *Phaeacea*,
Hym sent in shyp tyll he sayld home
To hys owne *Ithaca*.   25

    Who sleapyng styll was from the shyp
Layd foorthe vpon the lande:
Which whē he woke, what place it was
Dyd nothyng vnderstande.

                X.2.   Vntill   30

Vntill Minerua hym informde,
And gaue hym perfect viewe:
Howe soone he myght in presence be
Of *Penelope* true,   5

Hys wyfe most chast which fortune strange
To hys great griefe of mynde:
By dyuers lucke, long tyme with held,
In Homer as we fynde.

But *Philomela* busyly,   10
Recorded so her song:
That all my shyftes could wyn no slepe,
That would contynue long.

For as they feyne the thorne so sharpe,
Dyd seme to touche hyr brest,   15
For hyr shryll notes so perst myne eares,
That long I could not rest.

Yet in short slepes suche dredfull dremes
I gan to thynke and met:
That when I wakt besyde my wyt   20
It had me almost set.

Me thought I dyd in medowes walke
For my sport and solas:
Where syluer drops of dewe most swete
Dyd cleaue to euery grasse.   25

Wherby there ran a ryuer fayre,
Wyth streames so Chrystall clere:
That at the bothom myght be sene
The peble stones appere.

                                        Aboue   30

Aboue the medow was a rock,
And on that rocke a wood:
From whiche ran many pleasant springs
Into that ryuer good.   5

Crossyng the medes, they trickled downe
As lyfe bloud in the veynes
Dothe from the heart tyll eche member
Comfort therby atteynes.

Aboue thys woddy rocke there was   10
A Fielde most plesant grene:
Where the beautie of natures workes
Ryght aptly myght be sene.

There was no herbe nor plesant flowre
In suche a Fyeld to know: 15
But myght be sene most fruitfully
Within thys fielde to grow.

What should I name the *Hyacinthe,*
Or soote *Verbasculy*:
The *Clouer* swete of dyuers kyndes,   20
That caulde are trifoly.

The *Brunell* and the *Bugle* blewe,
Wyth fayre *Hieracium*:
The *Synkfoyle* and the *Betony,*
And swete *Origanum.*   25

The *Tutsane* and *Hipericon,*
Asciron, and *Paunsye*:
The *Vyolet* and *Simphiton,*
And the double *Daysye.*

      X.3. The 30

The *Hartes ease,* and the *Pacience,*
And crimsen *Pimpernell,*
The *Cammocke,* and the *Camomille,*
And *Canterbury bell.*   5

Rosecampany, *Maudlen,* and *Cost,*
And *London touft* so red:
Agrimony and *Lyons tooth,*
That Chyldren call *Pysbed.*

Odoriferous *Serpillum,*   10
And *lady Traces* fyne:
With *Yarow, Torne twyse, Strawberyes,*
And *Burnet* good with wyne.

The *Lunary,* the *Serpents tongue,*
And *Procerpinaca:*   15
The *Adder grasse,* the *Saxifrage,*
And eke *Veronica.*

It hedged was wyth *Honeysuckes,*
Or *periclimenum:*
Well myxed wyth small *Cotnus* trees,   20
Swete bryer, and *Ligustrum.*

The *whyte thorne,* and the *blacke thorne* bothe,
Wyth *boxe,* and *maple* fyne:
In whyche braunched the *Briony,*
The *Iuy,* and *wylde vyne.*   25

To long I should the tyme detract
And from my purpose stray:
If I should recken all the thyngs
Within the Fielde so gay.

                                      Beside   30

Beside the good prospect for those,
That knowe Astronomy:
I thynke no platforme in the worlde,
Where one myght more aptly   5

The rysyng see, and settynges bothe,
That Cosmike haue to name:
Acronyke to, and Helyak,
Of starres of noble fame.

About our Artick pole ye myght   10
The lyttle Beare fyrst see:
That called are, the guardes of those
That cunnyng saylers be.

The great Beare also in the whych
Charles wayne appeareth stoute: 15
Whych wyth the small Beare euermore,
Dothe walke the pole about.

Which Beares the Dragon dothe inuolue,
Then *Bootes*, and the North Crowne:
And after knelynge Hercules,   20
Is sene with great renowne.

Harpe, falling gryp, goate, swan, and he
That vse to dryue the cart:
The man that dothe the serpent beare,
The Egle and the dart.   25

Dolphin, forehors, and thother hors
That flyes, caulde *pegasus*:
The tryangle, and Andromede,
As some men doo discusse.

X.iiii.   The   30

The zodiake with hys .xii. sygnes
Where Planets haue theyr waye:
Wyth all aspects that may bechance
To any, nyght or day.   5

The Bulls eye, with the rest of sterres,
That caulde are *Hyades*,
Myght there be sene wyth the brood henne,
That some name *Pleiades*.

The Manger and the Asses twayne,   10
The Lyons hart, and tayle:
The virgins spyke, the scorpyons harte
And Water potte all hayle.

Whale, Oryon, and Golden yarde,
That ladyes Elle some call: 15
The ryuer, hare, and bothe the dogges,
As well the great as small.

The serpent of the southe, the Cuppe,
The Rauen, and Centaure:
The Centaures speare, & then the wolfe   20
And also the altare.

The South crowne also may be sene,
Wyth many other there,
As Tricars Constellation,
Or *Berenices* heare.   25

The shyppe that Argo poetes do name,
There myght a man beholde:
And many mo then I can name,
An hundred thousande folde.

                        There   30

There myght ye see ascensions,
Bothe oblique and ryght:
No secretes of Astronomye,
That were not there in syght.   5

And to be briefe it was the ioye,
Of Lady Vranie
Wherin to walke she dyd frequent
Wyth all her famylie.

But as I clymed vp the rocke,   10
As I had oft before:
Of that swete fielde to take the ayre
Whyche doth mans sprites restore,

I mette a man in garments long
Most decent to beholde: 15
His long beard gray, so was hys head
Which dyd declare hym old.

His countenance in sobernes,
All others dyd excell:
His gate and gesture semd ynough   20
All vyces to expell.

For from the rule of honestye,
In hym was nothyng sene:
His outward workes dyd explicate,
An inwarde conscience cleane.   25

He toke me by the hand, and sayd,
Dere frende howe farre away?
To yonder field father (I sayd)
A whyle my selfe to play.

X.5.   My   30

My frend alas (quod he) beware
Howe ye henceforth come there:
It wyll you els in hell confound,
Therfore I say forbeare. 5

What is your name my father fayre,
(Sayd I) doo it disclose:
Theologus I am (quod he)
Wyth thee I wyll not glose.

Why then (sayd I) do ye me warne, 10
From yonder plesant place?
Because (quod he) it late receaude
A chance of great disgrace.

Howe so (sayd I) then harke (quod he)
I doo not vse to lye: 15
I wyll the showe howe it befell,
And that ryght orderly.

A Heron foule, that hunger gutte,
Of all fowles at hys foode:
Most rauenous, insaciate, 20
And of most gredy moode,

Hard by the dolefull banks of Styx,
That fowle infernall flood,
To fyll hys gut, or take hys pray,
Styll watchyng late he stoode. 25

Where at the last, a serpent yong,
Of Plutos hatefull kynde,
Came craulyng out, whych gredy gut
Coulde very quickly fynde.

And 30

And thynkyng it had ben an eele,
He cobde hym up at ones:
And wyth that pray away he flewe
And made therof no bones.   5

Whyche crepyng in hys belly, dyd
To hym suche extreme payne,
Tyll in thys Field at last he lyght,
Thynkyng there to remayne.

And foorthwyth at hys fundament,   10
Put foorth hys forsayd meate,
Thynkyng as he was wont wyth eeles
The same agayne to eate.

But beyng quycke, the serpent streight,
Dyd crepe among the grasse,   15
Whyche long necke could no more espy,
Ne yet fynde where she was.

Wherfore to Styx he went agayne,
And lykewyse swalowed mo,
And to this Fielde styll toke hys flyght,   20
And there dyd let them go.

Tyll he at last so many brought,
Through thys hys frequent vse,
That now thys Field is marred quight,
Through most hatefull abuse.   25

And suche a numbre of serpents
In it doo dayly breede,
Whych on these herbes & pleasant gras,
Continually doo feede,

                                      That   30

That nowe it is not onely robde
Of euery plesant flowre,
But hatefull stynche may there be felt
At euery tyme and howre.   5

And Vranie hath it forsoke,
With holsome pleasant showres:
And naturall Astronomie,
With all her fauoroures.

And true Phisyke forsakes it to,   10
For why, clowdes infernall,
Are dayly blowne from Lethes floud
To water it wythall.

Which causeth nothing there to grow
But Superstition: 15
Of learnyng pure, and science good
The vyle obliuion.

Astrologye Iudiciall,
Therfore dothe it possesse:
Whiche is a strumpet counterfet.   20
And yet neuerthelesse,

Because some learned men to hyr
Do cast their myndes and loue:
That she is true Astronomie,
Ryght many she doth moue.   25

And vnder colour of that name
They vse Necromancye:
Wyth hatefull incantations,
And vyle Geomancye.

                                        Of   30

Of Magikes artes there are great store,
And Augures arte perdye:
Foredemyng as *Aruspices,*
And some as *Pyrethi.*   5

All wytchecrafte vyle, and Sorcery,
Of false *phytonicus,*
Although they geue themselues the name
Of graue *Philonicus.*

These are the fruites of *phlegiae,*   10
Or Sathans wycked broode,
That in thys Fyeld the Heron shyt
To ease hym when he stoode.

Alas, (quod I) hath this vncleane
And hatefull byrde done so: 15
And natures dearlyng thus defast?
To hym *Vae, Vae,* wo wo.

Then am I of my fantasy,
And my plesant delyght:
And holsome recreation   20
Robde, and depryued quyght.

Wyth hangyng head, and bashfull face
I turned backe agayne,
For grayberds counsell durst I not
Refuse or once dysdayne.   25

But with most lowly reuerence,
Wyth thanks and condigne prayse,
I serued hym, when as we went
Eche one hys sundry wayes.

But   30

But sorowfull syghyng I,
Went wyth my sory newes,
Enformyng my famyliar frendes
Wyth whome I dyd peruse   5

My study small, wherwyth I doo
My wytte styll occupy,
And doo with them communicate
My mynde continually.

Of whyche some dyd sorowfully   10
Wyth me thys chance lament,
And other some would not beleue,
But to the place they went.

Nor would not here *Theologus*
That frendly dyd them warne: 15
But nedes would go presumptuously,
The matter to decearne.

Whiche hath them so infected now,
And that most diuelyshly:
They are content to graunt it styll   20
To be Astronomye.

And necessary wyll it call,
Though by the diuels worke,
Vnder cloke of Astronomye,
These foule false faytors lorke.   25

So I be holpe of griefe (say they)
Or fynde that whiche I loste:
Or know my desteny to come,
Why should I count it coste?

God   30

God would not suffer (other sayd)
Suche thynges for to be wrought:
If he dyd not allowe the same,
Or knewe it to be naught.   5

It is a good worke (other sayd)
Men to health to restore:
Although it be by dyuels worke,
What nede I passe therfore?

To helpe a true man to hys goods,   10
Wherof he was depryude,
By fals theues and vyle barators,
That wrongly it atchieude,

It can not be but a good worke,
Thus beastly men and fond,   15
Do answer them that would instruct
Or make them vnderstand,

Not regardyng the law of God,
Nor hys commaundement:
That no yll thyng ought to be done,   20
Vpon a good intent.

Also yf Gods permission,
Were a laufull defence,
So were it for all kynd of synne,
And most wycked offence.   25

As whoredome, homicide and theft,
Wyth vyle Idolatry:
For treason, couetyse, and pryde,
And moste vyle simony.

                              May   30

324

May I not say, all these be good,
Sythe God dothe them permyt:
As well as those whom ye defende,
Oh men of beastly wyt? 5

His sufferance is to let your synne
Vnto full rypenes growe:
That in the lake of sulphure he
Most iustly may you throwe.

And so declare hys glory great 10
Vnto hys flocke electe:
That do by grace these wycked artes
Cleane from theyr heartes reiect.

Their counsels all at God they aske,
And doo at hym require, 15
Theyr sauyng health, and he doth geue
To them theyr whole desyre.

For why one heare shall neuer fall
From of theyr heads no tyme
Wythout hys wyll, whych doth impute, 20
To them no synne nor cryme.

For why they aske in lyuely fayth
All wherof they haue nede:
Whiche causeth them assuredly
Of theyr purpose to spede. 25

Therfore it must of force procede,
Of Infidelitie:
That ye at dyuels seke suche helpe
Through moste vyle sorcery.

As 30

As dyd kyng Saule that damned man,
When Gods sprite hym forsoke:
When God would hym no answer make
For wytchecraft gan he loke.   5

Which faithles shift, how much it dyd
Hym in his nede auayle
Dyd well appere: he slewe hym selfe
When foes dyd hym assayle.

And so do ye your selues declare,   10
Of that same very sect:
Whyle ye at Sathan seke your helpe,
And do Gods powre suspect.

For as to dyuels here ye sought,
As reprobates forelorne: 15
So shall ye be hys porcion,
Syth God ye haue forsworne.

Vnlesse in tyme ye may repent,
Whiche yf it be gods will,
He graunt ye all, that ye may hate,   20
And shonnyshe thys great yll.

For though on prudent Salomon
They father this theyr art:
They are the workes of wickednes,
And of eternall smart   25

The very cause: for why saint Iohn
As God dyd hym reueale,
Hath found their place to be in hell,
Where tormentes are eche deale.

                        Y   Con-   30

Confounded are these coniurers
Wyth conscience vncleane:
And all that vnto sorcery,
Or wycked wytchecraft leane.   5

For in theyr art they doo no dout,
The lyuyng God forsake:
Cleauyng to condemnation,
And therof hold doo take.

What nede I here recyte scripture,   10
Syth all men well do knowe:
That god so deadly doth it hate,
That neyther hygh nor lowe,

The same may vse, but that it wyll
To Sathan his soule gyue: 15
Or if Gods lawe obserued were,
Not one of them should lyue

That charmers are, or coniurers,
Wyth wytches sorcery:
Or suche as chosers are of dayes,   20
Markyng the byrdes that flye.

For why the faythfull that do feare
God ryghtly and beleue,
Assuredly do know that no
Suche thyng can once them greue.   25

And as for that Astrologie,
Iudicial that ye name:
Let learned Caluine satisfie,
All wyse men of the same.

                                But   30

But Phisike and Astronomy,
Alas is nowe the cloke,
For euery kynde of trechery,
That goodnes dothe reuoke.　　　　　　5

For wycked wandryng fugitiues
Or vagabundes most lewde:
Do now a dayes from shyre to shyre,
Wyth shyftes both false and shrewde,

Vnder colour of Phisikes arte,　　　　10
And noble Surgery,
Delude the common multitude
Wyth shamefull sorcery.

All secrete markes they wyll disclose,
And thynges long done and paste:　　　15
Whych doth with admiration
The people make agast,

In suche wise, that they streight beleue
That nothyng vnder sonne,
Dothe stande to hard or difficill,　　　20
Of suche men to be donne.

So that partly wyth Palmestry,
Or Chryromancies gaude:
And foolysh Physiognomye,
And wytchery that fraude,　　　　　　25

Vnto theyr wycked false purpose,
The people they allure:
More then can any godly art,
That perfect is and pure.

　　　　　　　Y.2.　　　For　　　30

328

For Bedlem baudes, & hatefull hoores
This is a common shyft:
Of ruffyen theues and murderers
It also is the dryft.   5

   Vnder suche cloke their companies
Together oft they drawe:
Free from danger of officers,
And punyshement of lawe.

   Alas that thys myght be sene to   10
With Iustice, powre, and myght,
That Vranie and Medicine,
Agayn myght haue theyr ryght.

   That nowe is by extorcion,
So fraudulently kept: 15
That for most true possessioners
The most part them accept.

   For how theyr Field was put them fro
Before I haue you sayd:
Desyryng now all learned men   20
In this to adde theyr ayde.

   That from the fylthy fruites of hell
It may once be purged:
That there the ryght inheritours
Agayne myght be lodged.   25

   That now be fayne to seke els where,
Some holsome place to dwell:
Where of the wyse they are accept
And entertayned well.

                          Among   30

Among these thoughtes most troublesome,
At laste I dyd awake:
Fyndyng my body sweatyng sore,
And all my synewes shake.   5

Where I long tyme lay syghyng sore,
Thynkyng of thys strange dreame:
Wyshyng for some interpretour
If any in thys Realme

Were full expert therin as was   10
Ferdinand Ponzetus:
Or *Artemidor*, whose syrname
Is sayd *Daldianus*.

But as eche thyng doth weare by time
So other thoughtes at last,   15
Abated this perplexitie,
And it began to wast.

And I agayne came to my selfe,
That I dyd shortly heare:
The warblyng notes & song so swete,   20
Of *Philomela* cleare.

Which counsayld me that slouthfulnes
I should from me expell:
Wherfore I rose, and wyth all spede,
I lyghted a candell.   25

So serude my turne my tynder boxe,
Whych stoode in my chamber:
Then toke I foorth my standyshe to,
Wyth pen, ynke, and paper.

                                    Where   30

Where I carude foorth yll fauoredly
Thys rough and ragged verse:
Wherin theffect of thys my dreame,
I rudely doo reherse. 5

Desyryng yet my readers dere,
To beare it paciently:
Syth it is but the buddyng flowre,
Of my poore infancy.

Whych as rypenes of knowlege growes 10
I shallbe glad tamend:
If any man shall me informe,
And thus I make an ende.

Esay.19.

When they aske councell at theyr Gods, at their 15
Prophets, at theyr Sothsayers and Witches, thē
wyll I bryng theyr counsels to nought.

Hieremie.10.

Ye shall not lerne after the maner of the heathen,
and ye shall not feare the tokens of heauen: for the 20
heathen are afrayd of such. Yea all the customes and
lawes of the Gentiles are nothyng but vanitie.

Esay.47.

Go now to thy coniurers and to the multitude of thy
wytches, whom thou hast ben acquaynted with all frō 25
thy youthe, yf they may heare thee or strengthen thee:
Thou hast hytherto had many counsels of them. So let
the heauen gasers & beholders of starres, come on nowe
and deliuer thee: yea and let them shew, when these new
things shall come vppon thee. Behold they shalbe lyke 30
straw, which if it be kyndled with fyre, no man may rid
it for

it for the vehemency of the flame. And yet it gyueth no
synders to warme a man by, nor clere fyre to sit by. Euē
so shall they be whom from thy youth thou hast frequen-
ted. Euery one shall shewe thee hys erronious waye,   5
yet shall none of them defend thee.

      ⟦ *A Ditie declaryng the risyng and setting*
      of the .xii. sygnes of the zodiake : one always
      opposite and goyng down at the same instant
      that an other ryseth.   10

    THE Sygnes do ryse and sette
    At iust instant of tyme,
    Eche hydyng hym selfe when
    His opposyt dothe clyme.
    For why the Ramme so soone,   15
    Appeares not in the east,
    But streyght the balance be
    Gone downe then in the west.
    The Scorpion rysyng,
    The Bull euen then doth fall :   20
    When twynnes come, the Archer,
    On thother syde the Ball
    Doth passe from vs, and so
    The Crabbe and Goate lykewyse
    The Lyon and the Water potte,   25
    Eche fall when thother ryse,
    The Vyrgin in the east,
    No sooner shewes hir face,
    But in Weste the Fyshes
    Them hyde, and so gyue place,   30
    Thus in lyke order as
    One in East dothe appere,
    The Opposite sygne then,
    Abstaynes from taryng here.

                        Y.iiii.   Ne 35

Ne yet can one of them
Declare hym selfe so bolde,
Aboue the Horizon,
His contrary beholde.   5

⟦ *A Ditie made to the prayse of God,*
   by the Author, for a pacient to vse after
   helth attayned, who contrary to all mens
   expectation, was in hys handes by the
   goodnes of God cured.   10

   Syng thys as, Of Ielousye who
   so wyll heare.

O LOUYNG God and myghty Lorde,
My maker and my gouernour,
My mouth and heart shall now accorde,   15
Thee to worshyp laude and honour.

   As Moses sung thy laude and prayse,
When through the red sea he had past,
And Pharao drownde as Scripture sayes,
As he pursude thy people fast.   20

   In many Psalmes as Dauid dyd
That kyngly Prophet prayse thy name:
When out of sorowes he was ryd,
He sung thy prayses for the same.

   As dyd good kyng Ezechias,   25
When thou dydst hym to helth restore,
Makyng hym whole as earst he was,
To lyue yet full fyftene yeares more.

                                     As

333

As Ionas brought from poynt of death,
Hym selfe adressed by and by,
As soone as he could drawe his breathe
Thy holy name to magnify.   5

And as thy Prophet Daniell,
From lyons mouthe delyuered,
For ioye thy prayse and powre dyd tell,
And Darius the worshipped.

So doo I wretched synner nowe,   10
Hauyng a cause as great as those,
In thys case execute my vowe,
Thy mercyes great Lord to disclose.

Thou bryngest downe to depth of wo,
Suche as thou myndest to correct,   15
And yet thou doste not leaue them so,
But doste to knowledge them direct.

As connyes myne, and theyr holes make,
In bankes where they delyght to brede,
Lyke order dyd my sycknes take,   20
Wythin my fleshe so dyd it fede.

Tyll at last I was consumed,
And nothyng left but bone and skynne.
My synnewes shrunke, my veynes were fled,
Not once possyble to be sene.   25

Incredible was my weakenes,
Consumed cleane wyth peyne and griefe,
But in greatest of my dystres,
Thy grace was sent to my reliefe.

                                        Wher-   30

334

Wherfore whyle breath within my breast,
May moue, I shall thy prayse declare:
And wyll shewe foorth to most and least,
Howe swete thy grace and mercies are.   5

And howe at nede thou art at hand
To helpe all that in thee doo trust,
And makest vs to vnderstand,
Howe faythfull thou art and how iust.

My holowe caues are fyllde agayn,   10
Those runnyng sores are whole and drye,
And I in ease ryd out of payne,
In health and strength ryght perfectly.

All honour prayse and great glory,
To thee therfore I styll shall gyue: 15
And wyll not put from memory,
Thy grace and mercyes whyle I lyue.

But wyll all other folke exhorte,
By all occasyons as I may:
To trust in thee, to theyr comforte,   20
And faythfully moue them to pray.

All honour therfore I render
To thee God, that of myght hast most.
O Father with thy sonne so dere,
And also to the holy ghost.   25

As hath ben is and shalbe styll,
To worlde of worldes for euermore,
Where angels euer with good wyll,
Doo prayse thee styll out of theyr store.

An   30

IF any man from wo,
And payne restorde to ease,   5
When griefe is gone hym fro,
With sycknesse and dysease,
Haue cause with prayse,
To laude thy name,
And shewe the same,   10
Wyth thankes always,

   Then I most wretched wyght,
Of all folke most am bounde,
To cause bothe daye and nyght,
Hys prayses to abounde,   15
Whyche at thys day,
Haue had reliefe
From all my griefe,
Wherin I lay.

   My pynyng payne and sore   20
Incomparable was,
As beastes in payne doo rore,
So dyd I wretche alas:
Almoste tyll death,
Would me haue caught,   25
At me he raught,
To stoppe my breath.

   For as a carkas dead,
I lay in wo and care:
I coulde not eate my bread,   30
So faynt was I and bare:

                But

But nowe beholde,
Howe God my Lorde,
Hath me restorde,
A thousand folde.　　　　　　　　　　5

For where before his rod
I carelesse was and wylde,
Forgettyng my swete God,
With all his mercies myld
I nowe am taught,　　　　　　　　　10
To prayse hys powre,
And kepe eche howre
The same in thought.

Thus may we dayly see,
He scurgeth vs for loue,　　　　　　　15
True christians to be,
His mercie dothe vs moue,
And euer styll,
Dothe vs procure,
Ay to indure,　　　　　　　　　　20
To doo hys wyll.

Wherfore I wyll not cease,
On earthe here whyle I dwell,
Hys kyndnes to rehearse,
And of hys mercyes tell:　　　　　　25
And howe that he,
When hope was past,
Yet at the last,
Restored me.

All godly men therfore,　　　　　　　30
That in hym hope and truste,

　　　　　　　　　　Prayse

Prayse hym with all honour,
For he is true and iuste,
And wyll not mysse
To helpe at nede,   5
And that wyth spede,
All that are hys.

Se that both day and nyght,
Whether ye worke or rest,
Ye prayse hym for hys myght,   10
All creatures moste and least :
Whether ye play,
Lye downe or ryse,
Styll exercise,
His prayse alway.   15

Whether ye syt or stande,
Whether ye ryde or go,
On sea or on the lande
What so euer ye doo.
Whether therfore,   20
Ye drynke or eate
After your meate
And eke before

All honour to hym gyue,
For he vs wrought and made,   25
And causeth vs to lyue,
Eche creature in his trade :
And dothe gouerne,
As shypmayster,
Dothe guyde and stere,   30
His shyppe wyth sterne.

Wyth

338

Wyth all our myght and strength,
Let vs hym magnifie,
Whych saueth all at length,
That loue hym faythfully: 5
Wherfore all thyng,
Wyth hart and voyce,
In hym reioyce,
And thys wyse syng.

Glory to the Father,   10
God that of myght hath moste,
And to the sonne so dere,
And to the holy ghoste:
As hath ben yore,
Is and styll shall   15
Be ouer all,
For euermore.   Amen.

⟦ *A ditie to be sung of musiciens in*
    the mornyng, at theyr lord or masters
    chamber doore, orels where of hym   20
    to be heard.

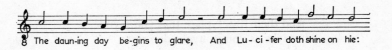

The daun-ing day be-gins to glare, And Lu-ci-fer doth shine on hie:

And

And sfaith that Phebus doth pre-pare,   To shew him selfe im-me-diat-ly.

And the most darke tenebrous nyght,
Is fayne to flee and turne her backe,
Whyche can in no wyse byde the lyght,   5
But beares away hir mantle blacke.

Wherfore in tyme let vs aryse,
And slouthfulnes doo cleane away:
Doyng some godly exercyse,
As seruantes true whyle it is day.   10

Let vs in no wyse tyme abuse,
Whyche is gods creature excellent,
All slouthfull sleape let vs refuse,
To vertuous workes let vs be bent.

Let vs commyt our selues to Christ   15
Wyth thankes & prayse him first to serue
Whyche dothe our deadly foes resyst,
And from all dangers vs preserue.

And then thys type se that you mynde,
That lyke as you in nyght doo rest: 20
And in the mornyng your selues fynde,
Awake and redy to be drest,

So shall our bodyes slepe by death,
And after be to lyfe restorde,
When Christ shall come & restore breth,   25
And Iudge vs all as sayth his worde.

Then

Then mekely let vs hym desyre,
That it may be hys blessed wyll,
That we thys day may well aspire,
By grace his seruyce to fulfyll.   5

So that we may do hurt to none,
Nor of none other hurt receaue,
But styll be kept by Christe alone,
That Sathan neuer vs deceaue.

But styll in christen godlynes,   10
By grace we may our selues prepare,
Of all offence and wyckednes,
For to escape the nette or snare.

Thys graunt vs Lord omnipotent,
For Christ his sake our mercy seate,   15
That we may tast ioyes permanent,
Before thy throne of glory great.
                              Amen.

[[*A ditie to be sung at nyght when*
   men go to bed. Syng this as,   20
   In sommer time when flowres gan
   spryng. &c.

NOWE that the day is wasted cleane,
And *Phebus* dothe hym self absent,
And *Hesperus* dothe downward leane :   25
And lurkyng nyght with darknes bent,
Her mantle darke abrode to spreade,
And hyde from vs the welkyn cleare,
And starres also are prepared,
With glystryng lyght nowe to appeare.   30

                        Ther-

341

Therfore of force we must nedes yelde
In bed to sleape and take our rest:
Forsaykng cleane both strete and field,
And other workes bothe most and least.   5
Wherfore to Christ now let vs call,
In thys our nede vs to assist,
From drede and feare and dangers all,
Defend our sely soules O Christ.

O Lord defend vs wyth thy grace,   10
In thys our nede when we do slepe,
Syth we are able at no space,
Our selues from dangers small to keepe,
O Lord that styll has wakyng eyes,
And knowst no sleape nor felest nyght,   15
Our humble sute do not despyse,
But vs defende now by thy myght.

Defende vs wyth thy grace and powre
To helpe our selues syth we ne can,
Nor haue no strength at any howre,   20
The same to doo so weake is man.
O let thy powre our feblenes,
Wyth helpe of grace this nyght supply,
O way our myserablenes,
And comfort vs wyth thy mercy.   25

O let vs then with mynde contrit
With prayse and prayer to Iesus,
Lye downe to rest, and so commyt
Our selues to hym that saueth vs.
O Lord forgeue vs all our synne,   30
And plant true fayth wythin our brest
And after cares that we are in,
Let vs ones tast eternall rest.   Amen.

                    z.1.   *A di-*

342

of Vertue

⟦ *A ditie to be sung at dyner tyme*
and meales. Syng thys as, If
truth may take no trusty holde. &c.

AS roote of tree dothe of the grounde,   5
Take moysture named radicall,
And causeth branches to abounde,
Wyth that he geues them ouer all,

 And suffreth no small twyg to want,
But naturally doth dispose   10
Suche as he hath plentie or scant,
Vnto the nutriment of those,

 As Nature by thys industry,
Dothe cause thynges vegitall to grow,
In other sort shee dothe apply   15
On animals good to bestowe.

 Among the whych we men mortall,
That formed are to Gods Image:
Wyth meate and drynke nutrimentall,
We maintaynde are from age to age. 20

 The myghty maker of all thynges,
Hys creatures leaues not destitute.
All that they haue is hys geuyng,
As well to man as beastes brute.

 Leste therfore we appere vnkynde, 25
Vnto this God that all dothe sende,
To prayse his name with thankful mynd
And gratfull harts now let vs bende.

        Let

Let vs not one morcell receyue,
Wyth forgetfull ingratitude:
Least to our owne lustes god vs leaue,
More wretched then brute beastes rude.   5

Ne yet let vs in any wyse,
Forget the nedy brethern poore,
The sycke and lame do not despyse,
Nor hym that goes from doore to doore.

For God hath made vs ministers,   10
That one an others nede should serue,
Wherfore we are but murderers,
If in our fault our neyghbours sterue.

And may be to that dogge comparde,
That lay vpon an heape of haye.   15
Spying the oxe come thitherwardt,
Wyth barkyng draue the same away.

Whyche nedes must be churlyshe enuy
Syth he hym selfe no haye could eate,
To stand at baye so frowardly,   20
And kepe the poore oxe from hys meate.

Let vs therfore doo otherwyse,
And from our bellies somwhat spare,
In loue to shewe some exercyse,
To brethern poore that nedy are.   25

For who so to the poore dooth geue
Dothe lend to God on vsury,
And shall receyue for hys releue,
Great gayne agayne abundantly.

z.2.   To   30

344

To hym therfore most gratefully,
Geue honour glory thankes and prayse,
To hym as one in Trinitie,
All honour be nowe and all ways.   5

⟦ *An other to the same purpose.*
  Syng thys as, Heare out O Lord
  the ryght request. &c.

WHEN ye take foode at any tyme,
Your bodyes to refreshe with ought   10
Remember Gods infynite powre
Which all hath made & formde of nought.

  Remember eke his prudent reygne,
His mercy and benignitie,
Who all his workes doth aye susteyne,   15
And gouerne styll continually.

  And consequently call to mynde,
Hys clemency and great mekenes,
Whych all creatures dothe fede & fynde,
Yea hys most foes in theyr dystresse.   20

  Ponder also the great meruayle,
How many great gyftes he ordeynes,
Sufficient foode and all victayle,
For all that this whole world conteines.

  Haue mynde how fast we do declyne,   25
How apt we are styll to decay,
Whiche only he by powre diuine,
Preserues, els were we gone away.

No

No mans wysedom nor angell bryght,
Were able this to take in hand,
In any wyse: or thyng more lyght,
The way howe once to vnderstande.   5

Sythe of hys gyftes therfore we lyue
Were it not cursed vnkyndnes,
That we due praise shold hym not geue?
Oh hatefull vile vnthankfulnes.

At thy table let sobernesse,   10
And wysedome be wyth talke most chast
Myndyng styll his pure holynes,
Whose gyftes this time in hand thou hast.

Let bytter wordes and backbytyng
From thy table secluded be,   15
Hys loue to thee rememberyng
Whose kyndnes is great towardes thee.

This place therfore contaminate
Not, wyth dysprayse of any man,
Syth thou feciste here for thyne estate,   20
Gods fauour, that no wyght want can.

Let therfore here no hate appere,
Where God so greatly shewes his loue,
But rather loue thy brother dere,
As gods great giftes here doo the moue.   25

Lorde graunt vs grace for euermore,
That we thy mercyes so muche mynde,
That hatred our heartes may abhore,
And neuer shewe our selues vnkynde.
                         Amen.

                   z.iii.   *An*   30

346

ALL folke that lyue in lyuely fayth,
Confesse wyth one accorde,
That all creatures are fed of God,　　　　　5
And prayse therfore the Lorde.

Lest then we shewe ingratitude
And mere vnthankfulnesse,
By lawe of loue graft in our heartes,
Let vs our fayth expresse.　　　　　10

And prayse the Lord for thys our foode
Here present to vs sent,
And for our helth whyche he to vs
Mercyfully hath lent.

And for hys worde to fede our soules,　　　　　15
We also ought to pray:
So shall we neuer dye, but lyue
Wyth God in blysse for aye.

Through Christ his death, who in thys worlde
Dyd take our fleshe therfore:　　　　　20
To whome be honour, prayse and laude,
Bothe nowe and euermore.
　　　　　　　Amen.

⟦*A sonnet inueyinge agaynst the*
abuses and pryde that reygneth a-　　　　　25
mong vayne women.

　　　　　　　　　Ye

YE women and maydes of Citie & country,
Leue your leude lightnes, lerne from honesty
If an of you the truth wyll regarde,
Spoke wyth simplicitie, let it be hearde.   5

And heare not only, but folowe the same,
Lest God discouer you to your great shame.
Remember your synnes, and rufully rue,
Lest after this barker a byter insue.

In Esay the prophete there may you fynde,   10
The plages y̆ for proude wome͞ God hath assignde.
The daughters of Syon (sayth he in that place)
Do tryp on theyr toes, wyth counterfayt pace,

Wyth stretched out necks, and nyce wanton eies,
But now wil I plage them for theyr proude guise.   15
They wold not my voyce here when that I cald,
Therfore for fayre heare they now shalbe bald.

For gyrdles of gold, they shall haue lose bandes,
Theyr husbandes shall fall in thenemies handes.
Theyr beautie shall fade, & they shall waxe dūne,   20
Theyr faces shall wyther, all burnt wyth sunne.

In stede of gay stomachers that thei now weare,
They shall weare sackloth in greate dread & feare.
Theyr brooches and ouches and garlandes gay,
Theyr partlets and pynnes I wyll take away.   25

Theyr hookes and hedbāds wherin they delight,
Hearlace and fyllets their heades wyth to dyght,
Perles & precious stones, gold wroght by mās art
Gold rings & iewels, wheron was theyr hart,

                              z.iiii.   Theyr   30

348

Theyr spāgs & their chains, their collers & hooues,
Theyr vales and theyr glasses, & theyr gay gloues,
Bonets and taches, and slyppers so thyn,
Settyng foorth beautie, and shewyng whyte skyn,　　5

Theyr smockes, theyr kerchers, & bracelets also,
And euery thyng els I wyll take them fro.
And for the swete smell that they do now vse,
They shall haue stynkyng that all men refuse.

For theyr great ryches and rayment costly,　　10
They shall be naked and in pouertie.
But leste ye should thynk this is but my mynde,
Reade Esay the third, and there shall ye fynde,

Whether that your lyfe from vertue rebell,
Or if it accord to Christ his gospell.　　15
For I can not thynke but then ye shall see,
That ten tymes as prowde as they were you be:

For whyche ye deserue (ye can not deney)
To be plagued ten tymes as muche as they.
For Christ in the Gospell playnly discust,　　20
Who so dothe a woman see, and doth her lust,

Hath presently in adultery done synne.
Then wo be to suche as trayne men therin.
For yf a mans eyes to lust do hym moue,
The woman dothe cause it, as I can proue.　　25

For Christ in the gospell also doth say,
Offences must nedes be, thys is no nay,
But wo be to them, through whō they be brought,
That is to say, suche as make men do nought.

　　　　　　　　　　　　　　　Let　　30

Let women in hart then ryghtly recorde,
If they cause not men to offend the Lord:
Whych all their whole lyfe for naught els prouide
But paynt out them selues of men to be spyde.   5

As men are adulterers, so are they whores,
That these wais mens souls consumes & deuoures.
If they commyt synne that doo but desyre,
Much more do those women through theyr attyre.

Whych curlyng theyr hear, & painting their face   10
Tempt and entice men, vayne loue to imbrace,
To daly and dance, suche women delyght,
Inuentyng newe tricks, from mornyng to nyght:

In pastyme and play theyr pleasure styll is,
And all the long day to clyp and kisse.   15
No good wyll suche doo wythin or wythout,
But dasse on theyr tayle, & pricke through a clout.

And some to be small, so streyneth theyr lace,
That they cleane depriue from colour their face:
The ryght course of bloud, so stoppyng wythall,   20
That often they faynt, and to the ground fall.

Yet though theyr smal wast ful oft make thē swoūd,
Theyr froks must haue buttocks most mōstrously roūd:
Lyke dancyng gyantes they go in the strete,
As though theyr hung houpes about theyr fine fete.   25

That Salomon sayth ryght true styll is it,
That recheles women doo by the way syt,
For suche as go by, they styll doo prepare,
The vnwyse to snarle in theyr wycked snare.

                                                  For   30

For women and maydens syt now adayes,
In wyndowes and doores, theyr beautie to praise,
The eyes of suche women thys is no nay,
Dooe wounde foolyshe men that passe by the way:　　5

Whyche is the whole cause (as semeth to me)
That men report of them worse then they be.
For why the scripture doth clerely preferre,
Our gate and behauour to teache what we are.

A tree by hys fruite men truly shall knowe,　　10
And dedes what man is, doo perfectly showe.
When suche perceaue men theyr pryde to despyse:
They leaue theyr old toyes, and new tricks deuise.

The fashion is changed, but streyght they wyll
Haue other newe fangles, worse or as yll:　　15
When I was a boy, I nowe well remember,
(Though I at that tyme of age were but tender)

That women theyr breastes dyd shew & lay out.
And wel was ẏ mayd whose dugs then were stoute.
Which vsance at fyrst came vp in the stues,　　20
Which mens wyues and daughters after dyd vse.

The preachers at that, then gan out to crye,
And honest men dyd it lothe and defye:
Wherfore they left of that foule synfull guyse,
But streight thei laid down their hear to their eies.　　25

So as fast as gods word one synne doth blame,
They deuyse other as yll as the same.
And this varietie of Englyshe folke,
Dothe cause all wyse people vs for to mocke.

　　　　　　　　　　　　For　　30

For all discrete nations vnder the sonne,
Do vse at thys day as they fyrst begonne:
And neuer doo change, but styll doo frequent,
Theyr old guyse, what euer fond folkes do inuent.   5

But we here in England lyke fooles and apes,
Do by our vayne fangles deserue mocks and iapes,
For all kynde of countreys dooe vs deryde,
In no constant custome sythe we abyde.

For we neuer knowe howe in our aray,   10
We may in fyrme fashion stedfastly stay.
But nowe to my purpose, I mynde not to put,
In no womans head to become a slut.

For though God to pryde haue geuen his curse,
I esteme sluttyshenes to be muche worse.   15
For cleannes is vertue none can denaye,
If pryde and excesse be banysht away.

But change of proude rayment now dayly vsed,
Ought of all good women to be refused.
Thys day my cassocke, to morow my frocke,   20
Next day my vardygue nyghest my smocke.

Thys day my kyrtell, wyth partlet and gowne,
To morowe a furred cap iust on my crowne,
Next day a veluet cap, or a frenche hoode.
Who can beleue that suche women be good?   25

Some weare a cheyne, and some a blacke lace,
And colours also to paynt with theyr face:
Wherwith they doo make theyr faces to shyne.
Since god made the world such pride was nere sene

    In   30

In doyng of the whyche this is no dout,
The Image of God they blot and put out.
Lo thus are they paynted out to be sold,
With many mo gaudes then here can be told:　　　　5

Forgettyng obedience, hatyng Gods lawe,
And lyue with theyr makes, without loue or awe.
And many oppressors thys day doth reygne,
That robbe & pyll poore men, wiues to maynteyn.

And fearyng least theyr great pride shold be lesse,　　10
The poore mans cause they wyll neuer redresse.
To mayntayne theyr wiues that proud are & nyse,
Lewde lubbers sometyme doo rebell and ryse.

A lowte with a lorde wyll proudely checkmate,
And is not content wyth hys poore estate.　　　　15
Agaynst men of honour, the person vyle,
Prowdly presumeth, wo worth the whyle.

Boyes agaynst elders preferment dyd take,
And at theyr own wyl wold magistrates make:
For by theyr apparell none can now know,　　　　20
The hygh estate from the most poore and low.

Eche lasse lyke a lady is clothed in sylke,
That dayly doth go to market with mylke.
Whych neuer theyr port could yet maynteyn well,
Vnlesse they were whores, & their husbands steale.　　25

Besyde the vndecent maner to see,
That eche one doth go in others degree,
Vayne women loue not the men graue and sage,
But rufflers that rudely raue can, and rage:

　　　　　　　　　　　　Whose　　30

353

Whose feruent desyre must always prouyde,
To set foorth theyr wyues in pompe and in pryde.
For so that suche women may haue theyr wyll,
They passe not although theyr husbādes doo spyll.   5

Such wepe when theyr husbāds be sick in bead,
And turne it to laughter when they be dead.
Wherfore suche proude women are lyke in hell,
To be rewarded with proude Iesabell:

Vnlesse they repent, and shortly amend: 10
Whyche God gyue them grace yet once to intend,
That I myght haue cause yet once in my dayes:
As muche for to wryte to theyr laude and prayse.

For blessed be they that hold them content,
With cleane apparell, honest and decent,   15
And women bearyng of beautie the name,
Without discrete maners ioynde with the same,

Salomon dothe them no better allowe,
Then a gold ryng in the nose of a sowe.
Therfore let old women honestly lyue,   20
And good examples to yong women gyue.

That one by an others conuersation,
May learne to leaue theyr abhomination,
That vertuous dedes in those of the Citie,
May be example vnto the countrey.   25

For they of the countrey euer take hede,
How they of the citie doo weare theyr wede:
Therfore I may say, and so I say wyll,
The Citie is fyrst the Author of yll.

                                        My   30

354

My prayer therfore shalbe day and nyght,
That eche parte may mende and walk here aright,
That I may report the maydes of my countrey,
Thankes be to God haue lerned honestye :   5
Whyche God graunt me grace, to see in my tyme,
Thus make I an ende, of thys symple ryme.

⟦ *The complaynte of a certayne famous*
   town for the death of an honest matron, wyfe
   to one of thinhabitantes of the same, wyth an   10
   answer to the sayd complaynt : & in fyne a generall prayse of all honest & vertuous womē.

FOORTH as I went my way of late,
(Whych was of Iune the .xvi. day)
After my due and wonted rate,   15
To set my worke in quyete stay :
A sodeyne voyce there dyd me fray,
And muche to muse dyd me constrayne,
So greuously it dyd complayne.

Merueylyng then I gan to saye,   20
What are you that doo sygh and grone?
Answere it made without delaye :
A famous towne dothe make thys mone,
For suche a losse as I haue one :
I thynke there hath in no place dwelt,   25
As Christes members haue well felt.

And why (quod I) what is the case?
What cause haue you thus to complayne?
Wyth greuous syghes it sayd alas,
Oh cruell death full of dysdayne :   30
Why dydst thou not a whyle refrayn?

                         But

But lyke a scadell vermyne styll,
Thou takste the good, and leaust the yll.

What gyrlyshe gylls, what wanton scoldes,
In me dothe reigne, to my great shame: 5
Whom honest men that them beholdes,
Reporteth in hurt of my fame:
Suche in his rage Death wyll not tame,
But modest matrons good and true,
In all the haste he dothe subdue.   10

For of the best the lest of all,
He hath not taken manerly,
But snatched hath the principall,
In all my ioy moste cruelly,
And turned to calamitie,   15
My staye, my health, and my delyght,
Whych reigned in that godly wyght.

She bare suche fauour to the truthe,
And beneficiall to the poore,
Hyr goodly traynyng vp of youthe: 20
As maydens sobre and demure,
And honest wyues some be you sure,
To whom she was a godly lyght,
And to theyr fete a lanterne bryght.

Her good constant womanlynes,   25
Hir obedience in her duetye,
Her lenitie and gentylnes
Her hate of vice in lyke degree
Her better sure I neuer see,
Her fayth was good, her lyfe also: 30
Her lyke there are not many mo.

                                        She

356

She loued truthe and godlynesse,
She gaue the hungry meate and drynke
She lothed vyce and wyckednes,
She was without all fault I thynke,   5
She holpe the poore, and dyd not shrynk,
She clothed the naked and colde,
She holpe the sycke many a folde.

Thus death hath taken hir away,
That mother was of modestye: 10
And none can tell the truthe to saye,
The losse that I susteyne therby.
Therfore I may well wepe and cry,
And say Alas wo worth the tyme,
That brought to me this wofull cryme.   15

Be styll thou towne thus sayd I then,
Beware, and harke, what I shall tell:
Thou maynteynest all wycked men,
Agaynst the good thou doste rebell,
Yea suche as preache the Lordes gospell.   20
Therfore no doubte come is the day,
God turnes his face from thee away.

Syth thou in tyme refusedst grace,
Thou shalte be left as one confusde,
Sythe thou doste wyckednes imbrace,   25
And godlynes thou hast refusde:
Before the Lord thou art accusde,
And he it is that in his wrathe,
Wyll take away thy frendes by death.

Therfore leaue of, thus death to blame,   30
And blame for it thyne owne offence:
And thyn inhabitantes by name,

                                        Whych

Whych are so full of negligence,
And also hate the diligence,
Of those that would haue them amende,
And seke vices to reprehende.   5

For lyke sayth God, as I dyd call,
And ye would not therto attend:
Euen in your nede when ye aske shall:
Myne eares to you I wyll not bende:
But as rebells you reprehende,   10
And take from you your hope and trust
Leauing you to your own harts lust.

Thy rulers folow not the truthe,
They set by theyr owne pryde and fame,
Theyr buyldynges gay to se is ruthe: 15
But none wyl help godes house to frame.
At Gods wysedome they iest and game,
Theyr worldly wyts they do exalt
With stomackes that be proud and hault.

I graunt thou hast a iewell lost,   20
Wherof thou knewest not the pryce:
Wherfore for thyne vnthankfull bost,
The Lorde hath take that matron wise,
Her corps to earth as colde as yse,
Hyr soule in blysse the Lord wyll saue.   25
Thou wast not worthy her to haue.

Lykewyse yf thou wylt not repent,
Thou shalt both lose and goe from all,
Thy ancient men learnde and prudent,
And men ecclesiasticall.   30

a   Thy

358

Thy courage god wyll so make fall,
As in the Prophete thou maist see,
That chyldern shall thy rulers be.

And as for her that is gone hence,   5
And changed hath for better boote,
She is full safe in gods presence,
Whiche loued hir at the hart roote :
The whiche shall thee nothyng promote,
No helpe it is for thee nor thyne,   10
Except ye folowe the same lyne.

I meane that ye should doo the lyke,
And folowe the lyke honestie,
Be humble, gentyll, good and meke,
With sobernes and modestie,   15
And with Christian seueritie,
Gods mercie then wyll on you rue,
And wyll agayne your ioye renue.

When that the town had hearde al this
All in hyr dumpes she gan to lowre,   20
And sayde nothyng therto I wys,
But stoutly stoode as a strong towre :
My gonshot could not make hir cowre,
But I pray God for Christes sake,
That she may this poore counsell take.   25

And now to you ye matrons all,
That fauor truthe and godlynes,
Vertuous iewels we may you call :
For fewe there be that doo profes,
Suche sapience and sobernes,   30
As manifestly doth appere,
In you, through Christ our lorde so dere.

                                        Be

359

Be of good chere I saye to you,
Though I expresse you not by name:
For knowne is your indeuor true,
To those that wyll set forth the same,   5
So that immortall is your fame:
Example as ye haue by this
Your syster, that departed is.

Whose worthy prayse shall neuer die,
But like is to indure for euer: 10
For why she lyued worthyly,
And to the ende she did perseuer:
God graunt vs all so to endeuour,
That we may liue whyle we be here,
With God in glory to appere.   15

Nomen authoris.

If any maruell, that the name
Of towne or corps, I not reherse:
Hatefull enuy causde the same,
Nought els kept them out of my verse.   20

Hate therfore here shall haue no cause
At any person to disdeyne:
Let all men flee from enuies clawes,
Lest she doo them some grefe and peyne.

a2   *An*   25

# of Vertue

⟦ An exhortacion for vertuous men
to perciste in vertue and to prayse Christ
the authour of vertue, to whom
be all honour and
glory. Amē.

5

Al ver - tuous men that ver - tue loue in ver - tue still re - ioyce,

and

—T.C.O.V.   361

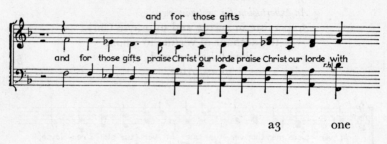

one hart minde and voyce with one hart minde and voyce.

For if as truthe is one good thought
Can not in vs once growe,
Without his grace that always doth   5
His mercies to vs shewe;

                              How

How can there any vertuous deed
At any time appere
In vs that are but vayne and nought
Saue for his mercies dere.   5

    Wherfore let none of vertue boste
As of his owne pure wayes,
But mekly thanke Christ for his giftes,
And geue him condigne prayse.

    Praise him therfore that first all made   10
And formed man of slime
And doth his worke most intricate
Preserue from time to time.

    Whiche also when as sinfull man
By fault fell into thrall,   15
Ordeined Christ our sauing helth
By death to heale vs all.

    Immortall thankes, eternall prayse
Euer now let vs giue
Vnto this lord of whom we are   20
And of whose grace we liue.

    Glory and prayse for euer more,
Therfore be to his name,
That vertue made for men to knowe
And to walke in the same.   25

FINIS

⟦ *Imprinted at London in fleete*
streete nighe vnto S. Dunstanes
churche, by Thomas
Marshe.
1565.
Mense Iulii. 16.

1. THE SURVIVING COPIES

THE four copies of *The Court of Virtue* now extant represent but one edition. To avoid repetition, therefore, I shall describe fully only the most nearly perfect copy, that in the British Museum, and shall supplement that description by noting variations in the other copies.

Title page: Lacking ['the Couurte of vertu contaynynge many holy or spretuall songes Sonettes psalmes ballettes short sentences as well of holy scriptures as others &c.' Title from *Stationers' Register*, I, 268].

Colophon: Imprinted at London in fleete | streete nighe unto S. Dunstanes churche, by Thomas | Marshe. | [rule] 1565. | Mense Iulii. 16. (Lacking in other copies.)

Collation: 8vo, 186 leaves, signatures B–z8, a8 (blank). Unpaged. Pressmark C.57.aa.33. All of sheet A is missing, except two unsigned leaves. These leaves are, moreover, consecutive, as is shown by the catch word on the verso of the first; that on the verso of the second is not taken up on B1, so that something must have come between the two leaves. The unsigned leaves cannot be 7 and 8, then, unless the preliminaries occupied more than 8 leaves. Since the printer customarily signs the first five leaves in each quire, it should follow that the two leaves in question are 6 and 7. But the chain lines of leaves 6 and 7 must match at the top of the page, and these do not. Indeed, the chain lines indicate that the first of the two leaves is one of the first four in the gathering, and the second leaf one of the second four; in other words, the two unsigned leaves ought to be 4 and 5 of an eight-leaf gathering or 2 and 3 of a four-leaf gathering. If so, the printer must have failed to sign the preliminary leaves as he did the leaves of the text. It is possible, then, that the unsigned leaves are 4 and 5, or (since it is unlikely that an eight-leaf gathering would lack signatures on 4 and 5) that the preliminaries were printed on a half-sheet, and that the leaves are 2 and 3. There is no sign of a watermark on either leaf.

Huntington and Bodleian copies: 181 leaves, B–z8, a6 (lacking a1).

Folger copy: same as BM, save that a8 is lacking. Thus Folger contains but 185 leaves.

Signatures: Normally, the first five leaves in each gathering are signed. However, the fifth leaf in gatherings N, Q, R, Y, z, and a is not signed, and Y3, z3, and a4 are not signed. M5 is signed

well Court. At the Britwell sale, April 2, 1924, *The Court of Virtue*, numbered 390, was acquired by the Henry E. Huntington Library. The copy is bound in an early binding of worn sheep over paper boards. A few leaves are loose; several are lacking: all before leaf B, including the title page, a1, a7, the colophon, and a8, probably blank. Inside the front cover is written: 'Trapworth [?] 1815,' and below it, in a different hand: 'Will: Thompson / Queen's Coll: Oxon: / 1750.' 'X.I.,' in another hand, follows after, and is itself followed by the notation, in a still different hand: 'This book was printed / in the year 1565.' At the bottom, in the right corner, appears a round white paper bearing the (unidentified) ms. number '1628.' Scribbling disfigures B1, B6v ('John Hall The Author.'), k6v, O8r, P1r ('John'), P1v ('Hall'), z1r. On the fly-leaf at the end of the volume is written, in a hand different from all the others: 'This book was intended as an antidote to a collection of licentious Songs, called "The Court of Venus." ' Condition is generally good, despite the missing leaves.

The Bodleian copy was owned by the collector, Francis Douce, who bequeathed it to the Bodleian Library. The earliest owner, so far as I can discover, was one Robert Hollinges, whose name appears in ink as 'Ro: Hollinges 1638. 2^d.' on B6v; and on P4v of *The Hymnes and Songs of the Church . . . Translated and Composed, By G*[eorge]. *W*[ither]. London, n.d. Wither's book is bound with the *Court*, preceding it. Since Hollinges' name appears in both volumes, they were joined, presumably, no later than the early seventeenth century. Ultimately, the *Court* passed to Topham Beauclerk, the friend of Dr. Johnson. On Beauclerk's death, it was sold at auction, as lot number 3299, on April 30, 1781. The new owner, I assume, was William Herbert, the historian of printing, whose hand is found on the first page of the Prologue. Douce may have had the book of Herbert, though Herbert's sale catalogues do not record any transaction. Douce died in March, 1834, leaving the greatest number of his books to the Bodleian, which issued, in 1840, a catalogue enumerating them. *The Court of Virtue* is listed therein. This copy is bound in a light brown speckled calf, with a gold border. The spine has recently been rebacked. The binding was probably done for Francis Douce, whose bookplate is pasted on the inside of the front cover. Condition is only fair: numerous pages are soiled and stained or slightly torn at the top; a6 has had a good piece of the top torn away. Scribbling in what looks to be an Elizabethan hand occurs on many pages. Some of the pages have been cropped. The note 'A[mes]. p. 300.' appears in ink on B1r. It is in Herbert's hand.

The Folger copy was acquired from the library of Lieutenant-Colonel E. H. Tomlinson-Harmsworth. Pasted on the inside of the front board is the notation: 'From library of Sir R. Leicester Harmsworth, Bart.' Earlier, this volume had been sold at Sotheby's as item 472 on April 6, 1925. In 1803 someone pencilled a word or two on a7v and L3r. On a3r is written: '179 Psalm.' The copy is bound in contemporary calf, with the initials M and C stamped in gold on either side of an ornate gold oval. This design appears on both covers. The condition is fair, with some leaves of the book having been mended. The binding has been repaired at the top and bottom of the spine, and reinforced at the hinges. The leather is still in one piece.

Press Variants: I have compared the different copies only with respect to bibliographical description. Observable variations are of two kinds: (1) accidental variation owing to displacement of type from the forme, and occasioned perhaps by inking; (2) deliberate variation owing to correction of type after printing has begun, and occasioned perhaps by the author's revision of proofs at the printing house. Under (1) I note the following variations: in the Huntington copy, a period follows the running title on D7r, and the numeral on O2r, the folio number is incorrect on F1, the signature is lacking on C5; in the Bodleian copy the conventional running title *Courte* omits the *e* on P1v and Q1v, the catch word is omitted on C7v, the folio number is lacking on C5, except for the tail of the numeral 7, the signature letter is lacking on I5, as it is in the Folger copy. Under (2), in the Huntington copy, several pages of text within the inner forme were interchanged in X and z gatherings. Thus X5r is followed by the series X7v, X8r, X6v, X7r, X5v, X6r; and z3r by z4v, z5r, z3v, z4r, z5v. I assume that the error was noticed while the book was being run off, and after the Huntington copy had gone through the press. Then the forme was unlocked, the units transposed, and the printing recommenced.

2. TABLE OF MISPRINTS

THIS table aims to cite every misprint in the Huntington (supplemented by the British Museum) copy of *The Court of Virtue*. Words out of alignment and broken fonts are, however, ignored. Punctuation and capitalization I have emended silently, where emendation seemed to me mandatory. The changes I have made are not recorded here. Numbers such as 158.15 refer to the page and line of the text.

6.27 *to to* for *to*

9.7 *haydy* for *handy* (corrected in 'Faultes escaped')

17.30 *The* (catch word) omitted

23.2 *Fayth* for *Faythe*

24.16 *ccondemne* for *condemne*

29.19 *sound* (catch word) replaces *heuen* in original because of revision of Hall's text

35.2 *Attende* for *Atende*

37.32 *By* for *Then*

40.18 *wisdom* (catch word) replaces *commen-* in original because of revision of Hall's text

49.2 *Howe* for *How*

62.1 *23* (folio number) omitted

68.9 *Wherin in* for *Wherin*

70.1 *72* for *27*

78.1 *31* (folio number) omitted

86.31 *O god* for *O God*

88.27 *omnipente* for *omnipotent*

91.26 *falfyll* for *fulfyll*

92.15 *howe* (catch word) replaces *and* in original because of revision of Hall's text

95.30 *I* for *If*

97.18 *What* (catch word) replaces *perfect* in original because of revision of Hall's text

98.2 *perfecte* for *perfect*

103.7 *faythfull* for *faythfully*

105.2 *Doynge* for *Doyng*

105.4 *is* for *his*

129.2 *lorde* for *lord*

132.5 *do* for *to*

132.9 *syug* for *syng*

133.2 *Which* for *Whiche*

140.2 *cried* for *cryed*

152.3 *suare* for *snare*

157.8 *broughst* for *broughtst*

158.15 *Descendyng did* for *Descendyng I did*

158.19 *brough* for *?brought*

160.16 *natures* (catch word) replaces *I wal-* in original because of revision of Hall's text

162.34 *Suche* (catch word) omitted

163.34 *But* (catch word) omitted

172.10 *to* (catch word) replaces *In* in original because of revision of Hall's text

174.21 *Bnt* for *But*

174.33 *M3* for *M5*

176.12 *howe* for *nowe*

178.28 *For* (catch word) replaces *alwayes* (omitted) in original because of revision of Hall's text

182.5–6 'Faultes escaped' notes that music preceding these two lines is incorrect; and goes on to 'correct' it without any alteration.

182.8 *Before* for *Study*

185.6 *fautsy* for *fantsy*

187.2 *Agaynst* for *Against*

190.30 *An* for *A*

192.11 *fashod* for *falshod*

194.29 *And* for *That*

203.2 *Saynt* for *Saint*

207.2 *Least* for *Lest*

209.28 *io* for *so*

210.22–23 *the the* for *the*

211.22 *peruayle* for *preuayle*

211.29 *how* (catch word) replaces *fect* (omitted) in original because of revision of Hall's text

225.24 *howe* (catch word) replaces

taught in original because of revision of Hall's text

227.2   *O* for *Oh*

227.10   *sayth* for *sayes*

228.2   *Like* for *Lyke*

238.1   *1011* for *111*

239.23   *abborde* for *abhorde*

239.32   *Thou* for *To*

242.30   *The* for *A*

245.29   *That* for *A*

247.20   *Expediente a* for *?Expediente is a*

248.29   *pnblique* for *publique*

249.19   *goo* for *god*

258.4   *dif-* for *de-* (corrected in 'Faultes')

258.5   *forheds* for *forheddes* (corrected in 'Faultes')

258.29   *So* for *To*

264.26   *Suche* for *Seneca*

267.30   *The* (catch word) omitted

268.30   *Suche* for *Such*

272.5   *adhorde* for *?abhorde*

273.13   *reuewe* for *renewe*

281.18   music omitted, but supplied in 'Faultes'

281.18   *It is* for *Is it*

281.19   Text indicates syllable *ed* (in 'wickedness') to be sung as b natural. ? Misprint for b flat.

305.30   *Whiche* for *Who*

308.30   *Knowe* for *Know*

309.30   *pack* for *packe*

313.2   *Vntyll* for *Vntill*

316.2   *Besyde* for *Beside*

320.1   *154* for *152*

324.1   *152* for *154*

335.6   *art hand* for *art at hand*

339.2   *With* for *Wyth*

339.23   *And* (catch word) replaces *doth* in original because of revision of Hall's text

346.30   *A* for *An*

347.25   *reygaeth* for *reygneth*

348.1   *158* for *166*

348.30   *They* for *Theyr*

352.1   *160* for *168*

354.5   *husbdāes* for *husbādes*

354.10   *Vulesse* for *Vnlesse*

356.1   *170* (folio number) omitted

357.2   *godlyuesse* for *godlynesse*

357.3   *hnngry* for *hungry*

359.33   *Be* (catch word) omitted

360.25   *An* (catch word) omitted

361.8   *and* (catch word) supplied because of revision of Hall's text

362.1   *173* (folio number) omitted

363.4   *ouce* for *once* (l. 9 in original text)

364.1   *174* (folio number) omitted

3. NOTES

IT is the aim of these notes to illuminate wherever possible the encyclopedic character of *The Court of Virtue*, a kind of *Speculum Mundi* reflecting a way of life, and a way of looking at life, now thoroughly vanished. Thus when Hall's reference is to botany, to astronomy or astrology, to costume, to proverbial lore, the reference is discussed in terms of its original context; in terms, that is to say, of the implicit assumptions on which it rests, the cosmology or psychology whence it derives.

References like 9.14 are to page and line of the text.

1.1–5   *The Couurte*, etc.: Title derives from *S.R.*, I, 268.

3.4   *Thomas Cole:* divine, d. 1571. A native of Lincolnshire, Cole held the mastership of Maidstone School in 1552, where perhaps Hall came under his influence: 'My yong, my frayle, and haltyng age, Fyrst cured was by you.' (3.28–29.) Cole was collated to the archdeaconry of Essex in 1560, and presented by 1564 to the rectory of Stanford Rivers, Essex. Hall describes him as 'archdeacon' in 1565. Cf. *D.N.B.* (1887), XI, 273f.

5.3   *good kyng Edwardes tyme:* 1547–53; and 'good' presumably because he favoured the Protestant party.

6.2–21   *A Mids the twynnes*, etc.: The seven planets, erratics or wanderers because of their journey about the heavens, are circling the world, according to pre-Copernican astronomy, from west to east. The sun itself ('Phebus bright') moves along an ecliptic circle (the name for its path through the heavens). Against that circle, the movements of the other planets, thought to wander no more than 6° above or below the circle, were referred. Enclosing the heavenly movements of all seven planets, then, is an imaginary band of 12°, bisected by the ecliptic circle. The band or path is the zodiac, divided into twelve equal parts of 30° each, each part corresponding to the distance the sun travels among the stars in one month (the sun's position changed about 1° every day), and to the (approximate) distance between those points in the heavens at which two successive like phases of the moon occur. The first of the twelve zodiacal parts began at the vernal equinox, the point at which the sun, in its northward course among the stars at the beginning of spring, crossed the celestial equator, an imaginary circle in the heavens, 90° from the celestial poles about which the heavens appear to revolve. In each division or house of the zodiac lodges one of the twelve zodiacal constellations, by which the stars, and particularly the seven planets which moved, came to be located. Here, the Sun has entered the third house, that of Gemini ('twynnes'). With the Sun in Gemini are the planets Venus ('Cithera') and Jupiter ('Ioue'). In the adjacent constellation, that of Cancer (the 'Crabbe'), are Mars and Saturn. Now each of the planets has its own peculiar nature, hinted at in Hall's choice of adjectives. But to each zodiacal sign or constellation is vouchsafed some quality, too. Manifestly, the interaction of the attributes of planets and signs will be of great consequence. Thus 'The Sun nourisheth every age and yet he is hot nd dry of nature, and the planet Saturn is to him full contrary,

373

for he is ever cold, and the noble planet of the Sun is hot and giveth all light . . . all thing is glad of the Sun.' (*The Kalendar & Compost of Shepherds* [1493], 1930, p. 144.) Venus is 'the gentle planet . . . moist and cold of nature . . . she causeth joy' (p. 145). 'The noble planet of Jupiter . . . is very pure and clear of nature, and not very hot, but he is all virtuous. . . . This planet may do no evil, he is best of all the other seven. . . . And evermore this planet doth good' (p. 142). Mars, conversely, 'is the worst of all others, for he is hot and dry, and stirreth a man to be very wilful and hasty at once, and to unhappiness. . . . And Mars mounteth into the Crab' (p. 143). 'Saturn . . . giveth all the great colds and waters, yet he is dry and cold of nature. And he cometh into Cancer. . . . When he doth reign there is much theft used and little charity, much lying, and much lawing one against another, and great prisonment, and much debate, and great swearing. And much plenty of corn, and also much plenty of hogs, and great travail on the earth. . . . For Saturn is enemy to all things that groweth and beareth life of nature, for the cold and stormy bitterness of his time' (p. 141). For the signs: 'Gemini signifieth large, good courage, wit, beauty, clergy' (p. 133). 'Gemini and Cancer will make thee glad' (p. 137). Cancer has no baleful significance, and so perhaps assists in mitigating the malice of Mars and Saturn.

Upon the positions of the planets in the zodiac, then, depends the character of their actions on human destiny. The conjunction of Mars and Saturn in Cancer, and the ascendancy or temporary leadership of these malicious planets bode ill for the affairs of men. Luckily, however, the Sun, Venus, and Jupiter, a better-favoured group, are in conjunction, too, and in Gemini. The influence of one grouping offsets that of the other. Thus is trouble 'mitigated.'

Next the Moon ('Lucina'), whose sidereal period or course about the world from west to east is less than that of any other planet, begins to overtake and then pass her fellow-wanderers. Her 'aspect' with them may be described as 'in conjunction,' for as she passes each one, she must run parallel to it.

As Hall completes the picture, God, enthroned in His Heaven above the *Primum Mobile*, has brought the seven planets within the three adjacent constellations of Cancer, Gemini, and Taurus (the 'Bull'). Since we have been told that the Sun is in Gemini, the third constellation from the spring equinox, we would compute the time as late June.

7 8   *Arete:* '*Arete*, in latine, *Virtus*, in Englyshe vertue,' C2v in Cooper, *Dict. Hist. & Poet.* The name also occurs in Homer, *Od.*, and in Palingenius, E4r–v. Arete, daughter of Aristippus, founder of the Cyrenaic school of philosophy, was supposedly the author of a treatise on Virtue, for whom she stands. Diogenes Laertius, with whose works Hall, on the evidence of his many 'sayings,' would seem to have been familiar, devotes a chapter to Aristippus and Arete in his *De Vita et moribus philosphorum*, Luguduni [Lyons], 1541, f5r–g4r. See also the *Apophthegmes* of Erasmus (Udall): 'His doughter, beeyng named Areta, he brought vp and enstructed with holsome doctrine, and preceptes of vertue, accustoming her in al cases, to refuse and renounce whatsoeuer passed the boundes of mediocritee' (1542), g2r–v.

9.14   *Fayre ladies three:* vertue, hope, and love; cf. 10.22.

15.27   *Venus court: The Court of Venus*, a popular poetical miscellany, issued first in the 1530s and, very probably, at intervals thereafter throughout the century.

20.24   *Gelasius:* Gelasius I, pope from 492 to 496, and the author of several religious works and numerous letters. See pp. 125f. in *De Scriptoribus Ecclesiasticus*, Roberto Card. Bellarmino, Lugduni, M.D.C.XIII, for an account of his writings. Four works of Gelasius are listed in the 1620 Bod. cat., p. 215: 'De 2. Naturis [*De duabis naturis in Christo*] Tig. [? Thiers] 1557 [1528 and 1556] and Bas [?Basle], 1528; Epistola Decretalis, MS; Testimonia veterum de 2. naturis [n.d., n.p.]. The writings of Gelasius were current throughout the century. See, for example, *Antidotum contra diversas omnium fere seculorum haereses*, Basle, 1528, in which both Gelasius and Justin Martyr are included. Hall therefore read Gelasius or a redaction.

21.3–5   *Tullie:* Cicero is given a chapter in *Apophthegmes* (1542), P6v–T4v: 'The saiynges of Marcus Tullius Cicero.' See also *Polyanthea*, Flv: 'Cicero lib. de amicicia. Qui autē summum bonum in virtute ponunt: preclare illi quidem.'

21.6–7   *Paule:* cf. *Polyanthea*, E8v: 'Paul. ad Galathas. c. ii. Iuuenilia aūt desideria fuge: sectare vero iusticiam.'

21.10–13   *Lactantius:* whose writings are noticed in Nannius Mirabellius, *Polyanthea*, Venetiis (1507); Bellarmine, p. 55; Baldwin, *Sayings* (1547); James, *Bod. Cat* (1620), p. 281: 'Opera, Paris, 1563 (with a commentary); Opera, MS; Opera Gallice, Paris, 1546.' For Hall's passage, cf. *Polyanthea*, Flr: 'Lactan. Fir. diui. institu. li.i.c.i. Virtus. n. colenda est: nō imago virtutis: et colenda nō est sacrificio aliquo: thure: aut p̄catione solēni: sed volūtate sola: atque proposito.'

48.4   *wysdome*, etc.: Cf. the praise of learning in *Zodiacus Vitae . . . Marcelli Palengenii*,Venice, B1v.

49.9   *To Ophir:* celebrated in the Bible for its gold. That the reference was familiar is attested to by a lengthy note in the dictionary of C. Stephanus (Starnes and Talbert, pp. 300f.). Cf. also Jonson, *Alchemist*, II, i, 3–4.

51.18–19   *For be . . . faste:* Cf. Stephen Hawes, *The Pastime of Pleasure* (1505–6), 'The Epitaph of Graunde Amour,' Capit. XLII, 11.61–3: 'After the day there cometh the derke night; / For though the day be never so longe, / At last the belles ringeth to evensonge!'

71.14–72.29   *Laudate pueri*, etc.: cf. *Primer*, Henry VIII, F3r–v.

76.10   *Non nobis Domine:* The Psalms, with Collect, Epistle, and Gospel, were embodied in the Introit. *Non nobis, Domine* (Psalm 115) was included in the Introit for St. Bartholemew's Day, and also in the Matins. Hall's habit of prefacing his versifications of the Psalms with their Latin titles derives from the Prayer Book and Primer, in which all those Psalms which he versifies are to be found. In *THE booke of the common prayer* printed by Whitchurche in 1549 is the direction: 'The Psalter shalbe red through, once euery Moneth.' A table is adjoined, giving 'The ordre of the Psalmes, to be sayed at Matins and Euensong.' The Old Testament, too, is appointed in this Prayer Book—the first of Edward's reign—to be read through once every year, and the New Testament thrice. Thus the familiarity of Hall and his audience with the Bible. By 1536, moreover, the English Bible was compulsory equipment for all churches.

79.18–81.5   *De profundis clamaui*, etc.: cf. Henry's *Primer*, K3r–v.

93.8   *And neuer change hym for no newe:* cf. 'Forsake me neuer for no new,' *Court of Venus*, p. 122, l. 11; 'Who likes that love, that chaungeth still for newe,' *The Paradise of Dainty Devices* (1576–1606), ed. H. E. Rollins (Cambridge, Mass., 1927), p. 41, l. 5; 'Or seeke to chaunge for any newe,' *A Handful of Pleasant Delights* (1584), ed. Rollins (Cambridge, Mass., 1924), p. 54, l. 1553; 'And chaunge mee for no new,' *A Gorgeous Gallery of Gallant Inventions* (1578), ed. Rollins (Cambridge, Mass., 1926), p. 25, l. 47.

97.17–100.21 *The syxt*, etc.: Hall versifies St. Matthew, vi. 5–9, but (characteristically) expands the original greatly. His ballad was appropriated subsequently by the printer Richard Jones. Cf. *S.R.*, I, 416.

100.22–102.9 *Pater noster:* Matthew, vi. 9–13. Part of Matthew, vi was sung at the Offertory. The Pater Noster began the Matins.

103.10–104.7 *Credo in deum*, etc.: the Apostles Creed is from Matins and Communion.

104.8–106.24 *The songe of prayse*, etc.: Hall versifies and expands Mary's song of thanksgiving, Luke, i. 46–55. The *Magnificat* is part of the Evensong. Cf. 'song of Mari,' Henry's *Primer*, G3v.

106.25–110.6 *The songe of prayse*, etc.: The *Benedictus*, a part of the Matins, is headed, in Henry's *Primer*, C4r, substantially as here, 'The songe of prayse and thankesgeuyng for the performaunce of Gods promyse.'

110.7–111.8 *The songe of prayse*, etc.: *Nunc dimittis* appears, in English with Latin title, in the evening prayer service in N. Hill's Bible of 1561. In this poem, as in the two that precede it, Hall incorporates a hortatory ending. The first two endings are variations one of another; thus the three versifications are unified.

112.2–114–13 *I am thy Lorde*, etc.: cf. Exodus, xx. 2–17 and Deuteronomy, v. 6–21.

114.14–119.13 *The prayse of God*, etc.: the *Te Deum* was ascribed to a joint extemporization of Sts. Ambrose and Augustine (cf. 114.15–17). Even in Hall's time, however, the legend was failing: in the *Psalterium Daudicum ad vsum ecclesie Sarisburiensis*, printed by Kingston and Sutton in 1555, is the rubric: 'Canticum beati Niceti,' and a note stating that the traditional account respecting St. Augustine's baptism is untrue. In the Breviaries, however, the reference to Sts. Ambrose and Augustine is general in some form or other.

A number of printed sixteenth-century versions were available to Hall. Thus the *Te Deum* appears in the *Prymer in Englyshe and in Latin sette out alonge; after the vse of Sarum*, Robert Valentin, 1504, where it is headed, 'The songe of Austyn and Ambrose.' Hall's model could not have antedated this version, which is the first (so far as I know) to read 'sabaothe' in verse V (cf. 115.16), and the first to make the modern mistake, 'Make them to be numbered with thy saints in joy everlasting' (cf. 117.26–31). Then follows the *Prymer* of 1535 (in *Three Primers of Henry VIII*, Oxford, 1834, p. 82), which takes over these peculiarities and adds its own (cf. J. Julian, *Dictionary of Hymnology*, 1892, p. 1129), but differs from Hall's version (*hosts* for *Sabaoth*). In the succeeding primers, those of 1539 and 1545 (*Three Primers*, pp. 337, 465), the titles read, *The Song of Augustin and Ambrose. Te Deum laudamus*, and *Te Deum laudamus. The praise of God, the Father the Son and the Holy Ghost* (cf. Hall's title). The last primer of Henry VIII (1546) and the first *Prayer Book* of Edward VI (1549) are like the modern prayer book. In Edward's second prayer book (1552), the heading reads simply, *Tdl*, as it does in the prayer book of 1560. Thus Hall's model fell between 1535 (the first post-Reformation text) and 1552. But the 1535 text differs from Hall's reading, and in Bishop Hilsey's Primer of 1539 the title is not given in full, and the book itself is behind the times, with respect to the Reformation, even though set forth at the command of Cromwell. It is likely, then, that Hall's verses derive chiefly from 'The Primer, Set Foorth by the Kynges

maiestie and his Clergie, to be taught lerned, & read: and none other
to be vsed throughout all his dominions,' R. Grafton, 1545. The 1539
primer, which mentions Augustine and Ambrose, he may have used
also, until the first complete English service, embodied in Edward VI's
first prayer book (1549), was produced.

119.2–13 *To the father*, etc.: Hall's habit of ending a number of his poems,
'Glory be to the Father,' etc., or, rather, versifying that conventional
ending, derives from Matins and Evensong. Cf.109.23–110.6.

119.16–17 *the songe of the three chyldren:* cf. Henry's *Primer* (1545), in which the
Benedicite is headed, 'The song of the three children, wherwith they
praised God, walkyng in the fyre.'

135.26–136.11 *Iob .i.*, etc.: cf. Henry's *Primer*, 2E3r.

136.12–137.13 *Prouerb .xxx.*, etc.: cf. Henry's *Primer*, 2E4r.

137.14–138.19 *Ecclesiasticus*, etc.: cf. Henry's *Primer*, 2H2r-v.

138.20–141.13 *Ego dixi in dimidio.*, etc.: cf. Henry's *Primer*, P2r-3r.

145.10–146.5 *Ieremie .xxxi.*, etc.: cf. Henry's *Primer*, 2E3v.

160.8–164.26 *A ditie of lamentation*, etc.: Hall's tune echoes the Doxology ('Old
Hundredth'). This most famous of the metrical psalm tunes was set to
the hundredth psalm in the 'old' version of the metrical psalms (Sternhold and Hopkins as opposed to Tate and Brady). The edition of this
version in which it first appeared was Day's of 1563. The history of the
tune goes back further, however, to Marot and Béza's Genevan Psalter
of 1551, in which it is attached to the 134th psalm. A form of the tune
appears even earlier, in the Antwerp collection, *Souter Liedekens*, 1540
(Percy Scholes). Hall levies on the 'Old Hundredth' again in tunes 19
(p. 191), 22 (p. 218), and 30 (pp. 339f.). He seems, moreover, in his
traditional May morning opening, to redact a popular poem, one included, perhaps (like 'Blame Not My Lute'), in *The Court of Venus*. Cf.
'In Summer time when flow'rs do spring' in Chappell, II, 541ff; and
pp. 392, 541. But see also Henry's *Primer*, A2r (1545): 'Now the cheerful
day doth spryng.'

161.14 *lord Christ help euery wofull hart:* surely the refrain derives from secular
verse: 'Sweete Themmes, runne softly, till I end my song.'

164.27–169.13 *A ditie named blame not my lute*, etc.: Wyatt's poem, here parodied,
derives from the Devonshire MS (Additional MS 17492). It does not
appear in Tottel or in *The Court of Venus*. Hall's source is thus to seek. Cf.,
however, *The Court of Venus*, p. 57.

169.14–172.3 *A song of the lute in the prayse of*, etc.: Wyatt's 'My lute awake,' also
parodied, is found in the Devonshire and Egerton MSS, in *Songs and
Sonnets*, and in two of the three fragments comprising *The Court of Venus*.

172.9 *wauer no more with eury wynde:* the ring of secular verse: 'Tell no more
of enchanted days.'

174.29–30 *Let not the common people deale*, etc.: cf. Richard Taverner's *Prouerbes or
Adagies, gathered oute of the Chiliades* (1552), C4r: 'The thynges that be
aboue vs. belonge nothynge vnto vs. This was the sayeng of Socrates . . .
it becometh not Iacke strawe to reason of princes matters.' Cf. also
Andrew Alciati, *Emblematum libellus*, Lyons (1551), number 102.

175.24–178.24 *A Ditie declaringe the daungerous*, etc.: ? parody of secular verse.

179.3 *venite ad iudicium:* Hall essays macaronic verse.

182.2–185.25 *Against pryde*, etc.: Each of the subjects against which Hall inveighs
(pp. 182–210) was noticed at length in contemporary primers. See, for
example, *The prymer of Salysbury vse*, printed by Thomas Petit, September
12, 1544, Y–Y2v; and F. Regnault's primer 'of Salysbury vse' (1538),

Y4. Hall's subject matter, and that of the primers, derives of course from the Catholic tradition of the seven deadly sins. For the sin indicted here, cf. Henry's *Primer*, 2H2v-3r.

184.21 *And fleteth faster*, etc.: A fine line, but made so, probably, by the unintentional dropping of a word: 'then [doth] tyme.'

185.26–186.29 *An inuectiue against . . . enuy*, etc.: cf. Henry's *Primer*, 2H3r-v.

186.10–13 *Within this worlde*, etc.; cf. *Polyanthea*, q2r: 'Cicero pro Lucio Cornelio. Est enim huius saeculi labes quaedam: et macula virtuti inuidere.'

187.2–188.9 *Agaynst slouthe*, etc.: cf. Proverbs, xxiv. 33–34. The proverbs of Solomon were among the most popular of the writings levied on by the florilegia.

188.2–5 *Who so to worke*, etc.: One need not go beyond the Bible, of course (II Thessalonians iii. 10); however, cf. *Polyanthea*, b5v: 'Paulus ad Roma. cap. i. xii. Sollicitudine no pigri. Pau. ad. Thessalo. scō [?] ae. c. iii. Si quis vult nō operari: nec manducet.'

188.11–16 *Saint Bernard saith*, etc.: cf. *Polyanthea*, e4r, 'Bern. super cantica sermone. xxxviii. Currus auaritie vehit rotis quattuor vitiorum: quae sūt pusillani mitas: inhumanitas: cōtēptus dei: mortis obliuio.'

190.14 *Our money (as sayth Seneca)*, etc.: cf. *Polyanthea*, e5r, 'Seneca in prouerbiis. Pecūiae si uti scias: ancilla ē: si nescias: dña [domina].' Cf. also *Mer. of Ven.*, III, ii, 103, 'thou pale and common drudge.'

191.4–193.20 *My pen obey my wyll a whyle*, etc.: Hall's parody of Wyatt's 'My penne take payne' is based on *The Court of Venus*. Cf. pp. 57, 113, 181.

193.21–202.4 *An exhortation to wrathfull men*, etc.: cf. Henry's *Primer*, 2H3v-4r.

193.26 *Apelles*: Hall could have read of the Greek painter Apelles in *The Apophthegmes of Erasmus* (itself based on Plutarch), trans. Udall, and published in 1542, and again in 1564; or in Pliny, Ovid, Cicero, Strabo. Cf. *Introducion to VVisedome* (which Hall used), H3v, 'What profyt shalte thou haue more of thy great fame . . . then the praysed pycture of Apelles.'

193.28 *Demosthenes*: Accessible to Hall in 'The saiynges of Demosthenes the Oratour,' *Apophthegmes* (1542), T4v-X1r; and in Burley. Demosthenes was prescribed at Harrow in 1590; a text probably in use there— Heliodorus, *De veterum scriptorum censura*—treats of him briefly, in company with Hesiod, Homer, and Isocrates.

200.13–14 *Therfore saynt Paule*, etc.: cf. *Polyanthea*, q3v, 'Paulus ad Ephesios. iiii. Sol non occidat super iracundiam vestram.'

200.15–18 *And Plato beyng demaunded*, etc.: cf. *Polyanthea*, q4v, 'Interrogatus Plato per quid cognoscitur sapiens: ait sapiēs quum vituperat non irascitur.' Cf. also Baldwin, N1v, 'Socra. A wyse man is knowen by iii. poyntes. He wyl not lyghtly be angry for ẙ wrong that is done him: neyther is proude whā he is praysed.' It is clear that, in this instance, Hall used Nannius.

200.21–24 *Byas also dothe*, etc.: cf. Taverner's Erasmus (1547), A3r, 'Wrath and rashenes be two the worst counsaylers that can be'; and *Polyanthea*, q4v, 'Laertius diog. . . . [*de vita . . . philosophorum*] Consilio maxime dicebat Bias contraria sunt festinantia et ira.'

200.27–30 *The chiefest helpe*, etc.: cf. *Polyanthea*, q4r, 'Maximum remedium ire est dilatio.'

201.16–19 *As sayth saint Iames*, etc.: cf. *Polyanthea*, s2r, 'Iacobus in . . . [General Epistle, i. 19] Sit aūt omnis homo velox ad audiē dū: tardus aūt ad loquēdu: et tardus ad iram.'

201.22–25 *By wrath as sayth*, etc.: cf. *Polyanthea*, q3v, 'Per iram sapientia perditur: vt quid quo ve ordine agendū sit nasciatur.'

202.20–23 *A drunkard (as saint)*, etc.: cf. *Polyanthea*, K6v, 'Ebriosus confundit naturam: amittit gratiam: perdit gloriã incurrit damnationem aeternam.'

203.2–5 *Saynt Ierome sayth*, etc.: *Polyanthea*, b2r–v ('Abstinentia'), and K6v ('Ebrietas'), gives a long series of quotations from Jerome, on which Hall's words may depend.

203.6–17 *Saynt Ambrose playnly*, etc.: cf. *Polyanthea*, n8r, 'Ambrosius in sermo de ieiunio. Male domine seruitur gulae: que semper expetit: nunque expletur. Quid enim [?] insatiabilius vẽtre? Hodie suscipit: cras exiget. Quum impletus suerit disputatur de otenentia [? continentia]: quum [?] digesserit: vale virtutibus dicitur.'

203.25 *Like as the fowler*, etc.: cf. 257.11, 16, 22, 29. The manner in each case is indebted to that of the volumes of 'Parables and semblables.' So Baldwin: 'Lyke as to a shrewde horse belongeth a sharpe brydle: so ought a shrewde wyfe to be sharply handeled' (Q3v–R4r in *Morall Phylosophie*, 1547). Baldwin had englished Erasmus, who had 'compyled a boke drawen (as he sayeth hym selfe) out from the purest of the Philosophers' (Q2v). Erasmus, and his redactors and imitators: Baldwin, Hall, Palfreyman, were forerunners of and contributors to the vogue of Euphuist writing.

209.10–13 *As Socrates hath sayd*, etc.: cf. Diogenes Laertius, *Vita*, p. 70; Erasmus *Apophthegmes* (1542), a2r–f1r, 'The saiynges of Socrates'; Baldwin, N8v, 'Socra. There is not a worse thyng, than a deceytfull and lying toung.'

209.23–25 *As Chilon dyd*, etc.: cf. Baldwin, N8v, 'Chilon. An euyll tongue is sharper than any swearde.'

210.22–23 *A ditie made in the tyme*, etc.: Perhaps the early date of this poem is significant of the date of the poems preceding it. For the plague itself: 'The 15. of Aprill, the infectious sweating sicknesse began at Shrewsbury, which ended not in the North part of Englande vntill the end of September. In this space what number died, it cannot be well accompted, but certaine it is that in London in few daies 960. gaue vp the ghost: it began in London the 9. of Iuly, and the 12. of Iuly it was most vehement, which was so terrible, that the people being in best health, were sodainly taken, and dead in foure and twenty houres, and twelue, or lesse for lacke of skill in guiding them in their sweat. And it is to be noted, that this mortalitie fell chiefeley or rather on men, and those also of the best age, as betweene 30. and 40. yeeres, fewe women, nor children, nor olde men died thereof. Sleeping in the beginning was present death, for if they were suffered to sleepe but halfe a quarter of an houre, they neuer spake after, nor had any knowledge, but when they wakened fell into panges of death. This was a terrible time in Londõ, for many one lost sodainely his friends, by their sweat, and their money by the proclamation. Seauen honest householders did sup together, & before eight of the clocke in the next morning, six of them were dead: they that were taken with full stomachs scaped hardly. This sicknesse followed English men as well within ỹ realm, as in strange countries: wherefore this nation was much afeared of it, and for the time began to repent & remember God, but as the disease relented, the deuotion decaied. The first weeke died in London 800. persons.' Thus John Stow, *The Annales, or Generall Chronicle of England* [continued and augmented by Edmond Howes] (1614), p. 605. Cf. also *A boke, or counseill against the disease commonly called the sweate, or sweatyng sicknesse. Made by Ihon Caius doctour in phisicke* ... 1552. 'Imprinted at London, by Richard Grafton.'

211.28   *Sith nothyng can be sure*, etc.: Surely the influence of Wyatt; cf. 'If fantasy
would fauour,' in *The Court of Venus*, pp. 124f.

225.20–227.27   *My harte constraines my mouth to tell*, etc.: A parody of the manner
of Wyatt? Especially remarkable is the picking up of the last line of one
stanza as the first line of the next ('So doe we must,' l. 4).

228.2–230.9   *Lyke as certain, the hart wold faine*, etc.: A parody of secular verse?
Cf. 'Like as the larke,' 233.12, and note.

233.12–235.13   *Like as the larke*, etc.: Hall redacts Tottel. Cf. Rollins's edition, I,
126 (for the poem), and II, 260f. (for notes thereon, and other versions).

237.19   *Why art thou to thy frend vnkynd?* The refrain echoes the manner of
secular verse.

239.2   *Thomas of Inde:* cf. John xx. 27–29. St. Thomas, the Doubting Apostle,
is supposed to have been martyred in India. On the site of his martyrdom,
Mylapur, now a suburb of Madras, the Portuguese rebuilt a shrine to
him in 1547, thus giving currency, perhaps, to this version of his name
in England. It is probable, moreover, that the fifteenth-century narrative
of Nicolo De Conti, otherwise Poggio Bracciolini (fl. 1419–1444), the
Venetian writer and explorer of southern Asia, who wrote of the shrine of
St. Thomas and the Christian tradition in India, was known in England.
Editions of Poggio's *Works* are listed in the BM Catalogue from 1513
forward. 'India Recognita,' the fourth book of the *De Varietate Fortunae*,
appeared first in 1492, and again in 1550, 1554, and 1563.

240.24–241.5   *As Phaeton prowde*, etc.: cf. *Metamorphoses*, i, 755 ff.; and 305. 17n.

246.2–259.5   With Hall's little verses: 'Of frendship,' 'Of vertuous exercise,' etc.,
cf. Henry's *Primer* (1545): 'Of the holy Trinite,' 'Of the holy Apostles,'
'Of the holy Martirs,' etc., D1v–D2r.

247.25–26   *For custome* (*Aristotle*, etc.: cf. Baldwin, N6v, 'Aristot. Custome is as
it were an other nature.'

249.19–23   *To Chilons answer*, etc.: cf. *Polyanthea*, m8v, 'La. Diogenes de vi. et mo.
philosophorum. Interrogatus Chilo quid est fortuna? ait ignarus medicus
multos enim excaecat.' Burley gives the same quotation.

249.24–250.7   *Or thus out of Iustinus*, etc.: The *Historiarum Philippicarum libri
XLIV* of the Roman historian Justin (Junianus Justinus), a capricious
anthologizing of the *Historiae philippicae et totius mundi origines et terrae
situs* of Pompeius Trogus, was much used in the Middle Ages, when its
author was sometimes confused with Justin Martyr. *Ed. princeps : 1470.*
Justin was read widely in sixteenth-century England (see Baldwin,
passim); the B.M. Catalogue lists eighty-nine editions of his work from
the fifteenth to the seventeenth centuries alone. Hall, by way of example,
might have used *Iustini Historici Clarissimi in Pompeii Trogi Historias*
(Venice, 1470, Liber XLIIII), an ancient history 'of the whole worlde:
from the beginnyng of the Monarchie of Assyria, vnto the reign of
Themperour Augustus'; or, what is more likely, a translation, printed
by Marshe in 1564, with—significantly—marginal observations and
gnomes: 'Thabridgment of the Histories of Trogus Pompeius, Collected
and wrytten in the Laten tonge, by the famous Historiographer Iustine,
and translated into English by Arthur Goldyng: a worke conteynyng
brieflie great plentie of moste delectable Hystories, and notable examples,
worthie not onlie to be read, but also to be embraced and followed of
all menne. . . . M.D.LXIIII. Mense Maii.' So Golding, B1r: 'Force and
wysdom geue place to Fortune'; C1v: 'A worthy example of the ficklenesse
of fortune, and of the frailnes of mans estate'; E1r: 'vnstablenesse of
fortune.'

250.8–12   *Of honor out of Tully*, etc.: ?cf. *Polyanthea*, r6v, 'Laeticia in animo est cōmotio suauis iucunditatis in corpore ... Ciceronem lib. ii. de finibus bonorum et ma.'

250.13–25   *Of glory*, etc.: cf. *Polyanthea*, n3v, for a possible correspondence: 'Gloria est illustris ac peruagata multorū et magnorū: vel in suos ciues: vel in patriā: vel in dē genus hoīum fama meritorū ... Cicero ... pro M. Marcello.'

251.15–21   *Of grace out of*, etc.: cf. *Polyanthea*, n6v, under Bernard, 'Gratiam in tribus consistere arbitror. In odio praeteritorum: contemptu praesentiū bonorum: et desiderio futurorum.'

251.22–252.6   *Of temperance out of*, etc.: cf. Holland's *Plutarch* (1603), G2r, 'Excessive sorrow and heavines, immeasurable ioy and gladnesse in the soule, may be aptly compared to a swelling and inflammation in the body, but neither ioy nor sorrow simply in its selfe. And therefore *Homer* ... doth not abolish feare altogether, but the extremitie thereof. ... And therefore in pleasures and delights, we ought likewise to cut off immoderate lust.' The first edition of the *Moralia* was printed by the elder Aldus (Venice, 1509). The *Apophthegmes* of Plutarch, engrossed in the *Moralia*, were quoted extensively throughout the sixteenth century. Cf. *Bod Cat.*, p. 395, for a list of works in print during the period. Hall, then, read Plutarch, probably the *Apophthegmes*, or a translation (as by Erasmus) or popularization of him.

252.7–24   *Of talebearers out of*, etc.: cf. *Polyanthea*, b7v, 'Hieronymus ad neporianum. Plus peccat detractor qui amorē proximi a corde alterius minuit: quam qui victū ab ore pauperis rapit. nā sicut aīa p̄ciosior est quam corpus: sic grauius est aīe victū auferre: quam corporis.'

252.25–31   *Of virginitie*, etc.: cf. 'Virginitas aequat se angelis, si veto exquiramus etiam excedit, dum in carne luctata, victoriam & cōtra naturam refert, quam non habent angeli,' X3r in *Opera Divicae ... Cypriani Episcopi Carthaginensis ... haec omnia nobis praestitit ingenti labore suo Erasmus Roterodamus ... Basileam ex officina Frobeniana. An. M.D.XXI.* The writings of St. Cyprian (*c.* 200–258), bishop of Carthage and martyr, were rather widely current in the Renaissance. James, *Bod. Cat.*, p. 154, enumerates Cyprian's works held by the Bodleian in 1620. For a further and more extensive list, cf. *De scriptoribus ecclesiasticis*, pp. 48–51. Hall therefore read Cyprian or a redaction, as did the Princess Elizabeth, assigned by her master Roger Ascham (in a letter to Sturm, on April 4, 1550, quoted in Baldwin, I, 259) to study 'Saint Cyprian ... as best suited, after the Holy Scriptures, to teach her the foundations of religion, together with elegant language and sound doctrine.' It is probable that both Elizabeth and Hall read the *De Disciplina Virginum*, Cyprian's most popular work.

255.2–21   *Lodouicus Viues in*, etc.: cf. *An Introduction to wysedom, made by Ludouicus Viues. Wherein is plentiful matter for al estates to gouerne thēselues by, to their synguler profytte and commodytye. Translated into Englyshe, by Richard Moryson. Imprinted at London by Iohn Daye* [1540?]: 'The opinions and common perswasions of the people, are pernicious: by cause for the most part they iudge of all thynges most fondlye.

Certes the vulgare people is a great schole master of great errours.

There is nothing that we oughte to seke for, with more study, than to bryng hym, that geueth him self to knowledge and wisdome, from the iudgemente of the rude multytude.

First let him suspect as mani things as the multitude, with great assent, and consent, doth approue, vntill he hath examined them after those mennes rule, whyche make vertue a measure to trye all matters by,' A6r–v.

255.22–33   *Agaynst vayne apparell*, etc.: cf. *Introduction to wysedom*, B2r–v, 'Necessitie fyrste inuented the profitable garmente, Riot and Ryches founde the[m] precious, which vanity fashioned vnto her trycke. Greate contention is in varietie of apparell, which hath taught men manye superfluous and hurtefull thynges, by reason that they seeke to be honoured euen for that, whych plannlye declareth theyr infyrmitie, follye, and weakenesse.'

256.2–17   *Agaynst anger out of*, etc.: *Introduction to wysedom*, D6r–v, 'The angry manne, for hys grymme countenaunce, hys sharpe woordes, and cruel dedes, ofte tymes looseth much of hys authoritye, muche beneuolencye is taken from hym, hys friendes forsake hym, no man wyl meete hym, he is left all alone, al men hate and abhorre him, wherfore great wyse mē neuer eschewed thynge more, or cloked thynge wyth greater diligence, then thei did Ire, and the works of Ire. In so much, that they not onely wrastled agaynst theyr owne nature, but in spyte of her bearde gaue her the fall.'

256.18–257.9   *Of frendes, out of*, etc.: cf. *Introduction to wysedom*, G7v–8r, 'Chuse no suche friendes, as lytle passe to iest of thy lyfe, to borde at suche thynges as thou wouldest haue kept secret, but most of al auoyd them, that for a thing of nought, wyl be at vtter defiance wyth theyr best friend, reuengyng them selfe more vpon suche, as they haue loued before, than vppon those, whom they alwaies hated: barbarousely perswading theym selfe, the iniurye done of a friende, lesse to bee forborne, then the iniurie done of their enemye, wherein they plainely declare that they neuer loued, for if they had, they woulde not so soone haue bene offended. It wer better to haue such persons for enemies, then for friendes.'

257.10–19   *Dulce bellum inexpertis*, etc.: cf. Vu2r, *Adagiorum Opus D. Erasmi Roterodami . . . Basileae*, 1526. Probably more accessible to Hall was Taverner's Englishing of the Greek and Latin sayings of Erasmus: *Prouerbes or Adagies, gathered oute of the Chiliades of Erasmus by Rycharde Tauerner*, 1552, London, Rycharde Kele. Cf. 13r: '*Dulce bellum inexpertis*. Batell is a swete thynge to them that neuer assayed it. He that lysteth to knowe more of this prouerbe, let hī go to Erasmus which handleth in his Chiliades this prouerbe both ryght copyously & also eloquent.' Gascoigne's 'corrected' *Posies of* 1575 includes the long poem entitled '*Dulce Bellum Inexpertis*.'

259.7–11   *Plato*, etc.: available entire in Ficino's Latin translation, 1551. But cf. Diog. Laert., *Vita*, p. 120; and Baldwin, O3r, 'Plato. Of all thynges the newest is the best, saue of loue and frendshyp: whiche the elder that it waxeth, is euer the better.'

259.12–16   *Seneca*, etc.: cf. Baldwin, N5v, 'Seneca. He is the very valiant, whiche neyther reioyceth muche, nor soroweth out of measure.'

259.17–19   *Socrates*, etc.: cf. Baldwin, O3r, 'Socrat. It is a poynt of madnesse, to be sorye, or to reioyce vnmeasurablye.'

259.20–22   *Plato*, etc.: cf. Baldwin, N7v, 'Plato. Idelnes engendreth ignoraunce, and ignoraunce engendreth errour.'

259.23–25   *Aristoteles*, etc.: cf. Baldwin, N8r, 'Aristo. Couetousenes taketh awaye the name of gentlenes, the whiche liberalitie purchaseth.'

259.26–28   *Bias*, etc.: cf. Diog. Laert., *Vita*, p. 44; and Baldwin, N8v, 'Byas. Fayre and flatteryng speache is an honnyed snare.'

260.2-4   *Salomon*, etc.: cf. Proverbs, xxvi. 1, 'As snow in summer, and as rain in harvest, so honour is not seemly for a fool.'

260.5-7   *Plato*, etc.: cf. Baldwin, O1v, 'Plato. Of small errours not let at the begynning, spryng great and myghty mischyfes.'

260.8-10   *Plutarchus*, etc.: cf. Baldwin, O1v, 'Plutarch. The wyttes whiche in age wyl be excellent, may be knowen in youthe by their honest delytes.'

260.11-13   *Chilon*, etc.: cf. Baldwin, O4v, 'Chilon. He is enuyous that is sorye for goodmennes prosperitie.'

260.14-16   *Socrates*, etc.: cf. Baldwin, O6r, 'Socra. He is an ignoraunt foole, that is gouerued [*sic*] by womens counsayle.'

260.17-19   *Aristippus*, etc.: cf. 'The saiynges of Aristippus' in Erasmus, *Apoph-thegmes*, 1542, f1r-i4v; Diog. Laert., *Vita*, p. 88; and Baldwin, P5, not under Aristippus, but 'Seneca. He hath ryches sufficient, that nedeth neyther to flatter nor to borowe.'

260.20-22   *Cicero*, etc.: cf. *Polyanthea*, Bbr, 'Sapiētia est rerū diuinarum et humanarum scientia cognitioque . . . Cicer. li. Tus. quaest.'

260.23-25   *Xenophon*, etc.: cf. Baldwin, I4r, 'xenoph. Be not to carefull for worldly ryches, for GOD hath prouyded for eche man sufficient.'

261.2-6   *Plutarche*, etc.: cf. Baldwin, M5r, 'Plutarc. Praye not to god to geue the sufficient, for that he wyll geue to eche man vnaxed: but praye that thou mayest be content and satisfyed with that whiche he geueth the.'

261.7-9   *Pithagoras*, etc.: cf. Baldwin, R3v, 'Pytha. It is aryght honorable and blessed thing to serue god, & sanctifye his sayntes. The worshippe of god consisteth not in wordes, but in deades.'

261.10-12   *Socrates*, etc.: cf. Baldwin, I4v, 'Socrat. Speke euer of god, and he wyll alwayes put good wordes in thy mouthe.'

261.13-15   *Solon*, etc.: cf. Diog. Laert., *Vita*, p. 26; and Baldwin, I6v, 'Solon. A cleane soule delyteth not in vncleane thynges.'

261.16-20   *Seneca*, etc.: cf. Baldwin, I6v, 'Seneca. The good soule graffeth goodnes, wher of saluation is the frute, but the euel planteth vices, the frute wherof is damuation [*sic*].' Cf. also k1r, 'Seneca. Truste not the worlde, for it payeth euer [? neuer] that it promyseth.'

261.21-23   *Pithagoras*, etc.: cf. Baldwin, k2v, '[P]ytha. True and perfect frendshyp is, to make one hart and mynde, of manye hartes and bodyes.'

261.24-262.5   *Xenophon*, etc.: cf. Diog. Laert., *Vita*, p. 82; and Baldwin, k3r, 'xenop. There is neyther frendshyp nor iustyce in them, among whome nothing is cōmon. There is no man that woulde chose to lyue wythoute frendes, althoughe he had plenty of al other ryches.'

262.6-12   *Socrates*, etc.: cf. Baldwin, k5v, '[So]crat . . . Make not an angrye man, nor a drunkarde, of thy counsayle, nor any that is in subiection to a woman: for it is not possyble y̆ they shoulde kepe close thy secretes.' Cf. also k6r, 'A wyse man ought to take councell, for feare of myxing his wyl wyth his wyt. Wrathe and hastynes, are very euyll counsaylours.'

262.13-15   *Isocrates*, etc.: Elyot's *The Doctrine of Princes* renders the exhortation by Isocrates to Nicocles, King of Cyprus. The 'admonition' *Ad Demonicum* was translated by John Bury in 1557, and prescribed at Shrewsbury and at Harrow (1590). Isocrates was read also at Westminster School. But cf. Baldwin, k5r, 'Isocra. He that geueth good counsayle to an other, begynneth to profyt hym selfe.'

262.16-20   *Seneca*, etc.: cf. Baldwin, k6v, 'Seneca. He is ryche that contenteth hym selfe wyth hys pouertie.'

262.21-25   *Hermes*, etc.: cf. Baldwin, p. 123, 'Receive patiently the words of correction; though they seem grievous!'

262.26–28 *Plutarchus*, etc.: cf. Baldwin, M5r, 'Plutar. Forget thyne anger lyghtlye, and desyre not to be reuenged.'

262.29–263.2 *Socrates*, etc.: cf. Baldwin, O2r, 'Socra. He is to be commended whiche to hys good bryngyng vp, ioyneth vertue, wysed[o]me, and learnyng.' 'Good bryngyng vp maketh a man wel disposed.' 'He is perfect whiche to his good bringyng vp, ioyneth other vertues.'

263.5–9 *Socrates*, etc.: cf. Baldwin, O6v, not Socrates (who appears, however, on the same page) but 'Plato. Eloquence is a goodlye gyfte, which in truth shyneth, but in falsehode corrupteth.'

263.10–14 *Pythagoras*, etc.: cf. Diog. Laert., *Vita*, p. 335; and Baldwin, P1v, 'Pythag. They that rob, and slaunder the dead, are lyke furyous dogges, which byte and barke at stones.'

263.15–19 *Plutarches*, etc.: cf. Baldwin, P3r, '[P]lutarch. Nothyng disprayseth a man so muche as his owne praysyng: specially whan he boasteth of his good deades.'

263.20–24 *Hermes*, etc.: cf. Baldwin, P4r, 'Hermes. He is a wiseman that doth good to his frendes: but he is more than a man, that doeth good to his enemyes.'

263.25–264.11 *As well men ought*, etc.: cf. Baldwin, P4v, 'Seneca. Benefits ought to be as well borne in mynde as receyued w̨ the hande.
The remembraunce of benefyttes ought neuer to waxe olde.
The wyl of the geuer, and not the value of the gyfte, is to be regarded.'

264.12–14 *Seneca*, etc.: cf. Baldwin, P4r, 'Seneca. He is worthy no wealth, that can suffre no woe.'

264.15–16 *Smalle knowledge*, etc.: cf. Baldwin, N2v, 'Seneca. A wyse man is knowen by silence, and a foole by muche babblyng.'
'Pytha. Muche bablyng is signe of smal knowledge.'

264.17–19 *Seneca*, etc.: cf. Baldwin, k6v, 'Seneca. A wyse man nedeth nothyng.'

264.20–22 *Hermes*, etc.: cf. Baldwin, M4v, '[He]rmes. By ware of spyes and talebearers.'

265.2–4 *Seneca*, etc.: cf. Baldwin, O1r, not under Seneca but directly beneath him, 'Plato. There is no goodnes in a lyer.'

265.9–12 *He is (as Chrysostome*, etc.: St. John Chrysostom was especially popular in the sixteenth century because of his ability as an orator (he is the 'golden mouthed'). James's 1620 *Bod. Cat.* devotes a full column to his works ('*De Sacerdotio*, The Statues [homiletic sermons], Matthew, Romans, Corinthians,' H8r, p. 127), ranging in date from 1487 to 1612. See also *De Scrip. Ecc.*, 1613, M3v–4v (94–96), for contemporary evidence of his popularity. Erasmus had recommended Chrysostom. William Hayne's *Certain Epistles of Tully*, 1611, mentions, among those tasks assigned to schoolboys, 'which I haue this twenty yeares and vpwards vsed,' the transposing from the Greek into Latin two orations of Chrysostom on prayer. Thomas Wilson in *The Art of Rhetorique* cites Chrysostom with approval. Hall's reference might depend on the homiletic sermons. But cf. *Polyanthea*, v7v, 'Io. chry. Super Mattheum. Ille clarus: ille sublimis: ille nobilis: ille tunc integrā nobilita tē suā patet: si dedignet seruire vitiis: et ab eis nō superari.'

265.13–30 *If thou (as Seneca*, etc.: cf. *Polyanthea*, v7v, 'Sen. ad Lucil. epla. xxix. Quū volueris verā hois estimationē videre: et scire qualis sit: nudū inspice. deponat patri moniū: deponat honores: et alia fortune mēdacia. Corpus ipsum exuat: et animū ītue re: qualis quātus quam sit: alieno an suo magnus.'

266.14–267.29   *The anotomy or particular description of a byrche broome,* etc.: Hall parodies a popular ballad. Cf. *S.R.,* I, 200.

268.2–270.13   *The description & declaration,* etc.: Hall's ballad may have been purloined by the printer William Lewes. Cf. *S.R.,* I, 310. With the ballad itself, cf. 'The forme and shape of a monstrous Child, borne at Maydstone in Kent, the xxiiij. of October, 1568,' pp. 288–92 in Huth's *Ancient Ballads and Broadsides.* With this ballad particulars of the incident are given, and the names of three witnesses are affixed. The ballad itself moralizes the immorality of the mother, and is entitled, 'A warnyng to England.' In his introduction (pp. xxx–xxxii) Huth discusses the prevalence of broadsides and their significance. Pp. 38–42, 66–71, 94–97, 163–65, 277–81, 299–303, 321–26, 360–64 print ballads similar in kind. Cf. also 'The thirtieth Chapter. Of a monstrous Childe,' for Montaigne's readiness to read a moral in deformity (Nn1r in *The Essayes or Morall, Politike and Millitarie Discourses of Lo : Michaell de Montaigne . . . done into English By . . . Iohn Florio . . . London by Val. Sims for Edward Blount . . . 1603.* For further examples cf. *The Pack of Autolycus,* ed. H. E. Rollins (Cambridge, Mass., 1927), pp. 185f.; and the jests of Autolycus himself (*W.T.,* IV, iv) and those of Trinculo (*Temp.,* II, ii). The moral persists: 'Strange wonders God to us doth send, / For to make us our lives amend,' p. 187 in *The Wonder of Wonders, or the Strange Birth in Hampshire* (1675?). *By T.L.* Cf. also pp. 139–45.

286.8–287.5   *A meruaylous dreame,* etc.: The 'lyon' is Leo, fifth constellation of the Zodiac, and comprised, like the others, in 30°. The Sun ('Phebus'), which moves along its ecliptic about 1° each day, beginning at the Spring Equinox, in Aries, has attained to the seventeenth grade, or completed 17°, in Leo. The time, therefore, is early August. The rest of the passage gives the position of the other planets, relative to the signs of the Zodiac: Jupiter ('Ioue') is in Taurus ('the bulles necke') but will soon enter Gemini ('twyns'); Saturn, slowest of the planets because closest to the Primum Mobile and thus most affected by its pull, has barely arrived in Cancer ('Crab'); Mars, but lately in Aquarius ('waterman'), has reversed his course and returned to Capricorn ('goate'). The progressive and retrograde movements of the planets, which Mars here illustrates, are now explained 'as the result of the earth's orbital motion about the sun, which causes the other planets, which are likewise circling about the sun, to undergo changes in the direction of their movements, as seen by observers on the earth.' (Johnson, p. 24). Venus also has taken a retrograde course, and returned for a time to the sign of Leo, where she was in conjunction with, and in close proximity to, the Sun. Mercury (here identified with the messenger of the god, Jove), who in May had been in Taurus, has now reached Virgo ('vyrgyn'); he will return back on his path in September, after completing his passage of that sign, and will thus meet the Sun who, in Leo, is directly behind him. Finally, the aspect of the Moon ('Diana') relative to the Sun ('her brother': Apollo) is described as 'tryne.' Now the benevolent or malignant influence of each planet is modified not only by the sign it inhabits, but by its 'aspect' or position with regard to the other planets, as well. The word 'tryne' denotes the aspect of two planets which are a third part of the Zodiac (120°) distant from each other. The Sun is in Leo; the Moon, 120° distant, must be in Aries ('ramme'), as in fact we are told that she is. That she no longer wears a 'tryne aspect' toward Venus indicates that Venus has left the sign Leo, and is no longer in conjunction with the Sun.

286.10 *When in the lyon Phebus*, etc.: cf. the Preface to Barnabe Googe's translation of Marcellus Palingenius, *The Zodyake of lyfe*, 1560, beginning,
'When as syr Phoebe with backward course. . . .'

289.6–9 *Which notwythstandyng of*, etc.: the kingdom won with blood and, despite
three heirs, rendered back again 'wyth losse and shame' may be France
or, simply, Calais, seized by Edward III after the battle of Crécy in 1346,
and retaken for France by Francis, duke of Guise, in 1558. Hall's poem
is dated 1561 (286.9). The 'iii. heyres' may refer to the three ruling
houses of Plantagenet, Lancaster, and Tudor.

290.8 *Epicure:* Epicurus, the Greek philosopher and founder of the Epicurean
school, which conceived of pleasure as the highest happiness, is the sub-
ject of Book X in Diogenes Laertius' *De Vita et moribus philosophorum*
(Lyons, 1541: the edn. consulted in this study). Possible sources of Hall's
reference, other than Diogenes, are Burley, Erasmus, and Palfreyman.
The sayings of Epicurus are given by Walter Burley (1510), fol. xxviii.
Cf. also 'The Epicure,' a colloquy between Hedonius and Spudeus: '*He.*
But there is no sect pleaseth me better, than the sect of the Epicureans.
Sp. Why but there is none among them all more condemned by the
voices of all,' in *The Colloquies, or Familiar Discourses of Desiderius Erasmus
of Roterdam, Rendered into English . . . by H. M. Gent*, London, 1671, p. 526.
The *Colloquies* of Erasmus (Basle, 1516) ran through ninety editions
before 1546 (cf. L. Einstein, *The Italian Renaissance in England*, 1902).
Palfreyman's *Heavenly Philosophy*, 1578, Oo7r, derides 'The Epicures of
this world, all worldlings, bellie gods, and the noysome route of voluptuous
persons.'

295.10–296.5 *Some gasyng vp*, etc.: with Hall's picture of the gulling of the
people by astrologers, compare Jonson's in *The Alchemist*, and especially
the gulling of Nab, the credulous Drugger, by Face and Subtle.

296.10–17 *And hatefull wytches*, etc.: cf. Agrippa, 'Of Witchinge Magicke,' Cap.
44.

296.22–297.9 *And some for gayn*, etc.: cf. *The Court of Venus*, ed. Fraser, p. 54; and
'Political Prophecy in "The Pilgrim's Tale," ' R. A. Fraser, *SAQ*, LVI,
no. 1 (Jan. 1957), 67–78 for comment on the 'trayterous kynd of prophesies' inveighed against in Hall's poem.

297.26 *Iuglers lewde:* cf. Agrippa, R2v, '*Of Iuglinge* . . . Magicke, wherof the
Iuglers skil is a parti also, that in illusions, which are onely done accordinge to the outwarde apparance: with these the Magitiens doo shewe
vaine visions, and with Iuglinge castes doo plaie many miracles, & cause
dreams, which thinge is not so much done by *Geoticall* inchauntmentes,
and praiers, and deceites of the Deuill, as also with certaine vapours of
perfumes, bindinges, & hangings, moreover with ringes, images, glasses,
& other like receites and instruments of Magicke, and with a naturel
and celestial vertue. There are many thinges done also, with a readie
subteltie and nimblenesse of the handes, as wee dayly see stage players
and Iuglers doo, whiche for that cause we terme *Chirosophi*, that is to saie,
hande wise.'

298.3–5 *And some with hoby*, etc.: cf. various accounts of the showman Banks
(*fl.* 1588–1637) and his dancing horse Morocco, whose most famous
exploit was the climbing of St. Paul's steeple, 'whilst a number of asses
stood braying [below].' Cf. *D.N.B.* under Banks; and *Maroccus Extaticus.
Or, Bankes Bay Horse in a Trance. A Discourse set downe in a merry Dialogue,
between Bankes and his beast: Anatomizing some abuses and bad trickes of this
age. . . . By Iohn Dando . . . and Harrie Runt* [*pseuds.*] *. . . Printed for*

Cuthbert Burby, 1595; and 'The Dancing Horse of "Love's Labour's Lost,"' R. A. Fraser, *SQ*, V, no. 1 (Jan. 1954), 98f.

298.6–9   *And many mynstrels*, etc.: cf. the description of Autolycus: 'He hath songs for man or woman, of all sizes, no milliner can so fit his customers with gloves. He has the prettiest love songs for maids, so without bawdry, which is strange, with such delicate burdens of dildos and fadings, "jump her and thump her." And where some stretch-mouthed rascal would, as it were, mean mischief and break a foul gap into the matter, he makes the maid to answer "Whoop, do me no harm, good man," puts him off, slights him, with "Whoop, do me no harm, good man."' (*WT*, IV, iv, 191–201).

298.10–13   *Yea popysh songes*, etc.: for an account of the prevalence of these, cf. Rollins, *Old English Ballads*, pp. xiv, xx, xxii–xxiv. Pp. 70–179 reprint fifteen Catholic ballads from Additional MSS. 15, 225; pp. 8–32 give five more Catholic ballads.

298.18–21   *And some agayn by palmestry*, etc.: cf. Vives, *Introduccion to Wisedome*, C3r, 'such craftes must therfor be shonned that fyght agaynste vertue, all craftes, that worke by vain coniectures as palmestry, pyromancie, Nicromācie, Hydromancie, astrologie, wherin much pestilent vanity lyeth hyd, inuented of y̆ deuyl, our deceitful ennemy.'

300.2–5   *Hou long shall suche*, etc.: cf. Matthew, vi. 19–20.

300.18–301.5   *Of these some cut the poore mans purse*, etc.: for complementary reports on the Elizabethan underworld, cf. Thomas Harman, *A Caveat or Warning for Common Cursitors, Vulgarly Called Vagabones* (1566); *A Manifest Detection of Dice-play and Other Practices* (*c.* 1552); Robert Greene, *A Notable Discovery of Cozenage Now Daily Practised by Sundry Lewd Persons Called Cony-Catchers and Crossbiters* (1591); the second and third part of *Cony-Catching* (1592); *A Disputation between a He-Cony-Catcher and a She-Cony-Catcher* (1592), *The Black Book's Messenger* (1592), on Ned Browne, a notorious English cutpurse. These pamphlets are reprinted by A. V. Judges, *The Elizabethan Underworld* (1930). Cf. also F. Aydelotte, *Elizabethan Rogues and Vagabonds* (Oxford, 1913); 'Cuthbert Cony-Catcher,' *The Defence of Cony-Catching* (1592); Thomas Dekker, *Belman of London* and *Lanthorn and Candle-Light* (1608).

301.7   *And suche as teethe dyd drawe:* Why drawers of teeth should be indicted I do not know, unless an amusing story in John Taylor's *Wit and Mirth* offers a clue. In 'Queen Elizabeth's days,' relates Taylor, a man availing himself of 'a brooch in his hat, like a tooth drawer, with a Rose and Crowne and two letters,' secured the Lord Chamberlain's licence to exhibit a performing ape. Wanting an audience, on a visit to Love in Cornwall, he wrote to the mayor: 'These are to will and require you, and every of you, with your wives and families, that upon the sight hereof, you make your personall appearance before the Queenes Ape, for it is an Ape of ranke and quality, who is to be practised throughout her Majesties dominions, that by his long experience amongst her loving subjects, hee may bee the better enabled to doe her Majesty service hereafter: and hereof faile you not, as you will answer the contrary.' The letter brought forward the entire population of the town (convinced largely, it would seem, by the tooth drawer's brooch), led by the penitent mayor, who 'put off his hat' to the animal 'because it was the Queenes Ape.' Cf. T. S. Graves, 'Tricks of Elizabethan Showmen,' *SAQ*, XIV, no 2 (April, 1915), 4f.

301.14–19   *And many wyth a pedlers packe*, etc.: Autolycus corroborates Hall: 'I have sold all my trumpery. . . . By which means I saw whose purse was best in picture. . . . 'Twas nothing to geld a codpiece of a purse. . . . So that in this time of lethargy I picked and cut most of their festival purses.' (*WT*, IV, iv, 606–626).

302.25 *Gelothophilis*: cf. *C. Plini Secundi Naturalis Historiae*, 'gelotophyllida in Bactris et circa Borysthenen. haec si bibatur cum murra et vino [cf. Hall's phrase], varias obversari species ridendique finem non fieri nisi potis nucleis pinae nucis cum pipere et melle in vino palmeo,' Lipsiae (1897), Lib. XXIV, 164, p. 108 in vol. IV of 6 vols.

305.17 *Midas*: It is interesting to speculate on the possible sources of Hall's knowledge of mythological character and story (he alludes in this poem to the Cyclops, 304.3; Bacchus, 305.20; Pactolus, 305.23; Circe, 305.29, as well as to Midas). He might of course have gone to *Ovid* (Met. XI), whose work was read in the schools; to Virgil (*Eclogues*, VI); or to the *Fabularum Liber* (191) of C. Julius Hyginus, a contemporary of Ovid, whose work, a series of 277 short mythological legends, was first published at Basle in 1535 in Greek and Latin. The Cyclops figure, moreover, in the *Georgics* and *Aeneid*, in Strabo, and of course in Homer, who tells also the story of Circe (*Od.* X. 135). I suggest, however, that Hall, though he may have read some or all of these writers, relied rather on one or more of the reference dictionaries so popular in the Renaissance. The lexicons which achieved widest circulation were those of Balbus (1460), Suidas (1499), Calepine (1502), Elyot (1538), Thomas (1587), the commentary on Martial of Nicholas Perottus (*Cornucopiae*, 1489), and, most important, the *Thesaurus* of Robert Stephanus (1531) and that of Thomas Cooper (1565). The compilers of these dictionaries were genuinely learned men; those who resorted to the dictionaries, to adorn their compositions, were learned, one suspects, in secondary sources only.

310.18–21 *Great tokens from the Lord*, etc: The reference to Kent may be paralleled by the subject of a ballad of 1561, entitled 'Newes out of Kent' and licensed to Ralph Newbery in that year. Cf. Hazlitt, *Hand-Book to the Popular, Poetical, and Dramatic Literature of Great Britain* (1867), p. 315; and *Stat. Reg.*: 'Receuyd of *Iohn Tysdale* for his lycense for pryntinge of iij ballettes the one intituled *newes out of Kent*.' (Arber, I, 181). In April of 1561 there was examined by the Justice of the Peace for Kent a priest named Coxe, alias John Devon, accused of celebrating Mass and, perforce, of magic and conjuration. A number of the gentry was involved in this scandal. Cf. *Calendar of State Papers, Domestic Series, Edward VI, Mary, Elizabeth, 1547–1580*, ed. Robert Lemon (London, 1856), pp. 173f.

310.22–25 *The elementes to repentance*, etc.: 'On Wednesday the 4. of June, betweene foure and five of the clocke in the afternoone, the steeple of Paules in London, being fired by lightning, brast forth (as it seemed to the beholders) two or three yardes beneath the foote of the crosse, and from thence brent downe the speere to the stone worke and bels, so terribly, that within the space of foure houres, the same steeple, with the roofes of the church so much as was timber, or other wise combustible, were consumed, which was a lamentable sight and pittifull remembrance to the beholders therof' (p. 646 in Stow's *Annales*, ed. Howes, 1614). Cf. also Stow's *Survey of London*, Everyman edn., n.d., pp. 296f. On June 8, the Sunday following the fire, a sermon was preached at Paul's Cross, in which the fire was seen as a promise of some greater evil to follow, unless the lives of the people were amended. Some suggested, however, that it showed God's ire at the reformation of religion. In any case, it was purposive and illustrative. Cf. *The True Report of the burnyng of the Steple and Churche of Paules in London*, printed by William Seres on June 10, 1561, and prefaced with a quotation from Jeremiah, xviii: 'I wyll speake suddenlye agaynst a nation, or agaynste a kyngedome, to plucke it vp, and to roote it out, and distroye it. But yf that nation, agaynste whome I haue pronounced, turne from their wickednes, I wyll repent of the plage that I thought to brynge vppon them.' Other notices of the fire: 'Did the Romans take it for an ill signe, whē their Capitol was strooken with lightning, how much more ought *London*, to take it for an ill signe, when her chiefe steeple is strooken with lightning?' Nashe, *Christs Teares*, z2v; *Brief Discours de la Tempeste et Fouldre Advenue en la Cité de Londres en Angleterre, sur le grand temple & clocher nomme de sainct Paul, le quatriesme Iuin. A Paris. Pour Christophe Royer, tenant sa boutique devant le College de Boucourt* [1561]. *Stat. Reg.* entries: 'Receuyd of I. Cherlwod for his lycense for pryntinge of a ballett intituled *a Diolige of the Rufull burr[n]ynge of Powles*' (I. 202, 1562–63). John Cherlewod was licensed again for the ballad 'whan yonge Powlis steple olde Powlies steples chylde &c' (I. 210, 1562–63). William Griffith was licensed for the ballad 'the incorragen all kynde of men to ẙ . . . buyldynge Powles steple agayne' (I. 263, 1564–65). Chappell, I, 117, mentions four ballads on the burning. Cf. also 'Documents Illustrating the History of St. Paul's,' pp. 120ff., Camden Soc.

311.24–25 *Necromancie . . . Iudiciall Astrologie:* cf. Caxton, *Mirror of the World*, f3v, 'Perse . . . conteyneth xxxiii regyons of whiche the first is the Royame of Perse / where as a science called Nygromancie was first founden / whiche science constrayneth the enemye the fende to be taken and holde prisonner.' Judicial astrology studied the influence of the stars on human destiny, whereas natural astrology predicted the motions of the heavenly bodies, and eclipses.

312.2–10 *From out the Ramme*, etc.: the Sun ('Titan') is proceeding from Aries ('Ramme') to Taurus ('Bull') along the ecliptic circle that is his path through the heavens. Cut by that circle are the twelve zodiacal constellations, extending 6° to either side of it, according to the theory of Hall's day, which held that the planets never wandered more than 6° above or below the ecliptic. The true value of the inclination of Mercury's orbit to the ecliptic is in fact 7°. Since the Sun has apparently just entered Taurus, the time is late April.

313.9 *In Homer as we fynde*, etc.: cf. *Od.*, bk. VI. Sir Thomas Elyot's *Boke of the Governour* advocated the study of the heroic poems of Homer (in Greek). Hall could not have read Homer's works in English, but a Latin translation would have been available to him: the *Iliad* in Greek and Latin appeared in 1523, the *Odyssey* in Latin alone in 1510. A Greek and Latin version of the latter was not published until 1574.

313.10 *Philomela:* cf. Apollod. iii.14.8; and Comes, p. 220 (I2i4r–v), who quotes as sources: 'Ovid, Lib. 6, Metam., Stra. [Strabo, the geographer of Pontus, who lived in the reign of Augustus, and whose *Geography*, 1516ff., is referred to here], lib. 9, Virgil in Sileno [*Eclogues*], Homer, Odyssey, lib. 7, Sophocles in Electra.' All of these writers and their work were accessible to Hall. But cf. 305.17n.; and the treatment of the lexicons in Starnes and Talbert, *Renaissance Dictionaries*.

314.19–315.25 *What should I name*, etc.: Hall's catalogue of plants is glossed by the descriptions and illustrations of the herbalists Turner, Lobel, Gerard, Willich, and Dodoens. Thus, *Hyacinthe* (314.18): 'The comune Hyacinthus is muche in Englande aboute Syon and Shene, and it is called in

Englishe crow toes, and in the North partes Crawtees.' (Turner, D6r; illustrated Lobel, *Stirpium Observationes*, London, 1581, p. 48; and described, Lobel, *Stirpium adversaria nova*, London, 1571, p. 46. Cited hereafter as *Obs.* and *Adv.*); *Verbasculy* (314.19): 'There are .iii. Verbascula. . . . The fyrste is called . . . a Primerose. The seconde . . . a Cowslip, or a Cowslap, or a Pagle. The third is called . . . Rosecampi.' (Turner, G7r; *Obs.* 305, 181; *Adv.* 243, 244, 142); *Clouer* (314.20): Gerard distinguishes numerous varieties of Trefoile or Clover, pp. 1020–26, and illustrates them. *Obs.* 493, *Adv.* 380; *Brunell* (314.22): '. . . is called in English Prunell, Carpenters herbe, Selfeheale, and Hookeheale, & Sicklewoort.' (Gerard, p. 508). It 'hath square hairie stalks of a foote high, beset with long hairie and sharpe pointed leaues, and at the top of the stalkes growe flowers thicke set togither . . . of a browne colour mixed with blew' (p. 507). It 'groweth verye commonly in all our fieldes throughout England' (p. 508; illus. p. 507); *Bugle* (314.22): 'Cōsolida media is called in english Bugle. It is a blacke herbe and it groweth in shaddowy places and moyst groundes.' (Turner, H2r; *Obs.* 252, *Adv.* 199); *Hieracium* (314.23): Turner distinguishes 'two kyndes. The one . . . may be called in englishe greate Hawkweede or yealowe Succory. . . . The second is like Dandelyon. . . . It maye be called . . . lesse Hawkeweede.' (D4v–5r; *Obs.* 119f., *Adv.* 88); *Synkfoyle* (314.24): 'Quinquefolium is called . . . in english Cynkfoly or fyue fyngered grasse . . . [and] is commune in al places.' (Turner, F5v; *Obs.* 393, *Adv.* 306); *Betony* (314.24): AS 'bishopswort'; identified after 1066 with the *vettonica* of the elder Pliny and became betony. 'Betonica . . . is named in englishe Betony or Beton . . . it groweth muche in woddes and wylde forestes.' (Turner, B5r–v; *Obs.* 286, *Adv.* 229); *Origanum* (314.25): ' . . . is called in englishe organ, howe be it I neuer sawe the trewe organ in England . . . our commune organ is . . . called origanum syluestre in latin, and in some places of England wylde mergerum.' (Turner, E7v; *Obs.* 262, *Adv.* 211). But cf. *Libellus*, B4r, 'Origanum . . . est herba quam vulgus appellat Peny ryall, aut puddynge gyrse.' Lobel describes the English 'Organe, or wilde Margerome' as *Origanum Heracleoticum*; *Tutsane* (314.26): 'Androsaemon is the herbe . . . whiche we call Totsan . . . it groweth in gardines in Englande and no where elles that I haue sene.' (Turner, A8v; *Obs.* 357, *Adv.* 279). Gerard illustrates, 435, and describes, 434f.: 'The stalkes of Tutsan be straight, round, chamfered or crested, hard and woodie, being for the most part two foote high.' It 'groweth in wooddes, and by hedges, especially in Hampsteed wood'; *Hipericon* (314.26): ' . . . is called of barbarus writers Fuga demonum, in englishe saynte Iohans wurte or saynt Iohans grasse. . . . It groweth cōmunely in al places of Englāde, & especially in woddes.' (Turner, D6r; *Obs.* 216, *Adv.* 172); *Asciron* (314.27): ' . . . is not very cōmon in England, howe be it I sawe it thys last yere in Syon parck, it hath a four squared stalke, & is like saynt Iohans grasse, but it is greater and not wyth suche holes . . . wherefore it maye be called in english square saint Iohans grasse or great saynt Iohans grasse.' (Turner, B3r–v; *Obs.* 216, *Adv.* 173); *Vyolet* (314.28): 'Viola nigra siue purpurea is called . . . in englishe a Violet.' (Turner, G8r; *Adv.* 266). Gerard illustrates and describes, 699: 'A beautifull flower & sweetely smelling, of a blew darkish purple, consisting of fiue little leaues, the lowest whereof is the greatest; and after them do appeere little hanging cups or knaps, which, when they be ripe, do open and diuide themselues into three partes'; *Simphtion* (314.28): ' . . . is of two sortes, the former is called Symphytum petreum,

and this herbe groweth about Syon, seuen myles aboue London. It is
lyke vnto wylde Mergerum, but it is neither so hote neither so wel
smellyng. It maye be called in english vnsauery Mergerū. The other
kynde called in latin Symphytum alterum, is called in englishe comfrey
or Blackewurt.' (Turner, G5v; *Obs.* 251, *Adv.* 198f.); *Daysye* (314.29):
'Bellis or Bellius named in Englishe a Dasie . . . growe[s] in al grene
places in greate plentie.' (Turner, B5r; *Obs.* 252, *Adv.* 199). Gerard, 510,
illustrates; *Hartes ease* (315.2): 'Viola alba is . . . [of] diuerse sortes. . . .
One is called in english Cheiry, Hertes ease or wal Gelefloure, it groweth
vpon the walles, and in the sprynge of the yere, it hath yealowe floures.'
(Turner, G7v-8r; *Obs.* 335, *Adv.* 266: 'Loue in ydle pances [pensees].')
Gerard, 703: 'The Hartes ease or Paunsie'; *Pacience* (315.2): *Libellus*,
B2r, 'Hyppolapathon, officine patientiam vocant, vulgus Patience.' (*Obs.*
152, *Adv.* 118.) Gerard illustrates and describes, 313f.: 'The garden
Patience [Munkes Rubarbe] hath very strong stalkes, furrowed or
chamfered, of ten or twelue foote high when it groweth in fertile grounde.'
It is found 'for the most part in ditches and water courses, very common
through Englande.' It is a species of Water Dock, and is known also as
'Bloudwoort, or bloudy Patience . . . [because] of the bloudie colour
wherewith the whole plant is possest'; *Pimpernell* (315.3): 'Anagallis, siue
Corchorus, is called in englishe pympernel . . . it groweth commonly
amonge the corne. The male hath a crimsin floure.' (Turner, A8; *Obs.*
247f., *Adv.* 194). Cf. also Gerard, 1088, who illustrates: 'It groweth likewise in a pasture as you go from a village hard by London called Knights-
bridge, vnto Fulham, a village thereby'; *Cammocke* (315.4): Gerard describes
and illustrates, 1141: 'Cammock or ground Furze, riseth vp with stalkes a
cubite high, and often higher, set with diuers iointed branches, tough,
pliable, and full of hard sharpe thornes: among which do grow leaues . . .
of a deepe greene colour: from the bosome of which thornes and leaues
come foorth the flowers . . . of a purple colour . . . the roote is long, and
runneth farre abroade, very tough and hard to be torne in peeces with
the plough, insomuch that the oxen can hardly passe forward, but are
constrained to stande still; whereupon it was called Rest Plough, or
Rest Harrow. We haue in our London pastures . . . one of the Rest
Harrowes'; *Camomille* (315.4): 'Anthemis . . . is called in englishe
Cammamyle . . . [and] is deuided into three kyndes . . . thys herbe
groweth on Rychmund grene, and in Hundsley heth in great plentie.'
(Turner, B1; *Obs.* 445, *Adv.* 342); *Canterbury bell* (315.5): Gerard distinguishes six kinds of this plant, 'called likewise throtewoorte,' illustrates,
and names the many places where it flourishes, 363-65; *Rosecampany*
(315.6): 'The first kinde of Rose Campions hath round stalkes, very
knottie and woolie; and at euery knot or ioint there do stand two woolie
soft leaues. . . . The flowers growe at the top of the stalke, of a perfect red
colour.' The second variety differs only in that it is white. 'The Rose
Campion groweth plentifully in most gardens.' (Gerard, 381, and
illustrated; *Obs.* 181, *Adv.* 142); *Maudlen* (315.6): 'Eupatorium Mesues
. . . is called in englishe Maudlene.' (Turner, D1r; *Obs.* 284, *Adv.* 208).
'Maudelein is somewhat like vnto Costmarie (whereof it is a kinde) in
colour smell, taste, and in the golden flowers, set vpon the tops of the
stalks in round clusters.' It grows 'euery where in gardens.' (Gerard,
523f., and illustrated); *Cost* (315.6): 'Costmarie groweth vp with round
hard stalks two foote high, bearing long broad leaues finely nicked in
the edges, of an ouerworne whitish greene colour.' (Gerard, 523; *Obs.* 38,

174, 259, 398; *Adv.* 34, 35, 136, 318); *London touft* (315.7): 'The narrow
leafed Sweete William groweth vp to the height of two cubits, very well
resembling the . . . [great Sweet William], but lesser, and the leaues
narrower. The flowers are of a bright red colour . . . [and] in English . . .
are called . . . London Tuftes.' (Gerard, 479f., and illustrated); *Agrimony*
(315.8): 'It groweth in barren places by high waies, inclosures of medowes,
and of corne fieldes, and oftentimes in woodes and copses.' (Gerard, 575,
and illustrated; Turner, D1r; *Obs.* 394, *Adv.* 308); *Lyons tooth* (315.8): 'The
herbe which is commonly called Dandelion; dothe sende foorth from the
roote long leaues deepely cut and gashed in the edges . . . vpon euerie
stalke standeth a flower . . . of colour yellowe and sweete in smell, which
is turned into a round downie blowball, that is carried awaie with the
winde. . . . [Dandelions] are found often in medowes neere vnto water
ditches, as also in gardens and in high waies much troden. . . . [They are
called] of diuers Pisseabed.' The name survives in New England still.
(Gerard, 228f., and illustrated); *Serpillum* (315.10): '. . . aliud hortense,
quae olim coronaria herba erat: aliud syluestre.' (Willich, h1r) 'Serpyllm
. . . is of .ii. sortes. The one is called . . . runnyng tyme. The seconde . . .
wylde tyme. The one groweth in gardines, & the other in sandy fieldes
and bare groundes.' (Turner, G2r; *Obs.* 230, *Adv.* 280); *lady Traces*
(315.11): 'Satyrion is very commune in Germany, and a certeyne
ryghte kynde of the same groweth besyde Syon, it bryngeth furth whyte
floures in the ende of harueste, and it is called Lady traces.' (Turner, F8v;
Obs. 97, *Adv.* 64); *Yarow* (315.12): 'Common Yarrow [or Nosebleed] hath
very many stalkes comming vp a white high, round, and somewhat hard:
about which stande long leaues . . . the flowers whereof are either white
or purple.' It 'groweth euery where in drie pastures and medowes . . .
[and] in a field by Sutton in Kent, called Holly Deane.' (Gerard, 913f.,
and illustrated); *Torne twyse* (315.12): ?Twice-writhen, a name invented
by Turner for *Polygonum Bistorta*. (Britten and Holland, *English Plant-
Names*, p. 477); *Strawberyes* (315.12): 'Fragraria is called in english a
strawbery leafe. . . . Euery man knoweth wel inough where straw beries
growe.' (Turner, D2v; *Obs.* 396, *Adv.* 308f.); *Burnet* (315.13): 'One of
the Burnets is lesser, for the most part growing in gardens, notwithstanding it groweth in barren fieldes, where it is much smaller. . . . [It] hath
long leaues made vp togither of a great many vpon one stem, euerie one
whereof is something rounde, nicked on the edges, somewhat hairie:
among these riseth a stalke that is not altogither without leaues, something chamfered: vpon the tops whereof growe little round heads or
knaps, which bring foorth small flowers of a browne purple colour. . . .
[Burnet] doth marueilously agree with wine; to which . . . [it] doth giue
a pleasant sent. . . . [Drunk with wine it] cureth the bloudie flixe, the
spitting of bloud, and al other fluxe of bloud in man or woman. . . . The
leaues of Burnet steeped in wine and drunken, doth comfort the hart, and
maketh it merrie, and is good against the trembling and shaking thereof.'
(Gerard, 880–90, and illustrated); *Lunary* (315.14): '. . . is of two kyndes,
the one . . . hath leaues lyke wylde Cucumer & coddes rounde almost as
the mone, and as thyn as a Cole leafe. It may be called in englishe great
Lunari. Some cal it Shabub. The other kinde . . . may be called . . . litle
Lunary or Maye Grapes. . . . The former herbe groweth onely in gardines,
the other in middowes and pastur groundes.' (Turner, H3r; *Obs.* 470,
Adv. 360); *Serpents tongue* (315.14): 'Lingua serpētina groweth in many
places of England. It may be called . . . Adders tonge. . . . It groweth

plētuously in middowes where as Lunary groweth.' (Turner, H3r–v; *Obs.* 471, *Adv.* 360); *Procerpinaca* (315.15) : 'The common male knot grasse creepeth along vpon the ground, with long slender weake branches, full of knots or ioints, whereof it tooke his name.' It grows 'in barren and stonie places almost euery where' and is called 'of *Apuleius Proserpinaca.*' (Gerard, 451f., and illustrated); *Adder grasse* (315.16) : Dogballocks (testicles). Gerard distinguishes four varieties: Great, White, Spotted, and Marish. 'These kinds of Dogs stones do grow in moist and fertill medowes. . . . They flower from the beginning of may to the middest of August.' (Pp. 156f., and illustrated); *Saxifrage* (315.16) : 'There are foure herbes, whiche al are called saxifragia. The englishe mens Saxifragia, which they cal Saxifrage, hath leaues lyke smal perseley, & groweth in middowes.' (Turner, H4v; *Obs.* 456, *Adv.* 183, 352); *Veronica* (315.17) : '. . . groweth in many places of England, and it is called in englishe Fluellyng.' (Turner, (H5r; for different varieties: *Obs.* 249, 50, 51, 186, 197; *Adv.* 197); *periclimenum* (315.19) : '. . . is called of the herbaries and poticaries Caprifolium and Matrisylua, in english wood bynde and Honysuccles. . . . Wodbyne, is commune in euery wodde.' (Turner, F2r; *Obs.* 357, *Adv.* 280.) 'Woodbinde or Honisuckle climeth vp aloft, hauing long slender woodie stalkes, parted into diuers branches: about which stand by certaine distances smooth leaues . . . of a light greene colour aboue, vnder neath of a whitish greene.' (Gerard, 744); *Cotnus* (315.20) : 'Malus Cotonea is called . . . in englishe a Quince tree.' (Turner, E3v; *Obs.* 580, *Adv.* 429); *Swete bryer* (315.21) : 'Cynorrhodus . . . is called in englishe a swete brere or an Eglentyne. . . . It groweth . . . in gardines in Englande.' (Turner, C6v). 'The sweete Brier doth oftentimes grow higher then all kindes of Roses; the shootes of it are hard, thicke, and woodie; the leaues are glittering, and of a beautifull greene colour . . . the Roses are little . . . tending to purple.' (Gerard, 1087, and illustrated); *Ligustrum* (315.21) : '. . . is called . . . in englishe Prim print or Priuet.' (Turner, E1r–v; *Obs.* 564, *Adv.* 420). 'Priuet is a shrub growing like an hedge tree: the branches and twigs wherof be straight, and couered with soft glistering leaues of a deep green color . . . the flowers be white, sweete of smell . . . which being vaded, there succeede clusters of berries. . . . The common Priuet groweth naturally in euery woode, and hedge rowes of our London gardens.' (Gerard, 1208); *whyte thorne* (315.22) : . . . or Hawthorne Tree, or May-bush, is 'very common in most parts of England.' It 'is a great shrub growing oftentimes to the height of the Peare tree: the trunke or bodie is great: the boughes and branches hard and woodie, set full of long sharpe thornes.' (Gerard, 1145; illustrated, 1146); *black thorne* (315.22) : Probably the wild plum tree, known as black thorn. It 'groweth not vp to the stature of a tree, but remaineth lowe by the grounde, lyke to a hedge bushe . . . it putteth vp many branches from one roote, set here and there with pricking thornes. . . . The wild Plummes do grow in feeldes and wayes, and other vntoyled places and in hedges.' (Dodoens' *Niewe Herball*, tr. Lyte [London, 1578], p. 720, and illustrated); *boxe* 315.23) : 'Buxus named in greeke Pyxos is called in englishe box.' (Turner, B7r; *Obs.* 562, *Adv.* 419). 'The great Boxe is a faire tree, bearing a great body or trunke . . . [and] beset with sundry small hard greene leaues. . . . [It] groweth vpon sundry waste and barren hils in Englande.' (Gerard, 1225, and illustrated); *maple* (315.23) : Not 'the great Maple' but 'a small Maple which doth oftentimes come to the bignes of a tree, but most commonly it groweth low after the maner of a shrub.' It is found 'almost euery where in hedges and lowe woodes.' (Gerard, 1299f.); *Briony* (315.24): '... groweth in many places of Englande in hedges.' (Turner, B5v, *Obs.* 344, *Adv.* 275); *Iuy* (315.25): 'Hederam greci ciffon vocant, angli Iuy.' (*Libellus*, B1v; *Obs.* 336, *Adv.* 269.) 'The greater Iuie climeth on trees, olde buildings and wals. ... The leaues are smooth, shining especially on the vpper side cornered with sharpe pointed corners. The flowers are verie small and mossie, after which succeede bundels of blacke berries, euery one hauing a small sharpe pointle.' (Gerard, 707); *wylde vyne* (315.25): 'Labrusca ... is of two sortes, the one kynde is so wylde that it hath onely floures and goeth no further. ... The other hath floures and also litle grapes. ... It may be called in englishe a wild vine.' (Turner, D7r–v; *Obs.* 345, *Adv.* 275). Lobel offers it as an alternative name for *Bryonie*, as do Britten and Holland (*English Plant-Names*, p. 480: *Bryonia dioica*), and Gerard: 'The blacke Bryonie hath long flexible branches of a woodie substance, couered with a gaping or clouen barke growing very farre abroad, winding it selfe with his small tendrels about trees, hedges, & what else is next vnto it, like vnto the branches of the Vine.' (p. 721, and illustrated).

316.6–9   *The rysyng see*, etc.: Hall refers to the two kinds of stellar rising and setting: (1) real, or imperceptible, (2) perceptible, or apparent. In the first class occur (1) the true cosmical rising: star and sun rise together, (2) the true cosmical setting: star sets as sun rises, (3) the true acronychal rising: star rises as sun sets, (4) the true acronychal setting: star and sun set together. In all four cases the star will be obscured by the sun. In the second class occur (1) the heliacal rising: the first visible appearance of the star on the eastern horizon before sunrise, (2) the heliacal setting: the last visible setting of the star in the evening, (3) the apparent acronychal rising: the last visible rising of a star in the evening, (4) the apparent cosmical setting: the first visible setting of a star in the morning. In the astronomical poem, *Phaenomena*, the Greek poet Aratus (fl. 270 B.C.) considers in detail what stars rise with a given zodical sign or set when the zodiacal sign is rising. (Cf. Acts, xvii. 28, 'For in him we live, and move, and have our being; as certain also of your own poets have said.') Aratus was first printed by Aldus in 1499 (Venice) in Greek and Latin, with the latter version by Linacre, and in a volume with the *Sphaera* of Proclus. This first edition was often reprinted and widely resorted to. (Googe's Palingenius, for example—a work Hall may have used—cites Aratus.) The *Phaenomena* parallels Hall's references to astronomy here, and may have suggested them (cf. ll. 559–732 in Aratus). I conclude, then, that Hall may have used the Aratus-Proclus volume, and derived a part of his knowledge from it. The conjecture is especially attractive since Proclus was one of the two principal Latin texts on elementary astronomy (the other being Sacrobosco's *Sphaera mundi*).

316.10   *About our Artick pole*: cf. *Phaenomena*, ll. 26–461, for an enumeration of the constellations paralleling that given here. With Hall's catalogue of the stars about the North Pole, and in the Northern Hemisphere generally, compare Proclus (Englished by William Salisbury, 1550), F1r–2v: 'The Sygnes that be blased with starres are deuyded into thre partes, some of them be placed in the Circle of the Zodiake. Some be called Northern, and some be called Southern. ... So manye are accompted for the Northern as be set betwyxt the zodiak and the North. And they be these.' Proclus gives the list substantially as does Hall. For the exact positions of these stars, and a diagram, see the article 'Constellation' in the 13th edn. of the *Encyclopaedia Britannica*; and an illustration from Ptolemy's *Almagest*, 1541, in *Sh. Eng.*, I, 449.

316.11–318.3 *The lyttle Beare fyrst see*, etc.: The descriptions that follow derive mostly from Robert Recorde's *The Castle of Knowledge*, 1556, the first original and really thorough treatise in English on the elements of astronomy. *The lyttle Beare*, etc. (316.11–13): 'The most northerly constellation is the lesser Beare, called Vrsa Minor. . . . This is the chiefe marke whereby mariners gouerne their course in saylinge by nyghte, and namely by 2 starres in it, which many do call the Shafte, and other do name the Guardas, after the Spanish tonge.' (Recorde, p. 263 [misnumbered 254].) Cf. *Othello*, II, i, 13–15; *The great Beare*, etc. (316.14–17): 'Nigh vnto . . . [the lesser Beare] is the greater Beare, called Vrsa maior, contayninge 27 starres, wherof 7 are moste notable, and are in latine named Plaustrum, and in english Charles waine, which serueth also well in sailynge.' (Recorde, 263); *Which Beares the Dragon*, etc. (316.18): 'Draco that lyeth betwyxt both.' (Proclus, F2r). 'Aboute these 2 Beares is there a longe trace of 31 starres, cōmonly called the Dragon.' (Recorde, 263); *Bootes* (316.19): '. . . whome Proclus and others doo name Arctophylax [or the Ploughman]. and it hath 22 starres, beside one very bryght starre called Arcturus, which standeth betweene Bootes legges.' (Recorde, 263f.); *North Crowne* (316.19): Corona borealis. 'By Arctophylax ryghte hande, is the northe Croune, called also Ariadnes Croune, and hath in it 8 starres.' (Recorde, 264); *knelynge Hercules* (316.20): 'Then foloweth Hercules, whom the greekes doo call Engonasin [as does Salisbury's Proclus], as it were the Kneeler, bicause of his gesture: and it containeth 28 starres.' (Recorde, 264); *Harpe, falling gryp* (316.22): 'By . . . [Hercules'] lefte hande, is there an other constellation, whiche is called the Harpe, in latine Lyra and Fidicula. and also Vultur cadens, that is the fallynge Grype, it comprehendeth 10 starres.' (Recorde, 264); *goate* (316.22): 'The cleare Starre that is set in the lefte shoulder of the Dryuer is called the Goote.' (Proclus, F2v); 'Then followeth Erichthonius, with the Goat and the 2 Kyddes, this constellation is also named Auriga the Cartar ["he That vse to dryue the cart," 316.22f.]: and cōtaineth 14 starres with one in his right foote, which is common to Taurus also.' (Recorde, 264); *swan* (316.22): 'By . . . [the Harpe] is the Swanne, named Cygnus, and Auis . . . it consisteth of 17 starres.' (Recorde, 264); *The man that dothe the serpent*, etc. (316.24): 'An other constellation is there which ioyneth heade to heade with Hercules, and is called of the Greekes, Ophiucus, and of the latines Serpentarius, that is the manne with the Serpente, or Serpent bearer: and it hathe 24 starres.' (Recorde, 264); *Egle* (316.25): 'By . . . [the Darte] towarde the southe, is the Egle, includynge 9 starres: hee is called not onlye Aquila in latine, but also Vultur volans, and in greeke Aetos.' (Recorde, 264); *dart* (316.25): 'Then is there an other small constellation of 5 starres, a lytle southe of the swannes heade, and it is named the Darte, Sagitta or Telum in latine, and in greke Oistos.' (Recorde, 264); *Dolphin* (316.26): Delphinus. 'A lyttle from . . . [Antinous] is the Dolphine, whiche hath in it 10 starres.' (Recorde, 264); *forehors* (316.26): Equuelus; 'Protome Hippi.' (Proclus, F2r) 'Then [after the Dolphin] foloweth the Forehorse, noted with 4 darke starres.' (Recorde, 264); *thother hors that flyes*, etc. (316.26–7): 'Harde by . . . [the Forehorse] is the Flying horse, named Pegasus: and doth consiste of 20 starres.' (Recorde, 265). The story of Bellerophon who, attempting to rise up to heaven, was thrown by his winged horse Pegasus, made furious by a gad fly which Zeus had sent, was doubtless familiar enough. It is interesting to discover, however, that the mythologer Hyginus, whose *Fabularum Liber* has been noted previously in connection with Hall (305.17n.), gives that story in his *Poeticon Astronomicon*, II, 18. Book II (of four books): *De Signorum Coelestium Historiis*, relates the legends connected with 41 of the principal constellations. Book IV, which ends abruptly, *De quinque Circulorum inter Corpora Coelestia Notatione, et Planetis*, treats of the circles of the celestial sphere, of the constellations appertaining to each, of their risings and settings (cf. Hall, 316.6–9n., 332.7–333.5n.), of the course of the sun and moon, and of the appearance of the planets. The *Poeticon Astronomicon* was first printed at Ferrara in 1475. Now it is remarkable that Hyginus, Proclus, and Aratus were all available to Hall in a single volume (Basle, 1535), which included also the *Fabularum liber* of Hyginus; the grammarian Palaephatus's *de fabulosis narrationibus*, a brief account of various Greek legends; the *Mythologiarum* (in three books) of Fulgentius, an ignorant rationalizing of Greek legends; and an 'Index rerum & fabularum.' Thus could the sixteenth-century reader find, within the covers of one book, all that he needed of mythology and astronomy; *tryangle* (316.28): 'By . . . [Andromeda's] lefte foot is ther a small constellation of 4 starres, which is commonly called the Triangle, and in latine Triangulus, but the greekes name it after one of their letters Delta and Deltoton.' (Recorde, 265); *Andromede* (316.28): 'Vnto . . . [Pegasus] ioyneth Andromeda, so that hyr headde lyeth on the nauell of Pegasus, and one starre is common to them both. This constellation dothe containe 23 starres.' (Recorde, 265); *The Bulls eye*, etc. (317.6–29): Hall passes now to a description of parts of constellations (asterisms), and individual stars in constellations, in the Zodiac. Cf. Proclus, F1r, 'In whiche .xii. beastes [of ẙ Zodiak] there ar certayne starres, who for certayne notable markes espyed in them, haue taken theyr proper names'; *Hyades* (317–7): 'Then Taurus whiche is adorned with 33 starres, wherof 5 be in his forhead and face, and are called of the Greekes Hyades, and of the latines Succule: amongest whiche, one is more notable then all the reste, and is called Oculus Tauri, the Bulles eye.' (Recorde, 265) 'The starres that be placed in the head of Taurus be .v. in nombre and are called Hyades.' (Proculs, F1r–v); *broode henne*, etc. (317.8–9): 'The fyxed starres that be in the backe of Taurus be called Pleiades.' (Proclus, F1r) 'Other 6 starres (as Proclus numbreth them, though other accompt them 7) ar in the backe of this signe, and be called Vergiliae in Latin, and in Greeke Pleiades, and also Atlantides: they are named in englysh the brood Henne, and the Seuen starres.' (Recorde, 265); *Manger* (317.10): 'That Cloudelyke substaunce, that is in Cancer, is called Prasepe [margin: The Crybbe].' (Proclus, F1v) 'Manger or Crybbe.' (Recorde, 266); *Asses twayne* (317.10): 'The two Starres that stande nygh Presepe ar called Asini.' (Proclus, F1v) 'Other two starres are called the Asses whiche seeme to stande at the Crybbe.' (Recorde, 266); *The Lyons hart, and tayle* (317.11): 'The bryght starre that is in the hert of Leo, (accordyng to the name of his place) is the Lyons herte, and it is called of some men, the Royall Starre, for that they that are borne vnder it, are thought to haue a royall natiuitie.' (Proclus, F1v) 'Then the Lion is nexte [after the Asses], as a princely signe, in whome are 27 starres, but two of them more notable then the reste: the one is in the tayle, and therefore is called Cauda Leonis, the other in the brest . . . and also the Lions harte, Cor Leonis in Latin, and

Basiliscos in greke.' (Recorde, 266); *virgins spyke* (317.12): 'The fayre
Starre that stycketh at fyngers endes of the left hande of Virgo, is called
the Spike.' (Proclus, F1v) 'Nexte after Leo, cometh Virgo, garnished with
26 starres, but one especially glystereth aboue the reste, and is called
Spica Virginis, the Virgins spike.' (Recorde, 266); *scorpyons harte* (317.12):
'Scorpius with his hooked tayle, and with his clawes doth reache as farre,
that two full signes he taketh in length and 30 degrees almost in bredth,
yet hath he but 21 starres beside those whiche bee in his clawes, and are
common to them & to Libra: amongest all which the principall is that,
which is called the Scorpions harte, and is named of the Greekes Antares.'
(Recorde, 266); *Water potte* (317.13): 'The .iiii. starres that be at the ryght
handes ende of Aquarius, are called Vrna [margin: The water pot].'
(Proclus, F1v) 'Aquarius . . . hath in him 22 starres peculiare to him
selfe, althoughe Proclus name 4 of them in hys ryghte arme, to be the
Water potte.' (Recorde, 267); *Whale, Oryon*, etc. (317.14-29): Hall now
turns to the Southern constellation. Cf. Proclus, F2v-3r: 'And all those
be Southerne Sygnes, that lye on the South syde of the zodiake. And theyr
names be these'; *Whale* (317.14): Cetus. 'Fyrste appeareth the great
Whale, contayning 22 starres.' (Recorde, 267); *Oryon . . . Golden yarde
. . . Elle* (317.14-15): 'Nexte foloweth Orion, the Stormy signe, and hath
diuers starres to the numbre of 38: but the moste notable are 6. . . .
Other thre stande as bullions set in his gyrdle, and are called of manye
englyshe men the Golden yarde.' (Recorde, 267f.); *ryuer* (317.16):
Eridanus. 'The floude of Orion.' (Proclus, F3r) 'Betweene Orion and
the Whale is there a great tract of starres, whiche represent the forme of
a Riuer: and therefore are they called the Ryuer. whiche some more
peculiarly name Eridanus, and other Nilus. Proclus calleth it Orions
ryuer, bicause it beginneth at his lefte foote and hath one starre in
common with his foote, but beside that it hathe 34 starres: wherof the
laste is one of the greatest lyght.' (Recorde, 268); *hare* (317.16): Lepus.
'By the beginninge of this Ryuer, vnder the feete of Orion is there a constellation of 12 starres, named the Hare.' (Recorde, 268); *bothe the
dogges* (317.16): Canis major and minor. 'And after . . . [the Hare]
toward the easte is the greater Dogge, (of whō the Caniculare daies bear
name) and is called of the grekes Sirius, and of the Latines Canis, hauing
18 starres, but one especially in bryghtnes more notable than anye of
the rest, and that is in his mouthe, and is called peculiarlye Sirius and
Canis, by the name of the whole Signe. . . . Northe almost from this
Dogge is ther a constellation of 2 only starres named Canicula, the lesser
Dogge: and in greeke Procyon, therefore dogge, whō Tully therfore
calleth Antecanis, and other name him Precanis.' (Recorde, 268); *serpent
of the southe* (317.18): 'Nexte after this ship [Argo] ther foloweth the
great Serpent whiche is called of the grekes and latines Hydra. it containeth 25 starres, and stretcheth in great lengthe by the space of 3
whole signes.' (Recorde, 269); *Cuppe* (317.18): Crater. 'On this Hydre
there resteth other 2 small constellations, the one named the Cuppe, and
the other the Rauen. The Cuppe includeth seuen starres all of one
bygnes. This Cuppe standeth on the Hydres backe, almoste in the myddle
of him.' (Recorde, 269); *Rauen* (317.19): Corvus. 'The Rauen standeth
on the same Hydre, more nearer towarde the pointe of his tayle: and it
is formed of 7 starres also.' (Recorde, 270); *Centaure . . . Centaures speare*
(317.19-20): 'Vnder the taile of this Hydre and those twoo other small
constellations, there standeth the centaure Chiron, lyke a lyghte horseman

with his chasinge staffe: he hath in him 37 starres, whereof 4 be in the garnishe or pensile of his spear, and them doth Proclus reckon as a peculiare constellation [as does Hall, who followed Proclus, then, and not Recorde], and nameth it in greeke Thyrsolochus.' (Recorde, 270); *wolfe* (317.20) Lupus: 'The beaste that Centaurus holdeth in his hande.' (Proclus, F3r) 'This Centaure with his righte hande dooth holde a Wolfe, whiche is a seuerall constellation made of 19 starres, althoughe Hyginus and others doo recked fewer in him.' (Recorde, 270); *altare* (317.21): Ara. 'Vnder that beaste [the Wolf] towarde the southe, harde vnder the Scorpions tayle, standeth the Altar, made of 7 starres, of the meanest lyght: but it is not seene in England aboue the Horizont.' (Recorde, 270); *South crowne* (317.22): Corona australis. 'By this Altar eastwarde betweene the two former feete of Sagittarye, there is the Croune of the southe, formed of 13 small starres . . . it riseth not aboue our horizont, but only toucheth it.' (Recorde, 270f.); *Tricars Constellation, Or Berenices heare* (317.24–25): 'Betweene the Lions taile and Vrsa maior . . . is . . . Berenices heare, some call it in latine Trica, and other Berenices crines. . . . The starres in it are 7. . . . Ptolemye . . . doth not accompte anye starre of Berenices heare, but called it the Traces of heare.' (Recorde, 271); *The shyppe that Argo poetes do name* (317.26): Poets like Aratus, in the *Phaenomena*, ll. 342, 348, 504, 604, 610, 686; Homer, in the *Odyssey*, XII, 69ff.; Apollodorus, in the *Bibliotheca*, I.9.16–27; and Hyginus, in the *Fabularum liber*, *passim*. 'At the tayle of the greater Dogge is the famous shippe Argo, whiche comprehendeth 45 starres, wherof 9 bee bewtifull but one in especiall which is in the foote of the roother [rudder] & is called Canopus. . . . This star is not seen in Englãd.' (Recorde, 268); *ascensions, Bothe oblique and ryght* (318.2–3): 'Ascension . . . doothe betoken the risinge of anye starres or signes (what so euer they be) aboue the Horizont.' (Recorde, 194). 'Horizon is a great circle that divideth the part of the sky that we see from that we see not. . . . All horizon is right or oblique. They have right horizon that habiteth under the equinoctial [p. 123: In the concave of the first mobile . . . be the two circles . . . the one . . . equinoctial, and the other . . . the zodiac. And these two circles divideth the one and the other equally, but not straight, for the zodiac crosseth crookedly and the places where it crosseth be said equinoctials.] and have their zenith [the point of the sky right over our heads] in the equinoctial for their horizon intersecteth and divideth the equinoctial . . . but they that habiteth other where than under the equinoctial all have their horizon oblique, for their horizon followeth and divideth the equinoctial all sideways, and not right.' Now (p. 127) 'our horizon is oblique and divideth the zodiac in two parts, whereof one is ever over our horizon and the other underneath . . . thus the zodiac riseth not regularly in these parts as the equinoctial [but obliquely].' (*The Kalendar & Compost of Shepherds*, p. 125).

319.8   *Theologus:* In Arthur Dent's *Plain Man's Pathway to Heaven*, the preacher, Theologus, takes part in a dialogue in which *The Court of Venus* and other 'vaine and frivolous bookes' are condemned (edn. of 1601, 2D5v–6r).

321.6–322.9   *And Vranie hath it forsoke*, etc.: *naturall Astronomie* (321.8), like *Phisyke* (321.10) or natural science, is a legitimate discipline (cf. 311.24–28n.), as opposed to *Astrologye Iudiciall* (321.18), defined and reprehended by Agrippa (1569), M8v–N1r. Despite the equivocal reputation of astrology, *some learned men* (321.22) devote themselves to it, like Dr. John Dee, in his younger days. Cf. Agrippa, O1r: 'And notwithstanding to these accursed trifles, & moste damnable opinions not without infamie of Heresie haue subscribed *Peter of Appona, Roger Bacon, Guido, Bonatus, Arnolde of Villa noua Philosophers,* the *Cardinal of Alia* a diuine, and many other Doctours of christian name.' Agrippa glosses also those kindred arts, each of them 'inhibited and out of warrant,' which Hall attacks in *A Visyon.* Thus, *Necromancye* (321.27): 'The partes of ceremoniall Magicke be *Geocie,* and *Theurgie. Geocie* is grounded vpon the entercours of wicked sprites made with the rites of detestable curiositie, with vnleful coniurations, and with defensiue prayers, bannished & accursed by the decrees of all lawes. Of this kinde be they, whiche at this daie we call Necromancers and En-chaunters. . . . These then be they whiche doe inuocate deade mennes soules . . . that inchaunted childerne, and caused them to speake oracles, and whiche beare about counsaylinge or helpinge sprites . . . and . . . feede sprites in glasses, by whom they auaunte to prophecie. And all these doo proceede in twoo manner of wayes. For some do endeuoure to coniure, and binde the deuill of hell. . . . Some other . . . submittinge themselues to sprites do Sacrifice to them and woorshippe them.' (Agrippa, Q1v–2r); *Geomancye* (321.29) is the art of divination by means of signs derived from the earth, as by the figure assumed by a handful of earth thrown down upon some surface. Hence, usually, divination by means of lines or figures formed by jotting down on paper a number of dots at random. Cf. Agrippa, H1v–2r, *'Arithmeticke* hathe brought foorthe the *Geomantical* Diuination. . . . Albeit, al for the moste parte doo attribute *Geomancie* to *Astrologie,* for the like manner of iudgemente, and also because they gette the vertue thereof, not so muche out of Numbers, as out of Mouinges.' *'Geomancie* . . . whiche castinge certaine poinctes made by chaunce, or by a certaine force, of the whiche by certaine equall and vnequall numbers: facioneth certaine figures attributed to the heauenly signes, by whiche they Diuine. There is also an other kinde of *Geomancie,* whiche *Almadal* the Arabian introduced and brought in, the which doth diuine by certaine coniectures taken of similitudes of the crakinge of the Earthe, of the mouinge, cleauinge, swellinge, either of it selfe, or els of inflamation & heate, or of thundringes, that happen, the whiche also is grounded vpon vaine superstition of Astrologie, as that which obserueth howers, the newe Moones, the risinge and forme of the starres.' (O3v) ; *Magikes artes* (322.3), natural, mathematical, and witching, are treated also by Agrippa, P2v–Q1r; as is *Augures arte* (322.3): 'Augures . . . were they that taught, that certaine lightes of diuination did descende from the heauenly bodies vpon all these inferiour liuinge thinges, as certaine signes and tokens placed in their mouinge, standinge, gesture, goinge, fleeing, voice, meate, colour, worke, and ende, naturally ingendred in them as it were by a certaine hidden force, and secreate consent & doo in such sort agree with the heauenly bodies by whose force they be moued, that they can after foretell al these thinges, what soeuer the Heauenly bodies haue intended to do.' (O3v–4r) ; The distinction between *Aruspices* (322.4) and *Pyrethi* (322.5) is not clear. The former, Agrippa defines as *a kinde of soothsaying.* (O3v) ; For the latter, cf. *Pythoni,* that is, soothsayers, oracles; *wytchecrafte* (322.6) is given a chapter by Agrippa, 'Of Witchinge Magicke. Cap. 44,' P4r–Q1r: 'Witchinge . . . is done with pocions, charmed drinckes for loue, and diuers poysoninge medicins suche a one as *Democritus* is reade to haue made, whereby happy and fortunate childerne maye be begotten, and an other whereby we maie well vnderstand the voices of birdes, as *Philostratus* and *Porphyrius* do recompte of *Apollonius.*' (P4r) ; By *phytonicus*

(322.7) is meant, presumably, phitonists, that is, soothsayers, conjurers (*O.E.D.* first cites in 1584), as opposed to *Philonicus* (322.9): (?1) artist. C. Cornelius Philonicus was a Roman artist in silver, M. Canuleius Philonicus a maker of little figures of genii. (2) followers of the Jewish philosopher Philo (Philo Judaeus, born *c.* 25 B.C.), who flourished at Alexandria about the beginning of the Christian era. Philo preached denial of the flesh, and accepted the belief in the power of the heavenly bodies as an inferior degree of wisdom. He exerted a profound influence on early Christianity, an influence still felt in the Renaissance, when his writings were widely current. See, for example, *Philonis Iudaei Alexandrini,* (*Cuius Doctrinae & orationis sublimitatem grauissimi autores etiam ipsi diuino Platoni aequarūt) omnes quae apud Graecos & Latinos extant, libri . . . Basileae* [1538].

325.18–20 *For why one heare*, etc.: cf. Matthew, x. 30, Luke, xii. 7, xxi. 18.

326.2–5 *As dyd kyng Saule*, etc.. : cf. I Samuel, xxviii. 7–25.

326.22 *on prudent Salomon :* For the fathering of witchcraft on Solomon, cf. Agrippa, Q2r: 'At this daye also there are bookes [of darkenes] caried aboute with fayned titles vnder the names of *Adam, Abel, Enoch, Abraham,* Salamon.' 'Naturall Magicke, wherein wee beleue that Kinge *Salomon* was verie excellente.' (Q4r). '*Salomon* was very wel learned in this science [of Cabala], and there by wrote an Arte againste Deuiles, shewinge the manner to binde them, & coniure them, and charmes also against diseases, as *Iosephus* testifieth.' (R1r).

326.26–29 *for why saint Iohn,* etc.: cf. Revelation, xxi. 10.

327.28 *Let learned Caluine satisfie :* in *An Admonicion against Astrology Iudiciall and other curiosities, that raigne now in the world : written in the french tonge by Ihon Caluine and translated into Englishe, by G. G[ylby],* 1561.

328.2–3 *Astronomy . . . is nowe the cloke:* 'The shameles deceiuers which wold vnder y̆ cloke of the science haue gone furder haue counterfeicted an other kynd whych they call Iudicialle [Astrologie].' (Calvin, B1r: almost certainly the direct source of Hall's attack.)

328.22–23 *Palmestry, Or Chyromancies gaude: 'Of Chiromancie or Palmestrie. Cap. 35. Chiromancie* dothe facion in the palme of the hande seuen mountaines, accordinge to the number of the planetes: and supposeth that shee is able to knowe, by the lines, which be there seene, what complexion a mā is of, his dispositions, his life, and fortune, by a certayne harmonicall agreemente of the lines, as by certaine celestial markes imprinted in vs there by God and nature, which God, as *Iob* writeth, hath set in mens handes, that thereby euery man may knowe his workes.' (Agrippa, O2v).

328.24 *And foolysh Physiognomye :* 'Phisiognomie therefore folowing the nature of these Artes [of Diuination] as guide (as shee saithe) doth presume that shee is able to finde out with probable signes, by vewing of the whole bodie, the dispositions of the minde & body, what mans fortune is, according to that she pronounceth this man a *Saturniste,* or *Iouialist,* that man a *Martialiste,* or *Solist,* an other, a *Venerean,* a *Mercurialist,* or *Lunist,* & by the forme and state of the bodie doth finde out their ascendentes passing by little and little (as they saye) from the effecte to Astrological causes, by the which she after warde dalieth vpon whatsoeuer she listeth.' (Agrippa, O2v).

329.2–9 *For Bedlem baudes,* etc.: With Hall's attack on whoring, winked at by the law, cf. Nashe, *Christs Teares Ouer Ierusalem* (1593), V1r–X1r, '*London,* what are thy Suburbes but licensed stewes. Can it be so many brothelhouses, of salary sensuality, & sixe-penny whoredome, (the next doore to the Magistrates) should be sette vp and maintained, if brybes dyd not bestirre them?'

330.11   *Ferdinand Ponzetus:* Ferdinand Cardinal Ponzetti was Bishop of Grosseto in Tuscany in 1522: 'a learned man but fond of wealth.' His *Libellus de venenis* [drugs] was published at Rome in 1521 and 1562, and the *Tertia pars naturalis phӱe* at Rome in 1515. James, *Bod. Cat.*, p. 400, contains the entry: 'Ferd. *Ponzettus* De venenis, Bas 1562.'

330.12–13   *Artemidor . . . Daldianus:* Artemidorus Daldianus of Ephesus, a professional interpreter of dreams, lived at Rome in the reign of Antoninus Pius and Marcus Aurelius. His chief work, the *Onirocritica*, was first published at Venice in 1518. Editions of the *De somniorum interpretatione* appeared frequently throughout the century (Basle, 1539, 1544, 1546, etc.). Translated into English by Robert Wood, it went through at least twenty-five editions, continuing in popularity to the nineteenth century. See also Agrippa, who devotes a chapter (39) to the interpretation of dreams: '*Baldian* and *Arthemidore* have written of the interpretation of dreames.' (P1r).

332.7–333.5   *A Ditie declaryng the risyng and setting*, etc.: cf. *The Kalendar & Compost of Shepherds*, p. 127, 'Zodiac . . . whereon the Signs be, riseth and resconseth ['to sconce' is 'to hide,' 1663] all on a day natural [as does the rest of the sky turn in its daily moving or diurnal from east to west] . . . our horizon divideth the zodiac in two parts, whereof one is ever over our horizon and the other underneath. Thus half of the Signs riseth over ou.' horizon everyday . . . and the other half by night.' When Aries the Ram, first of the twelve signs, has gone halfway about the heavens and is ready to rise above our horizon in the east, Libra the Scales or Balance, the opposite or contrary of Aries since it is number seven among the signs and thus half the zodiac away, must perforce be ready to fall below our horizon in the west. So, too, with the other ten signs.

336.2–339.17   *An other Ditie*, etc.: ?deriving from secular verse; cf., for example, 'During of payne and greuous smart,' a poem in the manner of Wyatt (*The Court of Venus*, p. 125).

339.18–21   *A ditie to be sung*, etc.: Hall's inspiration is Henry's *Primer*, 1545: 'A praier in the mornyng' (2C2); 'A prayer at your vprising' (2C2v).

341.19–20   *A ditie to be sung at nyght*, etc.: cf. Henry's *Primer*, 1545: 'A prayer before ye go to bed' (2C3).

341.21–22   *In sommer time*, etc.: cf. 160.8–164.26n.

343.2–3   *A ditie to be sung at dyner*, etc.: cf. Henry's *Primer*, 1545: 'Grace before dyner'; 'Grace after diner'; 'Grace before supper'; 'Grace after supper' (***3v–4r).

344.14–21   *And may be to that dogge*, etc.: Aesop's fable of the dog in the manger. Cf. the eleventh fable 'of the enuyous dogge' (m1r) in 'the book of the subtyl historyes and Fables of Esope whiche were translated out of Frensshe in to Englysshe by wylliam Caxton at westmynstre . . . M.CCCC. lxxxiii. [error for 1484].' Actually, these fables are a medieval compilation by Planudes from sources having no special connection with Aesop. Even in Elizabethan times the story may have been so common that one need not have read it. Aesop was, however, used in the schools. Cf. T. W. Baldwin, *William Shakspere's Petty School* (Urbana, Illinois, 1943), p. 84. James, *Bod. Cat.*, 1620, lists copies of Aesop ranging in date from 1490 to 1606. Editions of Aesop cover five pages in *List of English Editions and Translations of Greek and Latin Classics Printed Before 1641*, Henrietta R. Palmer (London, 1911), pp. 3–7.

345.6   *An other to the same*, etc.: cf. 343.2–3n.

347.2   *An other grace:* cf. 343.2–3n.

347.24–26   *A sonnet inueyinge*, etc.: Hall parodies the language of secular verse.

348.10–350.5   *In Esay the prophete:* Stubbes also, reviling woman's dress in *The Anatomie of Abuses*, 1585 (G1r–v), draws on the third chapter of Isaiah. The dress of a citizen's wife *c.* 1570 was composed of a jacket-shaped bodice over a partlet or neckerchief of linen headed by a small ruff, together with a kirtled skirt, often looped up to show another coloured petticoat (*Sh. Eng.*, II, 110). Cf. 352.22. Moralists like Hall objected, not only to the ornateness of costume and accoutrement (headbands, spangles, buckles), but to the desire of women to *paynt out them selues* (350.5): Face-painting, common among Elizabethan women and especially at court, was attacked by Nashe, Harrison, Stubbes, Stow, and Gosson. Cf. Nashe, *Christs Teares*, S3r–v, 'Lay not on your colours so thick, that they sincke into your soules. That your skinnes being too white without, your soules not be al black within.' Cf. also Stubbes, *Anatomi? of Abuses*, E8r, 'The Women of *Ailgna* (many of them) vse to colour their faces with certaine *Oyles, Liquors, Vnguentes*, and Waters.' (F1r–2r continues the attack).

350.10   *curlyng theyr hear:* Women's hair, from about 1560 until the end of the century, was worn curled and taken back from the forehead, dressed over a pad. Cf. Nashe, *Christs Teares*, S3r, 'Theyr heads, with theyr . . . Snow-resembled siluer curlings, they make a playne Puppet stage of.' Cf. also Stubbes, *Anatomie*, F2r, 'Then followeth the trimming and tricking of their heades, in laying out their haire to the shewe, frisled and crisped, laid out (a world to see) on wreathes and borders, from one eare to an other.'

350.18–21   *And some to be small*, etc.: The upper part of the figure was squeezed into a long stiff-pointed bodice, called the doublet both in men's and women's attire, stiffened with wood, steel, or whalebone, the lower part of the stomacher reaching below the level of the hips (*Sh. Eng.*, II, 95). Cf. *Pleasant Quippes for Vpstart Newfangled Gentlewomen*, London, 1596 (reference here is to a reprint, without date or place), p. 8: 'These priuie coates, by art made strong / with bones, with past, with such like ware, / Whereby their backe and sides grow long, / and now they harnest gallants are / . . . they doe only stay / the course that nature did intend, / And mothers often by them slay / their daughters yoong, and worke their end.'

350.23–25   *Theyr froks must haue buttocks*, etc.: During the latter part of the century the farthingale became enormously enlarged at the hips, the circumference there being as wide as at the hem. Farthingales were also made in semi-circular form, confined to the back of the skirt; hence the huge buttocks Hall mentions (*Sh. Eng.*, II, 95). Cf. Robert Crowley, *Epigram of Nice Rogues*, 1550 (in Morse, *Elizabethan Pageantry*, p. 112): 'A bombe lyke a barrell, with whoopes at the skyrte'; Thomas Lodge, *Wits Miserie*, 1596, C4r: 'There are boulsters likewise for the buttocks as wel as the breast, and why forsooth? The smaller in the wast, the better handled'; *Pleasant Quippes*, p. 9: 'These hoopes, that hippes and haunch do hide, / and heaue aloft the gay hoyst traine.'

351.2–5   *For women and maydens syt*, etc.: cf. Stubbs, *Anatomie*, G8r–v: 'Other some [women] spende the greatest parte of the daie, in sitting at the doore, to shewe their braueries, to make knowne their beauties, to behold the passengers by, to viewe the coast, to see fashions, & to acquaynt themselues with the brauest fellowes, for if not for these causes, I see no other causes why they shoulde sit at theyr doores, from Morning till

Noone (as many doe) from Noone to Night, thus vainely spending their
golden dayes in filthie idlenesse and sin.'

351.16–23   *When I was a boy*, etc.: 'Excessive exposure of the breast was peculiar
to England at this time; in a portrait of Lady Seymour of Trowbridge,
existing at Petworth, no concealment of it is attempted; portraits of
other noble ladies show that the taste was general, and divines devoted
many discourses to the obtrusive immodesty of women.' (*Sh. Eng.*, II, 94).
Cf. Nashe, *Christs Teares*, S3r: 'Theyr breasts they embuske vpon hie,
and theyr round Roseate buds immodestly lay foorth, to shew at theyr
handes there is fruite to be hoped'; *Pleasant Quippes*, p. 6: 'These naked
paps, the Deuils ginnes, / to worke vaine gazers painful thrall.'

351.25   *thei laid down their hear*, etc.: cf. Nashe, *Christs Teares*, S3r: 'Euen as Angels
are painted in Church-windowes, with glorious golden fronts, besette
with Sunne-beames, so beset they theyr fore-heads on eyther side, with
glorious borrowed gleamy bushes.'

351.28–352.11   *And this varietie of Englyshe*, etc.: Portia's satirical comment on the
borrowed attire of the Englishman echoes Hall (*MV*, I, ii, 79–82). Cf.
Stubbes, *Anatomie*, G7r: 'Our new fangles and toies are occasions why
all nations mocke and floute vs'; G8r: 'Thus be this people a laughing
stocke to all the worlde.'

352.18–353.5   *But change of proude rayment*, etc.: The farthingale (*vardygue*, 352.21),
with the ruff, became the principal characteristic of female dress during
the later Tudor period. A round petticoat made of canvas distended with
whalebone, cane hoops, or steel strips, it was covered with taffeta or other
material, the brocade, cloth, or velvet skirts being worn over it. (*Sh. Eng.*
II, 94f.). Cf. Florio's Montaigne (in Morse, p. 39): 'They make trunk
sleeues of wyre, and whalebone bodies, backes of lathes, and stiffe
bumbasted verdugals [the farthingale was invented by a Spanish princess
and called a *verdugado*: fitted with rods or sticks] and, to the open view
of all men, paint and embellish themselues with counterfeit and borrowed
beauties.'

Other articles of dress in Hall's indictment attracted the censure of his
contemporaries. For the *kyrtell* (352.22), cf. Stubbes, *Anatomie*, F7v: 'But
whiche is more vayne ... yet must they haue *kirtles* (for so they call
them) either of Silke, Veluett, Grograine, Taffatie, Satten, or Scarlet,
bordered with gardes, lace, fringe, and I cannot tell what besides'; The
gowne (352.22) also incurred the ire of Stubbes. Cf. *Anatomie*, F7r: 'Their
gownes be no lesse famous then the rest, for some are of Silke, some of
Veluet, some of Grograine, some of Taffatie, some of Scarlet, and some of
fine clothe, of x.xx. or xl. shillinges a yarde. But if y̆ whole gowne be not
Silke or Veluet, then the same shall be layed with lace, two or three fingers
broade, all ouer the gowne, or els the most parte. Or if not, so (as lace is
not fine enough sometimes) then it must be garded with great gardes of
Veluet, euery gard fower or sixe fingers broad at the least, and edged
with costly lace, and as these gownes be of diuers and sondry colours, so
are they of diuers fashions, chaunging with the *Moone*: for some be of the
new fashion, some of the olde, some of thys fashion, and some of that,
some with sleeues hanging downe to their skirtes trailing on the ground,
and cast ouer their shoulders, like Cowe tailes'; Included in Hall's
arraignment are *furred cap* ... *veluet cap* ... [and] *frenche hoode* (352.23–4).
A popular form of female head-dress was the coif, a tight-fitting cap
following the shape of the head. Fur was comparatively common for
trimming, but Hall's point is doubtless to the sumptuary laws prohibiting

its use by any below a knight or a dame. Cf. Stubbes, *Anatomie*, F3r–v: 'On toppes of these stately turrets (I meane their goodly heades . . .) stand their other capitall ornaments, as French-hood [a close-fitting bonnet, sometimes having a flat band of material laid from front to back and either trailing down the back or thrown over the head. Mary Stuart wore a french hood.], Hatte, Cappe, Kercher, & such like, whereof some be of Veluet. . . . And to suche excesse it is growne, as euery Artificers wife (almost) will not sticke to goe in her Hat of Veluet euery day, euery Merchants wife, and meane Gentlewomen, in her French-hoode'; Though the *cheyne* (352.26) is criticized, most citizens wore chains; those of ladies were of stones or pearls. (*Sh. Eng.*, II, 115); The use of *lace* (352.26) was also conventional. Cf. Stubbes, *Anatomie*, F4v–5r: Women 'are either clogged with gold, siluer, or silke lace of stately price, wrought all ouer with needle worke, spreckeled and sparkeled here and there with the Sunne, the Mone, the Starres, and many other antiques strange to beholde. Some are wrought with open worke . . . some with close woorke, some wyth purled lace'; Hall's reference to *gaudes* (353.5) is amplified by Stubbes, F2v: 'At their haire thus wreathed and creasted, are hanged *bugles* (I dare not say, *bables*) *Ouches, Rynges, Gold, Siluer, Glasses*, and suche other childishe gewgawes, and foolish trinkets besides.'

353.11–12   *The poore mans cause*, etc.: cf. Lodge, *Wits Miserie*, C3v: 'The almes that was wont to releeue the poore, is husbanded better to buy new Rebatoes.'

353.14–17   *A lowte with a lorde*, etc.: cf. Nashe, *Christs Teares*, K4r: 'From the rich to the poore (in euery street in *London*) there is ambition, or swelling aboue theyr states: the rich Cittizen swells against the pryde of the prodigall Courtier.' *Ergo*, L2r: '*London* looke to Ambition, or it will lay thee desolate like *Ierusalem*.'

353.20–21   *For by theyr apparell*, etc.: cf. Nashe, *Christs Teares*, T1v: '*England* . . . Scandalous and shamefull is it, that not anie in thee, (Fishermen & Husbandmen set aside) but lyue aboue their ability and birth; That the outward habite, which in other Countries is the only distinction of honour, shoulde yeelde in thee no difference of persons.' T2r: 'Those of thy people that in all other things are miserable, in their apparraile will be prodigal. No Lande can so vnfallibly experience this Prouerbe, *The hoode makes not the Moncke*, as thou: for Tailers, Seruing-men, Make-shifts and Gentlemen, in thee are confounded.' Cf. also Stubbes, *Anatomie*, C3v–4r: 'It is very harde to know, who is noble, who is worshipfull, who is a gentleman who is not: for you shal haue those, which are neither of the nobilite, gentilitie, nor yeomanrie, no, nor yet any Magistrate or officer in the common wealth, go daiely in silkes, Veluettes, Satens, Damaskes, Taffaties, and suche like: notwithstandyng, that they be bothe base by birthe, meane by estate, and seruile by callyng.'

353.22–23   *Eche lasse lyke a lady*, etc.: Silks and velvets came from Italy and France and were very costly. They were not manufactured in England until about 1604. Only the wealthy and eminent (presumably) wore silk stockings. Elizabeth, for example, wore the first pair of black silk stockings in 1560. However (Stubbes, *Anatomie*, F7v): 'So farre hath this canker of Pride eaten into the body of the Common wealth, that euery poore Yeoman his daughter, euery Husbandman hys daughter, and euery Cottager his daughter, will not stick to flaunt it out, in such *Gownes*, *Petticoates* and *Kirtles* . . . wherby it commeth to passe, that one can scarsly know, who is a noble woman, who is an honourable, or worshipfull woman, from them of the meaner sorte.'

361.7–363.3   The music appearing on these three pages represents a substantial revision of Hall's original version, which is written in four distinct parts: Triplex, Contra tenor, Tenor, and Bassus. The six lines of verse accompanying this transcription are repeated in the original, and with differences in spelling, for each of the four parts. The verse given here derives from Hall's Triplex.

The Table and *Faultes escaped*, which fill six and a half pages between the end of the text and the colophon, have been omitted.

4. GLOSSARIAL INDEX

EACH appearance in the text of all obsolete or esoteric words and phrases is noted here, by page and line, together with variant spellings. Obvious words and phrases, like *Noe, Phebus, for why* and *for the nones*, are not glossed. *I* and *J* are treated as a single letter, as are *U* and *V*.

abowght: about, 105.14

accept: accepted, 329.28

accompt: judgment, 224.7

admiration: wonder, 328.16

aduoyde: avoid, 268.12

affectionat: to regard with affection (O.E.D. first cites *c.* 1590), 281.9

agnise: acknowledge, 65.7

all and some: everyone, 117.19, 159.25, 251.21

all to wrake: into misery, 147.25

almyght: almighty, 113.7

alow: below, 308.12

an: one, 348.4

anoy: injure, 176.21

any tyme whan: at any time, 282.12

apalle: enfeeble, 8.17

Araons: Aaron's, 77.14

arke: the part of a circle which a heavenly body appears to pass through above (diurnal) or below (nocturnal) the horizon, 271.6

aspects: the way in which the planets, from their relative positions, look upon each other, but popularly transferred to their joint look upon the earth, 317.4

at: of, from, 56.15; 325.14, 15, 28

at any sted: anywhere, 95.16

ato: a-twain, 139.17

attaynt: condemn, 237.10

attende: tend, 231.15

Ball: Earth, 332.22

Barach: Barak, deliverer of the Israelites from Jabin, king of Canaan (Judges, 4–5), 27.19

barators: cheats, tricksters, 324.12

beareth roome: enjoys authority (O.E.D. last cites 1534), 266.10

bears the bell: takes first place, 272.21

becomde: befitting (O.E.D. first cites 1592), 74.10

bee: been, 180.11

beforne: before, 144.16

behoue: behoof, 259.8

belkyng: belching (Hall's sense, 'to boil', 'throb', not cited O.E.D. before 1648), 279.23

bewraye: expose, 12.2

bewyle: ?to lead by cunning (from v. 'wile'); or 'bewayle' (beguile). O.E.D. does not allow this meaning, but cf. Spenser, *FQ*, I, vi, i, 'As when a ship. . . . An hidden rocke escaped hath unawares, That lay in waite her wrack for to be waile.'

blesse: blessing, 117.6

blynde bayard: one who acts without consideration or reflection. Bayard was a horse famous in old romances. Originally the name denoted a grey horse, and then became generic for blindness, ignorance, recklessness, 17.20

blynne: cease, 13.8

bod: bade, 122.27

boord: board (assail), 256.21

boote: greave, 233.14; advantage, 359.6

botham: bottom, 99.6

boune: boon (request), 119.26

brute: report ('this is the way the world goes'), 231.21; brutish, 277.13

byde: remain, 260.9

bydyng: ?abiding, 251.3

Bygorne: ?bighorn; boggart, buggard, a spectre or goblin (O.E.D. does not cite), 306.21

ca: ?here, 285.8

cantell: cantle (portion), 120.19

canuys: canvass, to thrash (O.E.D. first cites 1590), 266.31

carein: carrion (flesh), 252.23

cassocke: a loose outward coat, 352.20

cease: put a stop to (trans.), 132.11

cease of: desist, 150.11

Ceraphin: Seraphim, 115.9

cest: ceased, 213.8

Chaldey: Chaldean, 119.23

chance: mischance, 319.13

chere: mood, 231.24

clout: cloth, 350.17

clyp: embrace, 350.15

cobde: var. of 'gobbled' (O.E.D. does not cite before 1601), 320.3

cockbeld: ?var. of 'cock-brain' (silly), 301.16

company: accompany, 248.13

coumpted: accounted, 81.24

countes to cast: accounts to cast up, 159.18

cowlyckt: plastered with a lock of hair, greased, curled, and brought forward from the ear (Partridge; not in O.E.D.), 258.10

coyle: disturbance (O.E.D. first cites 1568), 301.13

crall: crawl, 312.3

cubike: unpolished, rough, by analogy with 'cub' (as sb.) in its figurative sense (O.E.D. first cites 1601); or the conventional meaning (which makes little sense), 'of the form of a cube.' King James Version reads 'hewn stone' (III Jer., ix), 147.15

cure: heed, 50.13; care, 213.27, 292.4

cyse: size, 137.5, 283.9, 304.7

dasse: ?daze, i.e., 'remain inactive' or, more simply, 'sit' (O.E.D. last cites 1529), 350.17

decte: decked, 6.9

decyse: decide, 235.7, 248.8

deface: put out of countenance, 300.13

defast: defaced, 322.16

degrees: applied in the natural philosophy of the Middle Ages to the successive stages of intensity of the elementary qualities of bodies: heat and cold, moisture and dryness, 49.14

depnes: depth, 158.14

depryue: dispossess, 271.7

detest: detested, 224.30

detract: draw out (O.E.D. first cites 1569), 277.25, 315.26

did on: put on, 134.8

did why: gave cause, 234.13

difficill: difficult, 328.20

discent: dissent, 280.21

discusse, discust: make (made) known, 38.29, 349.20

doe: give, 11.11

dome, doome: judgment, 103.28, 200.5, 216.5

domifye: to divide the heavens into twelve equal parts or houses by means of great circles; to locate the planets in their respective houses, 295.25

dout: dread, 198.7

dryth: dry weather (O.E.D. first cites 1571), 232.10

dure: hard, 120.9

dyd: gave, 224.25

earst: erst, at first, 333.27

eche deale: every whit, 326.29

eche tyme and when: ?in every time ('when' is 'time'; O.E.D. first cites 1616), 119.10

Elias: Elijah, 30.3

endue: endow, 11.22; invest with honour, 223.19; instruct, 244.28

Enoch: who walked with God, and who, after 365 years, 'was not; for God took him,' 23.26

ensue, insue: follow, 4.25, 11.24, 24.17, 131.8, 175.23, 192.2, 239.27, 244.29, 248.12, 348.9

enterpryse: undertake, 15.15

except(ed): accept (ed), 47.28, 245.17

exercyse: the practice of virtue, 344.24

extincte: extinguish, 138.5

extold: celebrated (O.E.D. first cites 1607), 229.14

farsted: farced (stuffed), 203.14

fautes: faults, 285.3

fay: religious belief, 178.2

faytors: faitours, cheats, impostors, 323.25

feateously: handsomely, 258.7

feciste: ?fechest, var. of 'fishest,' 346.20

fende: fiend, 30.20

fermes: farms, 293.18

fetes: evil deeds (O.E.D. last cites 1559), 249.14

fleare: fleer, 284.2

forbeare: show mercy to, 126.27

force not: care not, 142.27

forlorne: brought to ruin (pa. pple. of 'forlese'), 164.8

forstallyng: buying up of goods beforehand, 291.20

foulers, fowler(s): bird catcher(s), 14.14, 203.25, 245.23

fray: frighten, 355.17

fro: from, 94.24, 98.22, 349.7

frocke: the outer garment, for indoor wear, of women and children, consisting of a bodice and skirt, 352.20

from pyller to poste: hither and thither (this common phrase is worth a note because it is originally a figure drawn from the tennis court—and so Hall uses it—and because in time the original order was inverted so that 'poste' might rhyme with 'toste,' as in fact it does here), 163.12

frumps: jeers (this precise form not cited by O.E.D., which first notices 'frumpery,' a cognate word, in 1583), 19.29

fyllets: headbands, of ribbon, string, etc., used for binding the hair, for keeping the headdress in position, or simply for ornament, 258.4, 348.27

fynde: devise, 249.14; supply, 345.19

fyne: free from impurity, 95.25

Gads: God's (an acceptable spelling, first cited O.E.D. 1611), 7.20

game: deride (O.E.D. first cites 1621), 358.17

gate: gait, i.e., course, 318.20, 351.9

geast: guest, 113.13

Gedeon: Gideon, who conquered the Midianites (Judges, vii), 27.18

glasses: ornaments of glass (O.E.D. does not cite before 1625, but cf. 352.18–353.5n., under 'gaudes'), 349.3

go: walk, 338.17

god: good, 51.10

gowne: an over-dress, 325.22

graffe: graft, 3.24

Gryp(pe): gripe, a vulture, 306.16, 316.22

guyse: manner, fashion, 200.9, 258.13, 351.24, 352.5

gylls: wenches (contemptuous), 356.4

had a ... stroke: were highest in excellence, 302.21

hault(e), haulty: haughty, 31.2, 87.7, 285.17, 358.19

hayle: whole, 317.13

hearlace: headband, 348.27

heauen blys (se): the bliss of heaven, 16.10, 279.29

hent(e): design (not cited O.E.D. before 1600), 121.27; seized, 134.11; seize, 306.17

hie: high, 71.27

ho: limit, 309.19

hold: prevail, persevere, 229.15

horne: emblem of power and might, 70.6

houe, hooue(s): coif(s), 134.14, 349.2

hoyse: lift, 266.23

hunger gutte: glutton, 319.18

Iephte: Jephthah, who conquered the Ammonites (Judges, xi), 27.20

in: ?of, 246.24

incident: likely to happen, 13.16

in couerture: covered, 176.12

in euery sted: everywhere, 121.3

instruct: instructed, 156.28

insue: cf. ensue

in the meane space: meanwhile, 270.13

inuent: plan, 228.12; plot, 249.15; contrive, 258.28

inuenth: inventeth, 105.16

in vre: into practice, 244.24

ioye: experience joy, 47.26

iust: justified, 76.5; exactly, 77.9; exactly the same, 332.12

kepe: care, 72.10

kerchers: kerchiefs, 349.6

kinreds, kynred(e)s: people, 104.25, 105.8; generations, 112.18

know(e)ledge: acknowledge, 66.29, 114.24

kynde: native place, 46.4; nature, 49.2, 238.7, 308.21

kyrtell: jacket with skirt attached and worn under the upper gown or robe, 352.22

leames: gleams, 287.9

leare: leer, 284.25

leche: physician, 249.22

let: forbear, 122.19; hinder, 207.20

lette slyp go: O.E.D. does not cite; cf. 'let slip': 'loose,' 301.27

leude: bungling, 249.22

lewdly: wickedly, 164.8

Libanus: Lebanon, 155.24

lurche: cheat, 278.24

lust(es): pleasure, 14.6; desire(s), 32.28, 149.17, 308.7, 344.4; lust after, 349.21

sweuen: vision, dream, 311.21

swynge: violent career (first cited O.E.D. 1570), 241.12

syche: such, 223.2

syght: skill, 14.16

tabrets: tabors (small drums), 145.11, 203.23

taches: buckles, 349.4

tacorde: to accord, 32.21

take: taken, 301.22, 358.23

tapere: to appear, 120.8

tauerne: to frequent taverns (O.E.D. first cites 1610), 291.12

than: then, 133.9

theyr: there, 350.25

third heuen: Heaven is divided in three. Cf. II Cor., xii.4 where the third heaven mentioned in II Cor., xii.2 is glossed as 'paradise,' 29.18

tho: then, 75.4, 140.6, 149.10

tholy: the holy, 34.3

thore: there, 17.14

timor: fear, 39.14

to: too, 137.3

to beate: belabour (last cited O.E.D. 1494), 196.24

to fell: fell down (last cited O.E.D. 1398), 241.4

to ryght: aright (intensive; not in O.E.D.), 293.20

to torne: torn, 303.9

trauell: travail, 147.5, 290.19

triplex: threefold (first cited O.E.D. 1601), 361.7

trust: trusted, 303.26

turmoyle: agitate (v.), 308.17

tyde: time, 44.27, 109.20, 242.16, 248.6, 256.22

type: symbol, 340.19

Vae: ah! alas! woe! 322.17

vardygue: farthingale, 352.21

vertue: of plants: efficacy arising from physical qualities, and especially the power to affect the human body in a beneficial manner, 49.17

vncouth: unknown, 308.13

vndo: undone, 139.15

vneth: not easily, 249.26

vnmete: unbecoming, 260.3

vntyll: unto, 11.27, 70.27, 78.9, 84.9, 219.22

vp: forward, 149.24

vse: keep, 352.3

vse to: is wont to, 316.23

vtred: vanquished (last cited O.E D. *c.* 1532), 234.8

wagde: employed, 293.3

warpe: contrive, 86.14

wayghtes: weights (i.e., onslaughts); or, less probably, 'creatures' (used often of preternatural beings), 86.7

wende: departed, died, 138.26

wene: ween (suppose), 94.29

weyght: wait, 207.23

weyte: weight (importance), 87.14

whan: one, 107.17

when: time (O.E.D. does not cite before 1616), 124.13

whoode: hood, 282.19

whot: hot, 8.7, 95.13, 119.18, 274.9

whyle: time, 353.17

whyster: whisper, 299.6

witsafe, wytsafe, wytsaft: vouchsafe, 53.28, 79.23, 137.24, 144.7, 305.20

wo: disease, 309.21

wonne: dwell, 116.25, 170.7, 309.27

worthe: happen to, 226.16

wo worth(e): cursed be, 180.26, 280.6, 353.17

wrath: wroth, 200.10

wryte: writ, 294.14

wunt(e): wont (accustomed), 87.25, 201.4

wyll, wylt: desire, 98.11, 239.3

wyth: withe, a tie or shackle used for binding, 266.19

yer: ere, 9.12, 182.6, 204.3

5. INDEX OF FIRST LINES

REFERENCES are to page numbers. Spelling is modernized, to facilitate reference by the reader. Those poems which are accompanied by music are italicized.

412

WORKS CONSULTED

AESOP, *The book of the subtyl historyes and Fables of Esope whiche were translated out of Frensshe in to Englysshe by wylliam Caxton at westmynstre* [1484].

AGRIPPA, Henry Cornelius, *Of the Vanitie and Vncertaintie of Artes and Sciences*, tr. Ia. San [ford]. Gent. London, 1569.

ALCIATI, Andrew, *Emblematum libellus*, Lyons, 1551.

Alumni Oxonienses 1500–1714, Oxford, 1891, 4 vols.

AMBROSE, ST., *Hymni de tempore et de sanctis*, Dauantriae [?1495].

APIANUS, PETRUS, *Cosmographiae*, Antwerp, 1524 [1532], 1539.

APOLLODORUS, *Bibliotheca*, ed. Benedicto Aegio Spoletino, Rome, 1555.

ARATUS, *Phaenomena*, Venice, 1499 [includes the *Sphaera* of Proclus]; tr. G. R. Mair, Loeb Classical Library, 1921.

ARBER, EDWARD, see *Stationers' Register*.

ARTEMIDORUS DALDIANUS, *De somniorum interpretatione*, Basle, 1539, *et seq.*; tr. into English as *Interpretation of Dreams*, 1644.

AYDELOTTE, F., *Elizabethan Rogues and Vagabonds*, Oxford, 1913.

BALDWIN, T. W., *William Shakspere's Petty School*, Urbana, Illinois, 1943.

————, *William Shakspere's Small Latine & Lesse Greeke*, Urbana, Illinois, 1944, 2 vols.

BALDWIN, WILLIAM, *A treatise of Morall Phylosophie, contaynyng the sayinges of the wyse*, London, 1547 [and ?1550]. 'Sayings of the Wise' reprinted in *The Christian's Library*, ed. Edward Arber, London, 1907, vol. III (of 12 vols., ed. A. H. Burton, London [1899]–1910).

BELLARMINE, ROBERT CARDINAL, *De scriptoribus Ecclesiasticus*, Lugduni, 1613.

Bible: editions of 1537, ?Antwerp (Tyndale-Coverdale); 1539, London (Coverdale); 1540, London (Coverdale); 1549, London ('Matthew's'); 1551, London, Nicholas Hyl (ed. Edmund Becke); 1551, London, John Day (Becke); 1552, London (Cranmer, 'Great Bible'); 1560, Geneva (Whittingham, 'Breeches Bible'); 1561, London (Cranmer).

Bibliotheca Beauclerkiana, London, 1781.

BOWERS, FREDSON, *Principles of Bibliographical Description*, Princeton, New Jersey, 1949.

BRITTEN, JAMES, and ROBERT HOLLAND, *A Dictionary of English Plant-Names*, London, for the English Dialect Society, 1886.

BURLEY, WALTER, *Vita omnium philosophorū & poetarū*, ?Cologne, 1515.

CAIUS, DR. JOHN, *A boke, or counseill against the disease commonly called the sweate, or sweatyng sicknesse*, London, 1552.

Calendar of State Papers, Domestic Series, Edward VI, Mary, Elizabeth, 1547–1580, ed. Robert Lemon, London, 1856.

CALVIN, JOHN, *An Admonicion against Astrology Iudiciall and other curiosities, that raigne now in the world . . . translated into Englishe, by G. G[ylby]*, London, 1561.

CAMPBELL, LILY B., *Divine Poetry and Drama in Sixteenth-Century England*, Berkeley and Los Angeles, 1959.

CAPELLI, ADRIANO, *Dizionario di Abbreviature Latine ed Italiane*, Milan, 1949.

CAXTON, WILLIAM, *The Myrrour of the Worlde*, Westminster, 1480.

CHAPPELL, W., *Popular Music of the Olden Time*, London, 1855–1859, 2 vols.

COLE, G. WATSON, *A Catalogue of Books, Consisting of English Literature and Miscellanea . . . of the Library of E. D. Church*, New York, 1909, 2 vols.

COMES, NATALES, *Mythologiae, siue explicationum fabularum*, Venice, 1568.

COOPER, T., *Thesaurus Linguae & Britannicae*, London, 1565.

Court of Venus, The, ed. R. A. Fraser, Durham, North Carolina, 1955.

CYPRIAN, ST., *Opera Divicae . . . Cypriani Episcopi Carthaginensis . . . Basileam . . . M.D.XXI; Works*, 1717.

DE CONTI, NATALE, see COMES, NATALES.

DE CONTI, NICOLO [Poggio Bracciolini], *De Varietate Fortunae* [Book IV: '*India Recognita*'], Milan, 1492, *et. seq.*

DEKKER, THOMAS, *The Non-dramatic Works*, ed. A. B. Grosart, London, 1884–1886, 5 vols.

DENT, ARTHUR, *The Plaine mans Path-way to Heauen*, London, 1601.

Dictionary of Archaic and Provincial Words, A, James Orchard Halliwell, London, 1901, 2 vols.

Dictionary of National Biography, A, ed. Leslie Stephen and Sidney Lee, London, 1885–1900, 63 vols.

Dictionary of the Bible, A, ed. James Hastings, Edinburgh and New York, 1898–1904, 5 vols.

DIOGENES LAERTIUS, *De Vita et moribus philosophorum*, Luguduni [Lyons], 1541; tr. as *Lives of Eminent Philosophers*, Loeb Classical Library, 1925.

DODOENS, REMBERT, *A Niewe Herball, or Historie of Plantes* [*Histoire des Plantes*, 1557], tr. Henry Lyte, London, 1578.

DOUCE, *Catalogue of the Printed Books and Manuscripts Bequeathed by Francis Douce, Esq. to the Bodleian Library*, Oxford, 1840.

DUFF, E. GORDON, *A Century of the English Book Trade*, London, 1905.

EINSTEIN, LEWIS DAVID, *The Italian Renaissance in England*, New York, 1902.

ERASMUS, *Adagiorum Opus D. Erasmi Roterodami . . . Basileae*, 1526.

——, *Apophthegmes*, tr. Nicholas Udall, London, 1542.

——, *The Colloquies, or Familiar Discourses of Desiderius Erasmus of Roterdam, Rendered into English . . . by H. M. Gent.*, London, 1671.

——, *Proverbs . . . from the Adagia of Erasmus*, R. Bland, London, 1814, 2 vols.

FERGUSON, ARTHUR B., 'Renaissance Realism in the "Commonwealth" Literature of Early Tudor England,' *Journal of the History of Ideas*, XVI, no. 3, June, 1955, 287–305.

FLETCHER, W. Y., *English Book-Collectors*, London, 1902.

FRASER, R. A., 'An Amateur Elizabethan Composer,' *Music & Letters*, XXXIII, no. 4, October, 1952, 329–32.

————, 'Early Elizabethan Songs,' *Musica Disciplina*, VII, 1953, 199–203.

————, 'Political Prophecy in "The Pilgrim's Tale," ' *South Atlantic Quarterly*, LVI, no. 1, January, 1957, 67–78.

————, 'The Dancing Horse of "Love's Labour's Lost," ' *Shakespeare Quarterly*, V, no. 1, January, 1954, 98f.

GELASIUS, ST., *De duabis naturis*, Basileae, 1528.

GERARD, JOHN, *The Herball or Generall Historie of Plantes*, London, 1597; revised edn., 1633.

GESNER, CONRAD, *Catalogus Plantarum . . . Tiguri . . . M.D.XLII.*

————, *De Raris et Admirandis Herbis . . . Tiguri*, n.d. [?1555].

————, *Opera Botanica . . . Norimbergae impensis . . .* MDCCLI.

————, *The newe Iewell of Health . . . corrected and published in Englishe, by George Baker, Chirurgian*, London, 1576.

GOOGE, BARNABE, see PALINGENIUS.

Gorgeous Gallery of Gallant Inventions (1578), A, ed. H. E. Rollins, Cambridge, Mass., 1926.

GRAVES, T. S., 'Tricks of an Elizabethan Showman,' *South Atlantic Quarterly* XIV, no. 2, April, 1915, 3–13.

Handful of Pleasant Delights (1584), A, ed. H. E. Rollins, Cambridge, Mass., 1924.

HAWES, STEPHEN, *The Pastime of Pleasure*, E. E. T. S., O. S., no. 173, London, 1927.

HAZLITT, WILLIAM CAREW, *Hand-Book to the Popular, Poetical, and Dramatic Literature of Great Britain*, London, 1867.

HERBERT, WILLIAM, *Typographical Antiquities*, London, 1785, 3 vols.

HEYWOOD, JOHN, *The Proverbs, Epigrams, and Miscellanies of*, ed. John S. Farmer, London, 1906.

————, *Two Hundred Epigrams*, London, 1555.

HOLLAND, JOHN, *The Psalmists of Britain*, London, 1843.

HOLT, ALFRED H., *Phrase Origins*, New York, 1936.

HUTH, HENRY, *Ancient Ballads & Broadsides*, London, 1867.

HUTH LIBRARY, THE. *A Catalogue of The Books, Manuscripts . . . Letters, and Engravings, Collected by H. Huth*, ed. F. S. Ellis, London, 1880, 5 vols.

————, *Catalogue of the Huth Collection of Printed Books & Illuminated Manuscripts*, London, 1911.

HYGINUS, C. JULIUS, *C. Iulii Hygini Augusti Liberti Fabularum Liber, ad omnium poetarum lectionem . . . Eiusdem Poeticon Astronomicon, libri quatuor . . . Palaephati de fabulosis narrationibus, liber I. F. Fulgentii Placiadis Episcopi Carthaginiensis Mythologiarum, libri III. Eiusdem de vocum antiquarum interpretatione, liber I. Arati . . . [Phaenomenae] fragmentum, Germanico Caesare interprete. Eiusdem Phaenomena Graece, cum interpretatione latina. Procli de sphaera libellus, Graece & Latine. Index rerum & fabularum in his omnibus scitu dignarum copiosissimus*, Basle, 1535.

————, *Poeticon Astronomicon*, Ferrara, 1475.

JAMES, THOMAS, *Catalogus vniuersalis omnium Librorum in Bibliotheca Bodleiana*, Oxford, 1620.

JOHNSON, FRANCIS R., *Astronomical Thought in Renaissance England*, Baltimore, Md., 1937.

JUDGES, A. V., ed., *The Elizabethan Underworld*, London, 1930.

JULIAN, JOHN, *Dictionary of Hymnology*, New York, 1892.

JUSTIN (Junianus Justinus), *Thabridgment of the Histories of Trogus Pompeius, Collected and wrytten in the Laten tonge, by the famous Historiographer Iustine, and translated into English by Arthur Goldyng*, London, 1564.

Kalendar & Compost of Shepherds, The, Paris [1493]; London, 1930.

LOBEL, MATTHIAS, *Plantarum seu Stirpium Historia*, Antwerp, 1576, 2 vols.

——, *Stirpium aduersaria noua*, London, 1571.

——, *Stirpium Obseruationes*, London, 1581.

LODGE, THOMAS, *Wits Miserie*, London, 1596.

LOWNDES, WILLIAM THOMAS, *The Bibliographer's Manual of English Literature*, ed. Henry G. Bohn, London, 1859, 11 vols.

LYTE, HENRY, see DODOENS, REMBERT.

MCKERROW, RONALD B., *An Introduction to Bibliography for Literary Students*, Oxford, 1927.

Maroccus Extaticus. Or, Bankes Bay Horse in a Trance. A Discourse set downe in a merry Dialogue, between Bankes and his beast: Anatomizing some abuses and bad trickes of this age. . . . By Iohn Dando and Harrie Runt [pseuds.], London, 1595.

MAUNSELL, ANDREW, *Catalogue of English Printed Books*, London, 1595.

MIRABELLIUS, NANNIUS, *Polyanthea*, Venice, 1507.

MONTAIGNE, MICHEL DE, *The Essayes or Morall, Politike and Millitarie Discourses . . . done into English By . . . Iohn Florio*, London, 1603.

MORSE, H. K., *Elizabethan Pageantry*, London, 1934.

NASHE, THOMAS, *Christs Teares Ouer Ierusalem*, London, 1593.

New English Dictionary on Historical Principles, A, ed. J. A. H. Murray, Henry Bradley, W. A. Craigie, C. T. Onions, Oxford, 1888–1928, 10 vols.

New Schaff-Herzog Encyclopedia of Religious Knowledge, ed. Samuel Macauley Jackson and George William Gilmore, New York and London, 1908–1912, 12 vols.

Old English Ballads, 1553–1625, ed. H. E. Rollins, Cambridge, 1920.

Pack of Autolycus, The, ed. H. E. Rollins, Cambridge, Mass., 1927.

PALFREYMAN, THOMAS, *A Treatice of Morall Philosophye*, London, 1567.

PALINGENIUS, MARCELLUS, *Zodiacus Vitae*, Venice [?1531]; tr. Barnabe Googe: *The Zodiake of life*, London, 1560 (3 books), 1561 (6 bks.), 1565, 1576, 1588 (complete work); described and partly paraphrased by Foster Watson: *The Zodiacus Vitae of Marcellus Palingenius Stellatus: An Old School Book*, London, 1908.

PALMER, HENRIETTA R., *List of English Editions and Translations of Greek and Latin Classics Printed Before 1641*, London, 1911.

Paradise of Dainty Devices, (1576–1606), The, ed. H. E. Rollins, Cambridge, Mass., 1927.

PARTRIDGE, ERIC, *A Dictionary of Slang and Unconventional English*, New York, 1950.

PHILO, *Philonis Iudaei Alexandrini, (Cuius Doctrinae & orationis sublimitatem grauissimi autores etiam ipsi diuino Platoni aequarūt) omnes quae apud Graecos & Latinos extant, libri . . . Basileae* [1538].

Pleasant Quippes for Vpstart Newfangled Gentlewomen, London, 1596; reprint, n.p., n.d., ?1841.

PLINY, *C. Plini Secundi Naturalis Historiae*, Lipsiae, 1897.

PLUTARCH, *Apophthegmata Regum & Imperatorum* . . . Paris, 1530; tr. Philemon Holland: *The Philosophie, commonlie called, the Morals* . . . London, 1603.

POGGIO BRACCIOLINI, see DE CONTI, NICOLO.

POLLARD, A. W., 'The Rowfant Books,' *The Library*, VI, 1905, 309–14.

Polyanthea, see MIRABELLIUS, NANNIUS.

PONZETTI, CARDINAL FERDINAND, *Libellus de venenis*, Rome, 1521, 1562.

Prayer Book and *Primer:* 'Prymer in Englyshe and in Latin sette out alonge; after the vse of Sarum,' 1504; 'Primer of Salysbury vse' (F. Regnault), 1538; Latin-English version (Henrician) of ?1540; 'Prymer of Salysbury vse' (Thomas Petit), 1544; Henry's Primer: 'The Primer Set Foorth by the Kynges maiestie and his Clergie, to be taught lerned, & read: and none other to be vsed throughout all his dominions,' 1545; *Three Primers of Henry VIII*, ed. E. Burton, Oxford, 1834; 'The Book of the common prayer,' 1549 (included as 'The First Prayer Book of Edward VI' in *The Library of Liturgiology and Ecclesiology*, vol. II, 1902); 'First and Second Prayer Books of Edward VI,' ed. E. C. S. Gibson, 1910; 'Book of Common Prayer,' 1552, 1560.

PROCLUS, *Sphaera*, tr. William Salysburye, *The Descripcion of the Sphere or Frame of the Worlde*, London, 1550.

Psalms: Thomas Sternhold, *Psalms of David*, 1551, 1553, 1561; *Psalterium Dauidicum ad vsum ecclesie Sarisburiensis*, 1555; John Day, *Medius of the psalmes*, 1563.

PTOLEMY, *Almagesti*, Basileae, 1541.

RECORDE, ROBERT, *The Castle of Knowledge*, London, 1556.

ROLLINS, HYDER E., 'An Analytical Index to the Ballad-Entries (1557–1709) in the Registers of the Company of Stationers of London,' *Studies in Philology*, XXI, 1924, 1–325.

————, 'Tottel's "Miscellany" and John Hall,' *London Times Literary Supplement*, January 14, 1932, p. 28.

Rowfant Books, The, a selection of one hundred titles from the collection of Frederick Locker-Lampson, New York [1906].

Rowfant Library, The, a catalogue of the printed Books, manuscripts, autograph letters, drawings and pictures, collected by Frederick Locker-Lampson, London, 1886; *An Appendix* thereto, London, 1900.

————: Dodd and Livingston, Catalogue 4: *Early English literature mainly from the Rowfant Library*, May, 1911.

RUTZ, CASPAR, *Habitus variarum orbis gentium*, ?Amsterdam, 1581.

SALYSBURYE, WILLIAM, see PROCLUS.

Shakespeare's England, Oxford, 1916, 2 vols.

Songs and Sonnets, see *Tottel's Miscellany*.

STARNES, DEWITT T., and ERNEST WILLIAM TALBERT, *Classical Myth and Legend in Renaissance Dictionaries*, Chapel Hill, North Carolina, 1955.

Stationers' Register: A Transcript of the Registers of the Company of Stationers of London. 1554–1640, ed. Edward Arber, London, 1875–1894, 5 vols.

STOW, JOHN, *Survey of London*, ed. Strype, London, 1720; Everyman edn., n.d.

————, *The Annales, or A Generall Chronicle of England*, continued and augmented by Edmond Howes, London, 1614.

STUBBES, PHILIP, *The Anatomie of Abuses*, London, 1585.

TANNER, THOMAS, *Bibliotheca Britannica-Hibernica*, London, 1748.

TAVERNER, RICHARD, *Prouerbes or Adagies, gathered oute of the Chiliades of Erasmus*, London, 1552.

Thesaurus Linguae Latinae, Lipsiae, 1900– (in progress), 8 vols.

TILLEY, MORRIS PALMER, *A Dictionary of the Proverbs in England in the Sixteenth and Seventeenth Centuries*, Ann Arbor, Michigan, 1950.

Tottel's Miscellany, ed. H. E. Rollins, Cambridge, Mass., 1928–1929, 2 vols.

True Report of the burnyng of the Steple and Churche of Paules in London, The, London, 1561.

TURNER, WILLIAM, *Libellus de re herbaria nouus*, London, 1538.

——, *The first and seconde partes of the Herbal . . . enlarged with the Thirde parte . . . Imprinted at Collen*, 1568.

——, *The names of herbes*, London, 1548.

VIVES, LODOVICUS, *An Introduction to wysedom*, tr. Richard Moryson, London, ?1540.

Vives and the Renaissance Education of Women, ed. Foster Watson, London, 1912 (translates Vives' *De institutione feminae Christinae*, 1523).

WARTON, THOMAS, *The History of English Poetry*, London, 1781, 4 vols.

WATSON, FOSTER, see PALINGENIUS, MARCELLUS.

WILLICH, IODOCUS, *Ars Magirica*, Tiguri, 1563.

WITHER, GEORGE, *Hymnes and Songs of the Church . . . Translated and Composed, By G. W.*, London, n.d.

Wonder of Wonders, The, or the Strange Birth in Hampshire, by T. L., ?1675

Zodiacus Vitae, see PALINGENIUS, MARCELLUS.

GENERAL INDEX